FOCUS ON EUROPE

A PHOTO-RECONNAISSANCE
MOSQUITO PILOT AT WAR, 1943–45

FOCUS ON EUROPE

A PHOTO-RECONNAISSANCE
MOSQUITO PILOT AT WAR, 1943–45

RONALD H. FOSTER DFC CdG

THE CROWOOD PRESS

First published in 2004 by
The Crowood Press Ltd
Ramsbury, Marlborough
Wiltshire SN8 2HR

www.crowood.com

British Library Cataloguing-in-Publication Data
A catalogue record for this book is available from the British Library.

ISBN 1 86126 718 5

Photograph previouts page: Ronald H. Foster and Francis H. Moseley,
Mosquito pilot and observer of RAF Benson's Photo-Reconnaissance
Unit, 1943–45, photographed at RAF Leuchars, Scotland, in March 1945.

Typeset by Textype, Cambridge

Printed and bound in Great Britain by The Cromwell Press, Trowbridge

Contents

Foreword

By Air Vice-Marshal C. L. Siegert, CB, CBE, MVO, DFC, AFC
Chief of Air Staff RNZAF 1976–79

Just before midnight on 3 September 1939 the cabinet of the New Zealand government agreed to follow Great Britain's lead and declare war on Germany. Two days later the prime minister of New Zealand, the Right Honourable Michael Joseph Savage, said that the time had come 'to overthrow the evil forces of aggression', and continued:

> With gratitude for the past and confidence in the future we range ourselves without fear alongside Britain. Where she goes, we go; where she stands, we stand. We are only a small and young nation, but we march with a union of hearts and souls to a common destiny.

There is no doubt but that the very great majority of New Zealanders, like teenager Ron Foster, was solidly behind Prime Minister Savage in his support of the 'Motherland'. Ron Foster's concern was whether the war would last long enough for him to play a part in it in the service of his choosing, the Royal New Zealand Air Force. When he was accepted for Air Force training, Ron volunteered for advanced training for his pilot's 'wings' in Canada, to ensure he was on his way to the big theatre of operations – Europe.

In the event, as this book tells, Ron Foster played a major part in the intriguing role of aerial photographic reconnaissance. His vivid descriptions of some of the more hazardous of the many perilous operations he completed are exciting and probably unique. The reader shares with him the pre-operation worries, the meticulous planning necessary for these dangerous flights, the techniques and mode of operating unarmed, high-flying aircraft against heavily defended targets, and the high skill and sustained courage displayed on these missions. Following this we become aware of the difficulties experienced in returning to the home airfield, sometimes in most adverse weather conditions and sometimes in a badly damaged and ailing aircraft. Then after each operation we can understand the feelings of exhilaration, and the satisfaction of successfully completing one's task against so many odds.

Foreword

Having portrayed how he played his part in, and survived the dangers of, World War II, Ron Foster looks at the post-war problems of Europe and the prospects for a permanent peace. But now he is seeing, through the eyes of a mature New Zealander, a very different Europe from that which, as a young and idealistic patriot, he had braved so much to help set free from tyranny. I believe that all right-minded people will echo his final sentiments that 'ultimately, there has to be a better way to obtain peace than by going to war'.

C. L. Siegert
Lower Hutt

Prologue

The wartime years of 1943, 1944 and 1945 focused our senses supremely well on the entire Continent of Europe. From our speedy and unarmed photographic reconnaissance Mosquito my navigator and I 'looked down from a great height': limitless panoramas from 40,000ft down to pulse-racing low-level flying over hostile territory at less than tree-top level. My eyes, and the lenses of the battery of cameras we carried in our aircraft, scanned every country of Europe except Greece and Portugal. We observed every aspect of towns and cities, mountains, rivers and lakes, countrysides and coasts. The coasts we flew over were of prime importance, especially those defining the barrier of sea, either English Channel or North Sea, that safeguarded the haven of Great Britain for my navigator and myself. After operational flights over enemy Europe we fought with all our effort to return to that matchless stronghold.

1
En Route to Europe

England has saved herself by her exertions;
And will, as I trust, save Europe by her example.
William Pitt, Prime Minister of Great Britain
(9 November 1805, nineteen days after the Battle of Trafalgar)

During my youthful days in New Zealand, the world we knew changed for ever in 1939 when war broke out around the world.

I was too young at that time to become directly involved until a couple of the war years had rolled by, and I had a secret concern that it might not last long enough for me to play my part in it. In December 1941 Japan entered the lists by attacking Pearl Harbour, and Kiwis and Aussies living in other Pacific countries had some of their attention and anxieties diverted from the European theatre of war. My parents eventually signed my application papers to volunteer for war service, but only under considerable protest. Many months of requests and confrontations had to be endured before I could persuade them to give their parental assent. One evening I remember saying bitterly to my mother: 'How would any country ever enrol its soldiers and sailors and airmen if all the mothers were like you?' And my mother replied with unanswerable motherly logic: 'If all the mothers were like me, son, there would be no wars!'

For the duration of the war I kept a small pocket diary each year, but I never looked at any of them again until I commenced the writing of this book. Occasionally time hung on one's hands, and the diary, or sometimes an old school exercise book, came in handy for jotting down some thoughts. I was always far too self-conscious to ever dream of showing these private thoughts to anyone else, but maybe this is now the time – sixty years later. These two extracts illustrate just how much times have changed, and personal attitudes along with them. How would a twenty-year-old British man word his innermost thoughts *now*, in similar circumstances, a couple of generations later?

This is what this young fellow thought as he worked as a clerical cadet in a large head office of a New Zealand government department while waiting to be called into Air Force camp. The date of writing, 21 January 1942, was a little more than a month after Japan had brought the United States into the war by its attack on Pearl Harbour.

9

. . . The office is now really dreary. Nearly all my pals have joined the Army, or the Navy or the Air Force. The place has filled up with uninteresting females, and to top it all, my work is keeping me far too busy. How can a fit young fellow who has been tumbling over himself for the past eighteen months to go away overseas, be expected to be content with pen-pushing eight hours a day? And in a dungeon-like room with incessant noise including the chattering of typewriters and typists – even the air we breathe is foul.

A man-sized job is waiting to be done nowadays for everyone who has any spark of pride, and interest in the protection of his family, friends, country and Empire. Oh! to be fully trained for this mighty conflict between Good and Evil: to have enjoyed the companionship that is bred when men and women of similar ideals share duty and danger together. Then, having entered the fight clean and confident, how much more soul satisfying it would be to fall, nobly and proudly, than to slowly decay away in this dull hole.

To quote the poet Thomas Mordaunt: 'One crowded hour of glorious life is worth an age without a name.' Colonel Theodore Roosevelt, president of the USA from 1901 to 1909, expressed my feelings clearly:

. . . Far better it is to dare mighty things, to win glorious triumphs, even though checkered with failure, than to take rank with those poor spirits who neither enjoy much nor suffer much because they live in the grey twilight that knows not victory nor defeat.

And the following extract reveals how this twenty-one-year old man felt while waiting, in Halifax, Nova Scotia, on 22 April 1943, for a convoy to transport him across the Atlantic to beleaguered Britain; if not torpedoed en route by U-boats, arrival in the European theatre of war meant flying as a pilot on operational sorties over Hitler's 'Fortress Europe':

About a year ago I had just entered RNZAF camp, an Initial Training Wing, at Rotorua, NZ. It was an anxiety to me whether I would ever make it as a pilot. There were then so many apparent obstacles in the way that it was desperately hard to be confident, but my keenness and determination must have overcome the apparent hurdles. Here I am wearing my officer's uniform with pilot's wings firmly sewn on.

At that time back in New Zealand, seeing so many of my friends going from civvy street into the Army or the Navy, or the Air Force, I was just longing to be able to prove, and chiefly to myself, that I, too, would be capable of playing my part in this second world war. It was a fierce urge in me that could not be quelled. It has been interesting for me to witness my own performance and development, and now, 13 months later, I am in the position of being nearly fully trained and will soon be doing the actual things that seemed so remote even a short time ago. As captain of an aircraft I will be responsible for other trained men, as well as the aircraft, and will be at the controls when enemy fighters are attacking, or while encountering a storm. Possibly the opportunity will present itself to fulfil orders completely, and strike a decisive blow for the family, country, and king I am fighting for.

I know now that I will not hesitate to do my duty, but will go in, still thoroughly believing in protection from above and not fearing as to the result. There cannot be anything to fear when so many of my fine comrades have given their all so unhesitatingly and willingly.

No, not really *giving* all, for they are *leaving* so much to those who are left. Is it possible to leave more than this perfect example of the spirit of faith and hope and courage? Their ideals and ambitions are completed in perfection, for in these past crowded months the proper fullness of life has been experienced.

Can life offer more that the bonds of comradeship, the absolute truth of ideals, and the beauty of having perfect peace of mind as to one's duty? To be sure we are not entering this conflict blindly and uncaringly. We believe and know that only by such efforts will humanity eventually be able to prosper on this earth ... Humanity ... people I love sincerely and who have much good in them. And this earth of ours, with its glorious peaks and lakes and green fields. The treasures abundant amongst us: our gift of Christian faith, the appeal of music, the spirit of adventuring, the joy and satisfaction of being in harmony with nature herself.

That I have so fully, though briefly, discovered all this, and feel thoroughly *alive*, is ample to show and justify what we must, and will do, to let others who come after us find the same youthful delight in living. Privileged indeed am I to be among this band that is truly discovering just what life really is. Goodness, Truth, and Beauty are apparent everywhere, and we are those fortunates chosen to realize these values most fully, and to defend them.

When World War II broke out, the New Zealand prime minister, Mr Michael Savage, said over the radio on 5 September 1939:

It is essential that we realize from the beginning that our cause is worth the sacrifice ... Both with gratitude for the past and with confidence in the future, we range ourselves without fear beside Britain. Where she goes, we go; where she stands, we stand.

11

During World War I, when New Zealand's population was one million, 99,000 servicemen left her shores: in 1914 that was 10 per cent of the total population, and 16,700 lost their lives on active service. And in the twenty-one years between the two wars, the basic attitude and feeling of New Zealanders did not change, so that in World War II, when the country's population had reached 1.7 million, the figures at the time of peak mobilization (1942) were as follows: servicemen and women in the army 126,000, in the Navy 6,000, and the Air Force 22,000. From that total of 154,000, 44,000 served overseas. This mobilization was huge in proportion to the country's population.

If, under those wartime conditions, the figures above can be taken as 'positive', let us look at the 'negative' side: more than 10,000 lost their precious lives, more than 2,000 were still 'missing', 8,500 were still prisoners of war at the end of hostilities, and more than 19,000 had been wounded. The figures for the RNZAF show that the numbers posted overseas peaked with 8,000 in the Pacific, and 7,000 mostly in Europe, but some in the Far East, Africa and India. By May 1945, nearly 11,000 New Zealanders had passed through the Empire Air Training Scheme as aircrew serving with the RAF. Casualties from this group of New Zealanders amounted to 3,320 killed, 282 missing, and 832 wounded, while prisoners of war peaked in 1944 at a figure of 501 . . . . One out of three of us 'went for a Burton'.

It is interesting to note from the *New Zealand Year Book – 1946* (from which these figures are extracted) that casualties for every 1,000 of the population were recorded in the following proportions: United Kingdom 19 per cent, Australia 13 per cent, Canada 9 per cent and New Zealand 24 per cent. In addition to those included in the above statistics, the New Zealand Home Guard peaked with a membership of 124,000.

To conclude all these figures, let us record how the RNZAF built up its strength in just one area of operations, the Pacific, while still maintaining its appreciable contribution to the European theatre of war: the RNZAF fielded twenty-six squadrons against the Japanese, comprising six bomber-reconnaissance, thirteen fighter, two flying boat, two torpedo-bomber, two transport and one dive-bomber squadron.

In World War II, New Zealand had the highest percentage of men in arms, the greatest percentage overseas, and the largest percentage killed, among the Allies. At an ANZAC day service in Wellington on 25 April 1990, Prime Minister Sir Geoffrey Palmer said: 'We are only now beginning to realize that war has done much to shape the New Zealand character, and to fashion our attitudes to the rest of the world.'

In March 1942 I entered the RNZAF camp in New Zealand as 'aircrew under training', with the rank of leading aircraftman. The training was conducted by the Empire Air Training Scheme. After completing Course No. 30, ITW, at Rotorua, I learnt to fly a de Havilland Tiger Moth at the EFTS at Bell Block, New Plymouth.

The next move was to Canada, by sea from Wellington to San Francisco, and train via Vancouver and Edmonton to Brandon in Manitoba. I spent nearly a year in Canada obtaining my pilot's 'wings', a commission as a pilot officer, and a navigator's certificate. The navigation course was at Charlottetown on Prince Edward Island. It was May 1943 by the time I crossed the Atlantic from Halifax to Bristol by way of an Elders and Fyffe banana boat in the middle of a convoy: the good ship SS *Cavina* of 4,500 tons.

How pleased I was to find myself one of two Kiwis who, together with forty-eight Canadians, made up a draft of fifty commissioned aircrew assigned to make the passage to England in the *Cavina*. During the preceding few months several ships carrying trained aircrew from Canada to Britain had been lost to enemy action while crossing the Atlantic. The authorities had accordingly stopped sending these men on troop-ships while they figured out how to counter the problem. When all the drafts came into Halifax the numbers quartered there mounted up until the facilities for accommodating them were full. As a result the overflow was despatched to the USA, and those men found themselves billeted in an American holding camp in the State of Maine. Parade-ground rumour had it that the total number awaiting transportation to Britain amounted to more than 3,000.

This huge and valuable pool of pilots, navigators, wireless operators and air-gunners – mostly from the UK, Canada, Australia and New Zealand – was eventually cleared with one stroke of initiative, although it was a decision that carried an incalculable risk. The transatlantic Cunard liner, *Queen Elizabeth*, was pressed into service, and the camp in Maine and the depot in Halifax were emptied – emptied, that is, except for fifty souls, of whom I was one – and for me, always well content to be at sea, the two exhilarating weeks of convoy life on a small ship suited me splendidly. Those who were crammed into the huge liner spent a long time each day queuing for the two meals that were served daily; nevertheless, the *Queen* rushed on at maximum speed straight through the packs of U-boats, and made the Atlantic trip in less than four days.

The Battle of the Atlantic was still being contested furiously by both sides, and U-boats were taking their toll of convoyed shipping. During the fourteen-day passage of our convoy we had our share of attacks, with ships sunk and damaged. In that month, May 1943, the Germans suffered forty-three U-boat losses, and this figure exceeded their replacement rate of construction by more than twice. We berthed in Britain on 23 May, and it was the day after, 24 May 1943, that Hitler's Admiral Donitz withdrew temporarily his fleet of submarines from the Atlantic because they could not continue to sustain those losses. (Post-war records disclose that out of 863 German U-boats in front-line service, 630 were sunk on operations.)

13

2

Training to Tackle Europe

Macte nova virtute, puer, sic itur ad astra.
Good luck to your youthful valour, boy.
Such is the way to the stars.

Virgil

My landfall on the other side of the world was my first step towards coming face to face with Europe. That Sunday in late May 1943 our convoy steamed around the north of Ireland and dispersed to various ports when we were off Belfast. The SS *Cavina* continued down the Irish Sea, up the Bristol Channel, and docked at Avonmouth; it would be another six months before Europe came into my view.

As the ship tied up I was filled with a surge of eager elation. At the stern of the ship the red ensign – called the 'red duster' by seamen – fluttered lazily in the fresh sunny air; it caught the eye as crisp and fresh, in contrast to the battered and rust-streaked appearance of the ship. An old docker of solid build handled the mooring warps with casual skill. He sported a large red rose stuck through the buttonhole of his ancient jacket and, with his weatherbeaten face, looked to be the epitome of John Bull himself. He glanced up and caught me studying him from over the rail above; my face was beaming with happiness, and he touched his cloth cap to me and gave a wink. From that moment I fell in love with England.

Our small company caught the train, destination Bournemouth on the south coast. This attractive seaside resort had been chosen as the base for all incoming aircrew from Canada, Australia and New Zealand; it had plenty of suitable accommodation, as well as good administrative and recreational facilities. In such glorious spring weather, the train trip was most pleasurable. We travelled first class, but I took off my uniform jacket and left the stuffy compartment, strolling out to the platform between the carriages and gazing at the beauty of the countryside; after seven months of North American winter, the sunshine and the green rolling fields, hedged and neat, provided a rare tonic. Being a Sunday, many people were walking along the

14

byways, and it gave my heart a lift to exchange waves with them.

Four hours after leaving Avonmouth we arrived at Bournemouth. But just as we were gathering our gear together on the road outside the station, the air was all at once filled with a violent roaring of engines and the spattering of machine-guns. People hurled themselves into the gutters at the roadside, myself included, though I didn't really comprehend what was happening until a Focke-Wulf Fw 190 fighter shot past, not much higher than the lampposts. At the General Reconnaissance School in Canada we had learnt aircraft recognition from models and photos – but here was a real Focke-Wulf, and its big black cross and swastika imprinted themselves in my mind as it zoomed over us.

This was a 'hit-and-run' raid, the planes coming across the Channel fast and low, shooting up civilian areas on the coast, and hoping to depart before the defence could be put into action. If the train journey had shown me one perspective of life in Britain, this was quite another, as I stared up from the gutter on this beautiful Sunday afternoon, and in glaring contrast.

The marauders had hit two or three hotels near the beach and esplanade, and there were people buried by rubble, a few of them aircrew; many of the airmen in residence helped to dig for survivors, but our draft did not have to do this. As soon as we had been allocated our quarters it was time for a much wanted evening meal.

Bournemouth appealed to me as a picturesque and colourful town, with its solid stone and cosy brick buildings, the perfect gardens loaded with blossoms and flowers, and the people plump and rosy. I was delighted to meet again some friends I had trained with in New Zealand, but who had not gone to Canada, having obtained their wings at home; we had many good old times to talk over. And my diary modestly records: 'Proud to observe that Kiwis are the most popular boys over here.'

The war came alive again that first evening. My room was in the attic several floors up, and was just big enough for one bed – which was fine by me, it suited me very well to be on my own. But no sooner was I comfortable in my bed than the unmistakable wail of the air-raid sirens shot me to my feet. The staff had already given us, as new arrivals, a short lecture on air-raid precautions: the procedure was to take one's greatcoat, boots, and all the webbing gear issued to us prior to embarkation at Halifax, which included an anti-gas respirator, a cape and a tin helmet, and then to proceed to the air-raid shelters down in the basements.

The little window in my room – as in all the rooms – was covered with a blackout shield, and without turning on my light I removed this and surveyed the scene. Searchlights weaved across the sky, and ack-ack tracer fire pierced the darkness. The view was absorbing, and so much held my attention that the long journey down all the flights of stairs to the air-raid shelters did not appeal at all (none of the lifts was operating); so I maintained my vigil from my watchtower until the 'all clear' sounded. The remainder of the night passed peacefully. My first day in the European theatre of war had come and gone.

After three days of attending lectures we were issued with clothing coupons, without which one could not buy clothes. Also most necessary to British wartime life were ration cards for the purchase of food and meals. RAF identity cards replaced our Canadian ones. And then came ten days' leave, a delight of anticipation.

During the next two or three days in London certain basic items had to be organized. Mail was the first priority, and for this, New Zealand operated a base post office in the Strand. Cox and King, an offshoot of Lloyds, handled the banking: our pay was lodged to our personal accounts, and payments made by cheque.

Throughout my stay in Britain I paid my mess bills, purchased civilian clothes and Air Force uniforms, entertained myself and my friends from time to time, and, as a pilot on operations, was able to buy an old car; in fact a total of three cars passed through my hands. It was only when I was in London on leave that I had the opportunity to call at the bank and enquire how my balance was doing; until then it never occurred to me to find out how much my rate of pay increased whenever I was promoted in rank. As regards the financial situation – and strictly from the financial point of view – those were halcyon days, and never since have I experienced a period in my life when the balance between income and expenditure was such a trivial priority . . . . Just pull out the cheque book and sign with a smile.

It was also important that we became familiar with the New Zealand Forces Club, an invaluable asset to all Kiwis; it operated from fine premises in Charing Cross Road, and was invariably packed out. What a pleasure it was to find one's arm nudged at the bar by your next-door neighbour at home, or the boy whom you sat next to at college, or perhaps a tennis champion whom you never thought you could meet, let alone on even terms. All that was the credit side; the debit side was to continually hear news of the casualties, army, navy, and air force.

An unofficial adjunct to the club was a nearby pub called The White Swan – although the Kiwis, who monopolized it, always called it The Dirty Duck. Later on, an unwanted female clientèle started to invade our favourite haunt, as a result of which the Kiwis gradually moved premises to The Tartan Dive, also handy to our club. And for me, there is an unsolved mystery regarding those two pubs: at night-time, blackouts and all, I could always, unerringly, find them, whereas on a bright sunny day with good visibility I would have to go round and round the blocks in bewildered fashion looking for them.

Those few days in London were good times. I fitted in the main sight-seeing attractions, and enjoyed a visit to the famous Windmill Theatre. My last diary entry before leaving the capital city for Scotland reads: 'London is a merry place!'

On return from my pleasurable Scottish interlude, I found that our previous base at Bournemouth had become far too crowded, with the result that only Canadians remained there. Kiwis and Aussies had moved along the coast to Brighton, another seaside resort, and so this was my new destination.

The following morning I had breakfast in the attractive hotel dining room, right on the sea-front, with a mass of glass windows along the side facing the beach, and overhead as well; it was like being in a large conservatory. Tucking in to the plateful of scrambled dried egg, I was my usual happy self, as I always am at meal-times, when a series of deafening crashes burst upon us. This is an air raid, thought I, and promptly took evading action under the table, well enveloped by the large tablecloth. But it was not an attack from the skies – it was a stray mine that had rolled up on the beach and exploded outside our dining room. All the glass was shattered and the entire floor covered by fragments inches deep. Fortunately no one was hurt, and best of all, in what I chose to think was in true British spirit, breakfast was re-served and I had a second plateful of dried eggs.

Waiting for a posting from Brighton was now the name of the game. My former comrades from course 30 in New Zealand were all posted the day after I returned from leave, many of them going on to bombers, the 'big stuff' with four engines. Back in Canada, my associates in the general reconnaissance (GR) course had mostly been posted to the west coast, to Vancouver Island, to train on torpedo bombers, Beauforts and Beaufighters.

A certain amount of choice had been offered us at the conclusion of that course; in particular I remember that a request was made for two friends to go to the Bahamas to learn to fly the big four-engined Liberators. Two of our Kiwis, close mates, shot up their hands to volunteer, and were chosen – but the joke is that many months later we heard that on arrival in the Bahamas they were measured, and were found to be too short to reach the controls of an American Liberator! Subsequently the war forgot about them for a while, and they had to be content with lying in the sun, eating and drinking whatever they fancied, and keeping up with the social life. It just shows that in wartime all is not super efficient and smooth running, and if you could question that elusive Irishman, Mr Murphy, he would enjoy telling you how frequently his law comes into operation.

The GR course was the entrée to Coastal Command. When requested to state, in order of preference, the three branches of Coastal Command we wished to be considered for, I had always written: '1. Flying boats 2. Flying boats 3. Flying-boats.' This was probably not helpful to the authorities, but it showed my one-track mind and my determination to be posted to these big, long-range craft. On graduating from that GR course in Canada, I and my best friend put up our hands when a request was made for two men to go to England. What type of posting it would be when we got there was not known. We were accepted; but the next morning there was a change of plan, and only one man was required to cross the Atlantic. Because everyone knew my keenness for flying boats, I was the one who went, and accordingly was separated from my friends.

On enquiring why no posting had come through for me at Brighton, I discovered that Coastal Command postings, for some reason unknown to me, came from the Air Ministry – another way of telling us to be quiet and just wait. Nine days passed by in relaxed and pleasant fashion; what a long time since I had piloted an aircraft: five months to the day.

Then twenty-three days after landing in England my posting came through. I travelled by train with seven Australians to an Advanced Flying Unit at Grove, near Challow railway station in Berkshire. My diary became unusually descriptive: 'Whoopee! Soon be flying again! Hurrah! Packed trunk, two kitbags and my handbag.' Grove was a wartime airfield with Nissen huts widely dispersed among the cornfields; the surrounding countryside was fresh and peaceful. Our quarters were arranged to take eight men in every hut, with two drawers for each, and space for our gear. Our hut was fortunate in having an excellent batman who kept our clothes well washed and pressed, and the meals were good, with large helpings: real English fare of pies with gravy, batters and puddings.

With my new Aussie mates we kicked a rugby ball about in the early evenings, and later played our mouth-organs, the twilight giving an intimacy to our little outside gathering; it reminded us of camping in our respective countries. In retrospect I am surprised the Aussies did not break up some of the few items of furniture and light a campfire for us to sit round and play and sing. We finished with *Waltzing Matilda,* and after a short but persuasive argument I taught them *The Maori Farewell,* and this stopped us from finishing with *Home Sweet Home* – that would have been too much to take.

Five weeks sped by, with the daily routine not varying much. We had to convert to an English twin-engined aircraft, the Oxford, which was straightforward enough; our initial difficulty was acclimatizing to English conditions after training in Canada. What a contrast, between clear blue skies over the prairies, few towns or settlements, and no other aircraft except those from our own airfield; and the haze and murk of English skies, with towns and villages in all directions, and airfields and aircraft scattered about in close proximity. With such a multitude of wartime airfields it was not unusual for an aircraft to find itself flying pretty close to another that was completing a circuit on an adjoining airfield – and tales are legendary about even the best of pilots landing on the wrong field by mistake.

Because the set-up was so dispersed, we were issued with pushbikes, and this was fun, speeding up the business of moving round to lectures, to flying, and to the mess – and even more useful in the evenings for exploring the beautiful countryside with its villages and pubs. Gradually I made some new friends. There were no Kiwis on this course, but the Aussies filled the bill. When New Zealanders and Australians are in their own countries, the rivalry in sports, business, and every conceivable activity is extreme; but away from the Pacific the members of the two nations are inseparable and as brothers. And if I needed to persuade an Aussie into friendship I had the perfect lever, because my father was born in Sydney – though he did have the good fortune to come to New Zealand when he was twelve years of age. My father's mother had arrived in South Australia from Devon in 1853 at the grand age of four, so I am a true Kiwi/Aussie. And if an Australian happens to be reading this, then of course I am a true Aussie/Kiwi.

One long evening in high summer I biked off on my own to explore and revel in the superb scenery. A couple of days earlier two Aussies and myself had walked to Wantage, a small market town that fascinated us: first, we had been told there were twenty-seven pubs; and second, there was a statue of King Alfred in the town square. This was all-important stuff, but we drank too much bitter and our heads had suffered the following morning; so here I was setting off solo on my bike, having decided that it would be best to give the beer a miss. The villages of Childrey and Sparsholt took my fancy, and being hot and thirsty, I entered a little pub – could it have been the 'Who-d-ha-thought-it'? Half-a-dozen Waafs were drinking and chattering, and I wished I hadn't come in; they wanted to be friendly and hospitable to this brand new young pilot officer from 'abroad', and suggested that I try a cider. This was something new for me, but I reasoned that a drink made from the juice of apples could not be as potent as best bitter, and I would be keeping to my pledge to give the beer a miss.

Every time I wanted to step up to the bar and pay for my shout, one of the girls would protest and come and take my money to the landlord, and then bring me my drink. So I just sat there, looked cheerfully at the company, admired the vista from the lattice windows, appreciated the colour of the cider, and drank up. In those days Britain had double summertime to assist the war effort, and it remained light to past closing time. Many hours slipped by, and at last it was time to go. I felt good and cheerful – but when I wanted to stand up, the odd thing was that my legs would not work, let alone support me. And this, apparently, was the time-honoured effect the girls and the landlord and the handful of local clients had wanted to bring about. Cider, or scrumpy, is a notorious drink. What was my next move?

The upshot was that I was helped on to my trusty old bike and two Waafs obtained some garden twine from the pub and tied it to my handlebars. I was then supposed to sit there and freewheel and keep my balance while

19

they provided the pulling power. The rest of the troupe were outriders. It was a long time before our airfield hove into view, and we crashed and fell off many times. My legs still did not work, and our slow convoy brought hoots of merriment from the members and, as we rode past the guardhouse, from the military policemen, and anybody else who was attracted by our entourage. The whole ride had been accompanied by the singing of a song that I could not fail to recollect as it was sung hundreds of times, with a chorus that may have sounded like 'roll me over. . .'.

My hut-mates delighted in telling me next morning what a pest I had been, and from then on dubbed me 'Ronnie the Romeo', having been escorted, bike and all, by six bicycling and singing Waafs right into our Nissen hut at the bewitching hour of midnight.

The flying progressed well; it took all my concentration, but I tried hard and enjoyed all aspects of it. Solo cross-country flights gave me satisfaction – it was good to fly up to the north of England, for example, and sometimes land at another airfield; some days we flew for six hours or more. One week was spent at a beam approach course at a nearby airfield, to improve and develop our instrument flying ability. As well as flying many hours in a short time, we did regular periods in the 'link' trainer, which teaches flying by instruments when the ground is not visible.

Some of us were then posted to another AFU at Ramsbury, near Marlborough, and big news greeted three of us there: Flying Officers Burfield and Vickers, both Aussies, and myself were told that we would be tested in a decompression chamber for selection to a PRU – a photographic reconnaissance unit – although at the time these letters did not mean much to me. This unit was based at Benson, between Oxford and Reading, and pilots there flew Spitfires or Mosquitos. This news put me in a whirl: was that what I wanted? What about my flying boats?

My flight commander, Flight Lieutenant Simon Templer, was a real 'gen man' – meaning that he was full of good information, and had a friendly attitude – so I approached him to ask for some advice and guidance. He had completed an ops tour flying Lysander aircraft at night to make landings in France, where they took in and brought out secret agents: a risky business. He thought PRU was 'the tops' in the RAF, and had applied several times to be posted there – and was surprised that Joe Burfield, Harold Vickers and myself had received the posting. Apparently up until that time all aircrew accepted at Benson had already completed at least one tour of ops in some other command. In a confidential gesture Simon showed me a summary of his report on me, which read: 'Good average. Very keen and intelligent pilot. Character and leadership = 90%.' I decided not to quibble with the posting. Many months later, Simon –'The Saint' – did manage to have himself posted to Benson, where he went to 540 Mosquito Squadron, and became a good friend. At a later date he received the same decorations that were given to me.

TEST CARRIED OUT AT R.A.F. ABINGDON.

MOBILE DECOMPRESSION CHAMBER.   (Ref:- M.D.C./1/15.)

STATION. R.A.F. RAMSBURY.

UNIT.... 15. P.A.F.U.

DATE... 28th JULY 1943.

RANK...... P/O.

NAME... FOSTER. R.H.

AGE...... 21.

NUMBER 47. 421695.

COURSE.

This Subject:-
Witnessed a demonstration of the
effects of Anoxia at high altitude.

Was rendered Anoxic at high altitude.

Was subject to an altitude of over
30,000 feet for... 120 ....minutes
Maximum height attained.. 32000 ..feet
                        and

Was entirely unaffected. ✓

Developed severe "Bends" necessitating
descent.

Suffered the effects of Gas expansion
in the bowels necessitating descent.

Suffered mild "Bends" which did not
necessitate descent.

Suffered mild Gas expansion which
did not necessitate descent.

Descended at an average rate of 3,000...
feet per minute without Ear of Sinus trouble

At more rapid rates of descent he had
difficulty with his Ears and Sinuses
apparently due to:-

Lack of skill in opening Eustachian tubes

Transient organic cause

Permanent organic cause

OBSERVATIONS.

.... This officer
experienced no difficulty
and is such passes
the P.R.U. Test.

[signature] Lt.
Medical Officer
i/c
MOBILE DECOMPRESSION CHAMBER.

Decompression test for PRU at Abingdon, 28 July 1943.

We three had our decompression tests at Abingdon, and these confirmed
our suitability and fitness to fly at maximum altitudes. We had all trained on
twin-engines, and guessed that we would be on Mosquitos, which turned
out to be correct. Although we did not realize it at the time, we should have
been well satisfied to have been chosen to pilot this thoroughbred of an
aircraft. Mosquitos were to earn renown as being by far the most versatile
military aircraft of the war, and possibly of all time; and they were the only
British-built, fully operational aircraft to be designed and produced between
the declaration of war in 1939 and the ceasefire in 1945.

The first Mosquito flew operationally on 17 September 1941, in a PRU
flight over Brest, on the French Atlantic coast. During the war, 125 RAF
squadrons flew the Mosquito in all commands, and 7,700 were built. Group

Captain John ('Cat's Eyes') Cunningham, CBE, DSO and two bars, DFC and bar, AE, DL, has written: 'The de Havilland Mosquito was the most outstanding aircraft developed during the Second World War.'

After clearance from Ramsbury we had a day in London before travelling overnight by train to Aberdeen; there was just time for a hair trim, a shave and a meal in the 'Granite City' of Scotland, and then the last stage by Station Transport out to Dyce RAF Station. From London, the trip had taken nearly twenty-four hours.

While we unloaded our piles of baggage, a Mosquito flying overhead took our attention – it was the first one we'd seen. It had one engine feathered: 'Flying on only one engine,' we said admiringly to one another. But a few seconds later it crashed on the runway, burst into flames, and the pilot was killed. No wonder my mind turned to flying boats again.

Both Station and mess were attractive, and it was great to feel that this was going to be my home for a reasonable period; the OTU course lasted eight weeks, as it worked out. My single room was fitted with bed, dresser, washstand, easy chair, stove, shelves, table, wardrobe, a reading lamp and two mats: excellent! The pushbike issued to me was number 544, and it was a strange coincidence that the same number later became important to me: on arrival at Benson I was attached to the second Mosquito Squadron, No. 544.

Filling in forms always occupied part of the first day at a new station, and following this we met the Chief Ground Instructor and the Chief Flying Instructor, the latter with a DSO. We were told that this was an individualist's job, which pleased me. My flying instructor wore the DFC ribbon, and was a nonchalant character; he had just finished a tour on Benson Mossies, and was showing a decided nervous twitch. Instructing, he made it plain to me, was not his cup of tea, and he would not be doing too much 'instructing'; in his book it was for me to do a lot of 'learning'. Parachutes, dinghies and Mae West life jackets were issued. Meals here were the best I had enjoyed in Britain, politely and pleasantly served, and mess rules dictated that we should change from our normal day wear of battledress, to full uniform for dinner. All of this suited me well.

On the airfield one particular open hangar attracted my attention, because inside were a Tiger Moth, a Cessna Crane (on which we had learned to fly twin-engines in Canada), an Airspeed Oxford that we had just been flying, and a de Havilland Mosquito. This was an unlikely quartet, and would probably not be seen together at any other airfield – but the combination seemed a good omen to me at that stage of my flying, because prior to arriving at Dyce I had had eighty pilot hours flying Tiger Moths in New Zealand, 150 hours in Canada on Cessnas, and fifty-six hours in the UK on Oxfords. Here at Dyce my Mosquito hours were to total forty-four, a grand total of 330 hours to prepare me for operational squadron flying.

Studying my logbook these decades later, I was surprised to realize that while at Dyce, I had already flown with sixty-five other men during my training.

The days sped by, with lectures, dinghy drill at the baths, link trainer, organized games (as the subject was cryptically called), and of course, plenty of flying. In our spare time we would hop into Aberdeen where the Caledonian Hotel became our unofficial headquarters, and Scottish girls offered us jolly hospitality. We used to go ice-skating when the bruises were not too bad, and often visited the cinema; amongst the films current then were *Gone with the Wind, Anthony Adverse, The Great Waltz, Colonel Blimp, Yankee Doodle Dandy* and *For Me and My Girl*. One evening in Aberdeen I missed the last bus to Dyce and had to walk the ten miles or so back; as I entered the camp and passed by the guardhouse I was not amused by the corporal of the guard dashing out with an energetic salute and a smirky smile shouting 'Good morning, sir!'. Tired, sore feet and a 3:00am return can try the patience.

Receiving and writing letters was one of my main occupations. As well as family and friends in New Zealand, my correspondence had grown – without any great effort on my part! – to include girls in Wellington, San Francisco, Edmonton, New York and Wiltshire. On camp we played a great deal of snooker and some table tennis.

On 3 September 1943 we attended a rare church parade to commemorate the conclusion of the fourth year of the war. But the Allies were invading Italy at that time, and my diary note asks 'How many more years?'.

The more enjoyable outings were called 'commando afternoons'. One that occupied all the daylight hours and more was known as an 'escape exercise', in which the Scottish Home Guard, liaising with the police, prided themselves that any 'enemy' spy would be caught within hours. On one particular occasion we aircrew were bundled into covered transports in the dark of the early morning, and dropped in pairs at different stages at a radius of 15 miles from the camp. We had no idea at which point of the compass, and the game was to get to the airfield control tower and leave a scrap of paper, which represented a bomb. All this was practice for a sojurn in Germany or occupied Europe, and certainly for me, it was no trouble to enter into the spirit of this sort of thing.

No holds were barred. We could commandeer citizens' bicycles, but were not permitted to converse in any language with anyone. It was a real challenge. With my Kiwi 'outdoors' background, and fired by growing hunger, I and my navigator threw ourselves into the challenge with intensity. Suffice it to say we were apprehended after a heart-stopping chase when only a mile or two short of the airfield, in the gathering dusk. My battledress was ruined, but by a stroke of good fortune – together with the popularity of Kiwi airmen with most Waafs – I managed to obtain a new issue at no cost from the clothing stores. We had forded rivers, hidden in railway coal wagons, stolen bikes, unintentionally frightened little schoolgirls, and run many of the Home Guard off their feet before we submitted to capture. It gives me a good smile now to picture the middle-aged gamekeepers of the Home Guard who eventually nabbed us. They clung to our arms to support themselves, and all four of us were so exhausted that we were quite unable to utter a word between us for what seemed a long time. Eventually we did manage to exchange compliments.

Learning to fly a Mosquito, at that time the fastest-flying piston-engined aircraft at its optimum altitude, was exhilarating for me. During the two and a half years that I flew Mosquitos, I flew nearly every 'mark' built, from Mark 1 to Mark 32; the machine in which my navigator and myself flew our first trip together was a Mark 1, No. 4059, the ninth Mossie constructed. My instructor at Dyce had a slight stutter, and after a few dual hours he said to me: 'If you w-w-want to g-g-go and k-k-kill yourself, off you g-go!' – or words to that effect.

So I went – for my first solo, that is. It was only for twenty-five minutes, but such is the cruising speed of the Mosquito that I soon found myself racing up the east coast of Scotland and out over the North Sea. Back in New Zealand when taking the medicals required to enter the air force I had been super fit, but because I was in such a keyed-up state wanting to pass, my nerves had made my pulse far too rapid. The army doctor pointed to propaganda posters on the wall, which questioned and admonished 'Can *you* control 3,000 wild horses?' (referring to the horsepower of aircraft engines), and 'Beware of the Hun in the sun!' He said to me, 'What will *you* be like with your fast pulse?' And all I could say was, I hadn't the slightest idea. So when the Mosquito was again heading south towards Dyce, I held the control column with my knees and proceeded to take my pulse: and it was good, plodding on serenely – even the landing was OK.

About half way through the course, a bunch of navigators turned up. At that stage of the war, instead of wearing the letter 'N' in their half wing, these fellows had 'O', for observer – like the new pilots, they had been more broadly trained and specially chosen for long-range PRU, and it was my hope to be matched with someone friendly and capable. All but one were sergeants. Francis Harold Moseley became my steadfast crew, companion and life-long friend. Frank was a sturdily built English gentleman of the highest order, with flaxen hair and moustache in striking contrast with his steady blue eyes, and an appearance and calm casual manner that never failed to inspire me with confidence. My diary reminds me that crewing up with Frank gave me a good feeling. He was a year older than I, married to a Wren, with his nest in Coventry. Years later Frank confided in me that while observers and pilots were mutually summing each other up, he looked at me and thought: 'How can that Kiwi be old enough to be a commissioned

YEAR 1943		AIRCRAFT		PILOT, OR 1ST PILOT	2ND PILOT, PUPIL, OR PASSENGER	DUTY (INCLUDING RESULTS AND REMARKS)	SINGLE-ENGINE AIRCRAFT					MULTI-ENGINE AIRCRAFT							INSTR/CLOUD FLYING
							DAY		NIGHT			DAY		NIGHT					
MONTH	DATE	Type	No.				Dual (1)	Pilot (2)	Dual (3)	Pilot (4)	Dual (5)	1st Pilot (6)	2nd Pilot (7)	Dual (8)	1st Pilot (9)	2nd Pilot (10)	(11)	Dual (12)	Pilot (13)
—	—	—	—	—	—	TOTALS BROUGHT FORWARD	37·05	19·65	2·40	·20	100·50	86·60	3·10	7·45	3·20	—	86·00	46·00	2·55
		NO. 8 (COASTAL) O.T.U.— DYCE — ABERDEENSHIRE — SCOTLAND.																	
AUG.	6	MOSQUITO III	873	W/C YOUNG. D.F.C AND BAR	SELF	DUAL DEMONSTRATION.					·40								
AUG.	8	MOSQUITO III	873	W/C YOUNG.	SELF	DUAL					·40								
AUG.	19	MOSQUITO III	861	F/O STEWART. D.F.C	SELF	DUAL					1·40								
AUG.	21	MOSQUITO III	861	F/O STEWART	SELF	DUAL					1·05								
AUG.	23	MOSQUITO III	898	F/O STEWART	SELF	DUAL					·45								
AUG.	23	MOSQUITO III	898	F/O STEWART	SELF	DUAL					1·00								
AUG.	23	MOSQUITO III	898	F/O STEWART	SELF	DUAL					1·00								
AUG.	27	MOSQUITO III	898	F/LT. VANDAMM.	SELF	DUAL CHECK					1·30								
AUG.	27	MOSQUITO III	262	SELF		FIRST SOLO					·30	·25							
AUG.	27	MOSQUITO III	262	SELF		LOCAL FLYING						·45							
AUG.	31	MOSQUITO I	4059	SELF	SGT. F.MOSELEY.	CROSS COUNTRY (2000').													

SUMMARY FOR MONTH OF AUGUST - 1943.
UNIT : NO. 8(C) O.T.U.   TYPE : MOSQUITO
DATE : 31/8/43.   J.H. *
SIGNATURE : *

O.C. 'C' FLIGHT.

SEPT.	2	MOSQUITO I	4059	SELF	—	LOCAL FLYING													
SEPT.	2	MOSQUITO IV	538	SELF	SGT. MOSELEY	CROSS COUNTRY (25,000').													
SEPT.	4	MOSQUITO IV	699	SELF	SGT.MOSELEY	LOCAL FLYING													
SEPT.	8	MOSQUITO IV	280	SELF	SGT. MOSELEY	LOCAL PHOTOGRAPHY (~)													
						GRAND TOTAL [Cols. (1) to (10)] 302 Hrs. 25 Mins.								8·20		8·00			
						TOTALS CARRIED FORWARD								8·20		8·00			

MOSQUITO AIRCRAFT UNDERCARRIAGE DRILL

You can have sure that your undercarriage is down and locked by:-

(a) MOVING UP-LOCK COCKPIT LIGHTS ARE GREEN.

(b) MOVING THAT THEM DOES NOT SOUND WHEN YOU THROTTLE BACK.

IF YOU ARE UNDERCARRIAGE WHETHER UNDERCARRIAGE IS DOWN, RETURN UNDERCARRIAGE LEVER TO NEUTRAL AND PUSH EMERGENCY SELECTOR DOWN, AND PUMP UNTIL A STRONG RESISTANCE IS FELT.

NOTE: (1) THIS WILL NOT LOWER THE TAIL WHEEL.
(2) IT TAKES APPROXIMATELY FOUR MINUTES TO PUMP DOWN THE UNDERCARRIAGE WITH THE HAND PUMP.

THEN MOVE EMERGENCY LEVER UP AGAIN.

THEN USING THE HAND PUMP (a) SELECT FLAPS DOWN AND PUMP DOWN THE FLAPS.
(b) SELECT UNDERCARRIAGE DOWN, AND PUMP TAIL WHEEL DOWN.

N.B. IT IS IMPORTANT TO OPERATE THE EMERGENCY SYSTEM IN THE ABOVE ORDER. FAILURE OF UNDERCARRIAGE TO LOWER BY ENGINE POWER PROBABLY MEANS A LEAK IN THE HYDRAULIC SYSTEM, AND USING THE HAND PUMP IN SUCH CIRCUMSTANCES WILL MERELY WASTE THE FLUID.

Logbook 27 August 1943, showing my first solo flight in a Mosquito, at No. 8 (Coastal) AFU Dyce, Scotland. Note the signature of Fl/Lt Vandamm of the *Windmill*. Also note Mosquito No. 4059, the ninth one built – Frank is a sergeant.

pilot? He looks young enough to be a schoolboy!' Ah – happy days! It is my sad duty to record that dear Frank died in Coventry on 6 April 2001, at the age of eighty.

When we teamed up together, my flying hours totalled about 300, and Frank had about 275, which was a lot for his job. Our first few trips at high altitude were on the casual side, and it seemed to me that not much instruction was ever received – it was rather left to us to experiment with oxygen, high-level navigation and photography. Nevertheless, for whatever reason, we did all right. Both of us were exceptionally keen, and because I was so determined to excel, and well prompted by the instincts of self-preservation, I spent hours in the Intelligence Library, the Tactical Library, and talking to those officers in the mess who had already flown on PRU operations. They were all very ho-hum about it.

One of our 'cross-country' flights took us up to the Orkneys and the Shetlands, but the British fleet anchored there in Scapa Flow gave me such a fright that I turned back and left well alone. Next we sat exams in the subjects we had been studying. Ship recognition, signals and Aldis lamp tests all appealed to my maritime instincts, but the weather had adversely affected our flying hours and we did not know when the course would finish. Although we did know we would be posted to Benson, it was not clear whether we would stay there for operations over Europe, or be sent out to India to cover the Japanese scene of warfare.

Without much notice we were told that we were 'trained'. A departure date to Benson was fixed, but as Benson accommodation was temporarily full, a few days of leave were granted to us. My diary comments: 'What amateurs!'

Since even before the outbreak of war, RAF Station Benson had been developing into an outstanding top-level unit, and its activities became vital to the overall effort of winning the war in Europe. HM King George VI and HRH the Duke of Kent had already visited it during this war, and in my stay there Lord Trenchard, Marshal of the Royal Air Force, and known as 'the Father of the RAF', paid us a visit. Less welcome visitors were German aircraft that attacked the airfield on a number of occasions.

Benson had been the home of the King's Flight, and later the Queen's Flight, and as such it was responsible for providing the royal family with air transport – and for teaching some of them to fly. . . . And back in 1943 a couple of novices were about to be let loose from within its perimeters. . . .

3

At Last! Europe in our Sights

In ranks and squadrons and right form of war.
William Shakespeare

Ops Nos 1 & 2, 25 & 29 November 1943

On 6 October 1943, I and my Aussie cobbers Joe and Vic, together with our sergeant navigators, arrived at Benson RAF station, and the next day received the 'pukka gen': we were posted to a newly formed Mosquito squadron, No. 544, for operations over Europe. The first practical step towards operations was a daily issue of a glass of milk and a vitamin B pill – at mealtimes this would surely identify us as 'operational types', at least embryo.

A newcomer to this peacetime station could not fail to be well impressed, its officers' mess an attractive brick building covered with Virginia creeper and surrounded by immaculate lawns and flower gardens. Driving up to the front entrance of the mess was a surprise in itself, as the number and quality of the cars parked there certainly did not reflect the austerity of wartime. Operational aircrew could own cars, because they had the privilege of being issued with a ration of petrol coupons. By custom the better cars parked at the front, while the others, like mine, parked at the back near the kitchen and boiler house; thus near the front entrance one could see a Rolls, a Bentley or two, an Alvis, a Morgan and several MG coupés. This was certainly a place for individualists, and for their vehicles.

Once inside the mess, especially if one was accustomed to visiting Air Force messes, the first and most striking impression was of the unusually large number of men wearing ribbons of the DSO and DFC: Freddie Ball, George Singlehurst, Tim Fairhurst, Dicky Blyth and Frank Dodd are the names of a few of these outstanding pilots. Frank Dodd, the flight commander of our 'A' Flight, had a famous career in the RAF, rising to the rank of air vice-marshal and earning the DSO, DFC and AFC and two bars. As well as two Spitfire and two Mosquito squadrons, this airfield also accommodated the headquarters of an entire group, No. 106, PRU, under Coastal Command. The station CO, instead of holding the rank of group captain, was an air commodore, and was therefore our AOC; the man in charge at the time of my arrival was John Boothman, a former winner of the Schneider Cup for Britain. He later became Sir John, and rose to the rank of air chief marshal, heading Coastal Command. Our men in charge of squadrons were wing commanders in rank, while our flight commanders held the rank of squadron leader. Conversely men who, before coming to Benson, had held a higher rank, often voluntarily dropped a rank or two so as to fit into the scheme of things. An example of this latter case is the man who was later in charge of my flight, Lord David Douglas-Hamilton. He had been a wing commander when leading 603 ('City of Edinburgh') Squadron of Spitfires during the defence of Malta, but dropped his rank two notches to flight lieutenant in order to join our squadron. On his promotion to flight commander, he rose in rank again to squadron leader. His older brother, Lord Malcolm, a wing commander, was the CO of the other Mossie squadron, No. 540.

The leaders of the Spitfire squadrons and their flights were outstanding men, experienced, brave, humble, and all real characters in their own ways. I looked up to them, and wondered how Frank and I would fit in to this expert and illustrious company. Our 544 Squadron, still in the early stage of its formation, had John Merifield as its CO; in Professor R. V. Jones' *Most Secret War* he is described as 'the best Mossie pilot in the Air Force', and the man who, after the war, 'for many years held the transatlantic crossing record of, I think, five hours and forty minutes'. In the same book Professor Jones refers to Geoffrey Tuttle who commanded PRU in 1941. He comments that Squadron Leader Tuttle, DFC, later to become Sir Geoffrey and an air marshal, 'set a splendid example, and . . . was able to call on the most able pilots in the RAF to join his unit'.

During my tour of ops I was happily eating my lunch in the mess one day when the 'Spit' squadron commanders and flight commanders suddenly burst into the dining room, clutching pints of beer and in riotous mood, even though it was still only near midday. The occasion was the unexpected arrival of the most dashing and exuberant character that I ever observed during the whole course of the war: the very presence of Wing Commander Adrian Warburton created an electric atmosphere. His reputation had been built in the Middle East and Malta, where although a PRU pilot, he had still managed to shoot down many enemy aircraft. The Americans gave him their DFC. Lord Tedder, Marshal of the RAF and Eisenhower's deputy, described him as the 'most valuable pilot in the RAF'; he flew nearly 400 ops, and was awarded the DSO twice, and the DFC three times.

I will never forget the impression Warburton made on me, sitting at the next table. A bowl of vitamin pills was on his table, and he scooped up a small handful and chucked them into his mashed potato; with huge laughter all round, he then gobbled the lot, washing it down with his pint of bitter. Later in the war, this buccaneer from the skies disappeared in mysterious fashion, having taken off on 12 April 1944 in an American Lightning twin-boom aircraft from Mount Farm airfield, very close to Benson. Much research was carried out post-war to try and fathom what had happened. Then about two years ago the remains of Adrian Warburton and his identified aircraft were discovered in southern Germany; they were removed to England where an official RAF funeral has finally honoured this remarkable English hero. The facts of his life read like exaggerated fiction, and I can only guess that he was the right man in the right job at the right time. . . . To see our 'gen' men paying him homage was a rare experience.

Information given us at Benson indicated that more than 80 per cent of all intelligence during the 1939–45 war came from aerial reconnaissance. Summaries for the 1914–18 war show that the RAF began that war with sixty-three aircraft, and had 22,500 by its end. Although it was 1915 before aircraft commenced taking photos from the air, it was estimated that aerial photos during World War I gathered 66 per cent of all intelligence.

Our squadron in its early days consisted of only a handful of crews, but it was still divided into two flights: I went to 'B' Flight, and Joe and Vic to 'A' Flight. A new squadron crest was chosen that pictured a soaring albatross, with the motto 'Quaero', meaning 'I seek', or 'search out'. It appealed to me: I was ready and willing, and hoped to be able – and secretly, I also believed I was a 'seeker'.

Squadron Leader Bill Aston commanded 'B' Flight. His navigator, Felix Fielding, sported what must have been the longest and most untidy moustache in the whole Air Force. Fellows used to watch him when he donned his flying helmet, and would ask him where he put all that hair on his upper lip – and a demonstration would follow, of how he folded it up in zigzag fashion until it did not project outside his oxygen mask; though when he landed a few hours later, it used to have kinks in it for a while. Without kinks, if you were walking along behind him the famous moustache could be seen sticking out on each side.

Bill and Felix pioneered flying photographic operations at night using the most powerful lighting methods, a practice that made the exercise dangerous in the extreme. Three months later they failed to return from a night op.: Felix was killed, but Bill became a POW and was awarded a DFC. These many decades later, Frank showed me a report describing Bill's aviation exploits after the war; he has clocked up a huge total of flying hours, and is one of the few, to my knowledge, who has defied the conclusion that I sadly, but accurately, came to in those early 1940s – that there was no future in flying (applying to people who follow flying as a career). Some sage and venerable pilot once declared: 'One can be a bold pilot, and one can be an old pilot; but one cannot be a bold *and* an old pilot!'

Most unhappily my observations did indicate that many did not last the

The 544 Squadron crest: 'Quaero', meaning 'I seek'.

distance. Another notable exception to this maxim, and whom it is a pleasure to mention, is Larry Siegert who most kindly agreed to write the 'Foreword' to this book. Air Vice-Marshal Siegert, a pilot with a record second to none, retired after serving in the RNZAF for thirty-seven years, and is one of the longest-serving members in the history of the New Zealand armed forces. But an example to the contrary was Wing Commander Donald W. Steventon, who later became my CO, of No. 544 Squadron. He was a most distinguished officer and pilot, pre-war trained at Cranwell, and many times decorated. When my posting from 544 Squadron came through just before the end of the war, Steve had been awarded the DSO and bar, the DFC and bar, and the American DFC. He took the strain of sending out hundreds of sorties, as well as doing more than his share of the dicey trips.

Five or six years after the war, when visiting Britain, I called at the Air Ministry to search out some comrades; once 'vetted' there, I was over-whelmed by the service and courtesy offered to me. In answer to my query as to where Steve was stationed these days, the reply came: 'He was one of our finest young officers; but I am sorry to have to tell you that he ejected from a jet fighter just recently, but he was too low, and he was killed. He was due to be married.' So many of those whom I considered to be far better pilots than I ever was, did not complete their circuit.

Those early days at Benson were disjointed and casual; no doubt our superiors wondered, as we did, how this little intake of inexperienced crews, even including a couple of rough Aussies and a quiet Kiwi, were going to fit into the routine. We enjoyed a squash court and table-tennis facilities, and at times the gymnasium became the scene for highly strenuous activities, and these, combined with endless rough-and-tumbles in the crewroom, kept us fit. In the evenings a fine theatre-cum-cinema on the station was a pleasant asset, and our mess had an admirable billiard room.

There were no parades for us to attend, and apart from occasional days as duty officer, there were no bounds or restrictions on us. In theory we had a week off the station every six weeks, but when the pressures of D-Day came along, this was abandoned. On the one hand, our days passed with keeping fit, and keeping clear of too much mischief, while on the other hand we had to be instantly ready for an ops trip. The crew-room had a 'tennis ladder' arrangement whereby the top listed crew did the next trip, and then their names dropped to the bottom of the ladder, and they could afford to relax for a few days. However, pressures overtook this comfortable system, and conditions reached the point where the number of serviceable aircraft determined how many trips went out each day; on many days, all fit kites and crews became airborne over Europe.

Each of the four squadrons was a complete unit. In the mess we did have the opportunity to fraternize, but any closeness or intimacy occurred within the members of one's own squadron. This grouping did not appear to manifest itself to any marked degree in the Spitfire squadrons; at least with the Mosquito, every pilot had a navigator to make a small team. At the beginning of my tour most of the navigators were sergeants and therefore living in their own mess, and so even the Mossie pilots were often just individuals. But as the months and years passed, navigators tended to obtain their commissions, and thus we then had their company in our mess and our rooms. I had the pleasure of seeing 'my' Frank progress from sergeant to flight sergeant and then to warrant officer, and on being granted a commission he became a pilot officer, and by war-end, a flying officer.

One day in the mess, we spotted 'DDH' who had been on leave, and whom we had not met, although we knew he had been posted to 'B' Flight. He was drinking a beer, leaning on the mantelpiece at one end of the ante-room. Joe and Vic and I eyed him up from a distance down the room. Joe – whose full name was Norman Milton Burfield, although he was invariably known as Joe – was a tall, rangy, craggy man from the outback. He looked a rough diamond, his eyes a sharp blue, with the tell-tale crow's feet of an outdoor man at their corners. A Chips Rafferty type, with the full Australian flow of vocabulary. But over a period of more than two years I came to know he was the finest of men, in character a shining knight. He was married to a pretty Australian girl whose large framed photograph accompanied him on all his moves. Most of the English thought Burfield was uncouth, though they took care not to offend him: he was different from them, and they could not easily or comfortably figure him out. Even so, the senior officers held him in high esteem, and he was the first of our little gang to receive a DFC. In a similar sort of way the English did not know how to easily relate to the aristocracy – namely, DDH.

Vic, the other Aussie, whose full name was Harold Rupert Vickers, was just as stalwart a character as Joe. The three of us strolled up the room and approached Douglas-Hamilton, and Joe said, 'How about shouting us a beer, mate?' At which DDH put down his pint on the mantelpiece, turned towards Joe and put up his hands, adopting the boxing pose. Said he, 'Want to go a round or two for a pound or two, old chap?' This was dramatic stuff, and the whole room focused on the by-play. Everyone knew that DDH had been an Oxford boxing blue, and that he had represented Scotland in the Empire Games at the sport.

But Joe was equal to the occasion. Affecting an upper-crust English accent, he replied, 'I don't mind if I do, sir!' and the two of them shaped up to each other and lightheartedly gave a shadow display of belting each other. It was enormous fun and broke the ice beautifully. All four became good friends: we had no hang-ups, and DDH found it easy to relate to us with our banter and mischief.

Vic was of medium height, deceptively wiry, and handsome with his blond hair, ruddy complexion, and ice-blue eyes. He had already been a captain in the Australian army in the Far East, before transferring to the Air Force. His eldest brother was a founder member of the 'flying doctors'. Vic smoked a lot, and was typically seen leaning against a post or a wall, feet crossed, blowing smoke rings up to the ceiling, probably just waiting for any pretty girls to pass by. 'Nonchalant' describes him, or in modern parlance, 'cool'. During our times on leave, we three occasionally had to use a little force to extract ourselves from an unsavoury situation, and in these circumstances Joe and Vic were the best of companions, and their ability to offer me protection when necessary, and to teach me how to cope, was invaluable. At that time I was about twenty-two, and they were about thirty-one, and men of the world: to them I was a mere boy. We were a good trio – good for one another and, if I may say so, good for Britain.

At intervals every few months our wingco would declare that the squadron would hold 'an aircrew party' on a certain evening, and these occasions were highlights in many ways. We had much fun and drank too much, but the net result formed closer camaraderie and raised morale. In between these parties I made a habit of not drinking alcohol: orange juice suited me well, and that way I was always fit for flying.

It was very good news to find that several new crews were now posted to 544 Squadron: up to this stage we had been a small nucleus. One of the pilots was Flight Sergeant Max Bartley, a New Zealander. He and I had never met, but my brother had crewed for him on his yacht when they sailed races on Auckland harbour before the war: what a small world. But within two months he and his navigator, Don Penman, failed to return from an op: Max was killed, and Penman became a POW. Sometimes we received reports from intelligence sources indicating whether a crew was alive or dead, but more often than not there wasn't even the slightest information: one day a friend might eat his breakfast with you, but at dinner-time you didn't see him – nor ever again. It became my duty and wish to write to Max's mother, and she subsequently kept up a correspondence with me, and sent me welcome parcels of food.

The autumn brought bitter cold weather with conditions that frequently prevented flying, and this became a tedious and anxious period. They packed us off on more leave, and I went to London, only fifty miles down the road, and saw Ivor Novello's show *The Dancing Years* at The Adelphi. Then it was back to the next slice of 544 reality.

The following day our recently appointed squadron CO, Wing Commander Walker, with whom I had only briefly shaken hands, had a dicey-do in which his navigator, Henderson, was killed. Walker then crewed up with a new navigator, Jimmy Crow, an experienced Scot who already had a DFM, and a week or so later they set off on an op. down to the south of France. But they ran into big trouble and had to bale out. The wingco was a well built man, and as pilot he had to wait for his navigator to scramble out first, the cramped confines of the cockpit offering no other options. (At that stage we had never practised baling out by parachute, even while sitting in the aircraft in the hangar.) The navigator got clear, landed, and struck out for 'neutral' Spain by way of the Pyrenees, but poor Walker was jammed in the exit trapdoor of the cockpit and was killed in that position when the kite hit the ground.

Brave French patriots guided Jimmy Crow over the mountains, but the unfriendly and manifestly un-neutral Spanish chucked him into a filthy gaol. British pressure effected his release, and in due course he arrived back at Benson via the Navy from Gibraltar. While he was convalescing, Air Ministry sent him round operational stations where he gave lectures to the personnel there concerning what to do and what to avoid should they ever have to try getting back to Britain from the Continent.

Jimmy was then once again crewed up with another pilot on our squadron; but twelve months after his experience in Spain he was killed on ops – and this, too, was a sorry tale. His pilot was called Olson, and he was the only other New Zealand pilot, apart from Max, to come to either 544 or 540 in my time; he had already completed a tour of operations and earned a DFC in some other command of the RAF. At the end of 1944 when the war in Europe was only a few months from its conclusion, this crew was shot down over north Germany; the two men baled out. The pilot landed in a haystack with a broken leg, and then could only watch as poor Jimmy was attacked by farm workers and killed. What an expression: 'The Fortunes of War!'

Squadron Leader Steventon next commanded our squadron. He was a 'gen' man, having completed tours on PRU Spitfires, and he held his position until the end of the war, which at least gave us a feeling of some stability and continuity. His promotion to wing commander soon came through. The day after Steve took charge we were told that an op. was scheduled for us the following morning. It wasn't the done thing, but I invited Frank to my room for the evening and we spent a profitable three hours organizing ourselves. Usually we would have an idea that we were due a trip in a day or two, and it would be confirmed the afternoon before.

When we received instructions about any trip scheduled for the following day, a time was given for take-off which was worked out so that the aircraft was over the target area at a particular time of the day. From that information the cameras were prepared and set precisely for the anticipated conditions over the targets, and from this it was worked out at exactly what time we would need an early morning call. Two service policemen, one usually a sergeant, would stamp along the long corridors of our mess at the agreed hour and, book in hand, stop at our door. Knock! Knock! And in they would march: 'Good morning sir, six o'clock, please sign.' I would struggle awake, and sign to the effect that I had been woken up, and enter the time. With the help of a little bribery in the shape of a large slice of home-made fruit cake, sent to me frequently from my homeland, I organized a system whereby these two worthies came back to my room after a further ten minutes and made sure I was out of bed!

Early breakfast was at 6:15am, but the officers' mess was not open for meals at such an early hour, and all pre-op meals were therefore served in the airmen's mess. A real egg or two was the attraction at these early breakfasts, though sadly my stomach did not welcome a big fried meal at that stage of the day; however, being a good Kiwi I forced it down. But not too much to drink – that was a trap for young players. In theory, in a Mosquito the pilot could fish out from under his seat a funnel attached to a flexible tube, and if he could fight his way past the seat harness and his parachute straps – we sat on our 'chutes – and then unbutton his fly, he could relieve himself. On one urgent occasion I did try this impractical system, but the funnel could not be brought close enough, and the liquid went on the cockpit floor. There it froze solid, and the problem appeared to be over. However, on descending to land, the warmer temperatures melted the frozen liquid, and the pilot was decidedly unpopular with the groundcrew. From then on I endured the trips of six hours or so, and put up with the stress and strain. . . . So only one cup of tea at breakfast. . . .

After breakfast Frank and I hurried off to the operations' room for briefing, and were all set to crack off at 8:15am, which was 'first light' at the end of November. A postponement for one hour, but then off we climbed to the south England coast. Good so far, though our instructions were to abort the sortie if we made condensation trails at 22,000ft or less. And sadly we did, so full of disappointment, back we flew to base. It was a relief to learn that two experienced crews from 540 Squadron had also returned for the same reason.

Undaunted, Steve detailed seven crews to fly a long cross-country exercise around Britain. When over northern Scotland we had serious engine problems, and much as I hated not going back to base, I decided not to take an unnecessary risk, and landed at Leuchars in Fifeshire. And here I was much relieved to find DDH, who had experienced the same fuel supply problems as ourselves; in fact he was having high tea in the Leuchars' mess by the time I caught up with him. It made me feel much better to see that he had made the same decisions.

In fact when we returned to Benson the next day we learned that four of the seven aircraft had not got back to base the previous day. To cap it all, Joe and his young Scottish navigator, Alec Barron, had lost both their engines and had had to bale out over Loch Ness. Joe said the water had looked softer, though he landed on *terra firma*. Well, that proved it could be done successfully, which was great – especially as Joe was a big, broad fellow. He did make us laugh: when he and Alec had to bale out, he had said to Alec, 'Beat it, my wee mannie!'; apparently Alec had replied, 'I don't think I want to go, Joe!' – at which point Joe's unspoken answer was to place a large, strong hand on Alec's head and give him a suitable push down through the hole. His farewell was, 'Bye-bye, my wee mannie!'

During that period we had a great deal of trouble with fuel of inferior octane, which caused the Rolls-Royce Merlin engines to cut out. It was unpleasant and occurred without warning, and Mosquitos were lost because of this fault. At Benson a conference was held to discuss the troubles, and we completed lengthy reports. To indicate the wild swings within our daily lives, I see that after the meeting some of us repaired to the Riverside Café for the luxury of real eggs and bacon. We then became ensconced in a room occupied by Waaf motor transport drivers, where we sang and had our fortunes told. After that there was high tea, and the evening wound up with a mess dance.

On 29 November 1943 Frank and I completed our first successful op., a trip to the French Mediterranean coast; it was my first look at the Riviera, and a worthwhile introduction to the Continent. We flew over 10/10s cloud for 700 miles on the way out, but on the return trip had a clear view of Paris: Europe at last, six months after landing in England, and twenty months since first entering camp.

One incident is amusing, in hindsight. Somewhere over France we spotted a formation of aircraft many thousands of feet below us, probably a training flight with no idea of, or concern regarding our presence. My reaction was to ask Frank to turn up the small steel panel that hinged at the top of the back of the pilot's seat, the theory being that this metal would deflect bullets or shrapnel and prevent the pilot from being decapitated. In reality, however, those training aircraft probably could not climb much above 10,000ft, while we were cruising along at about 25,000ft. But at least I had read the instructions, and now felt better prepared for the worst. Our trip covered all targets, and the job was removed from the programme; a diary entry noted that 'Frank did a fine job!'. I now had a total of 6hr 25min operational hours.

The next day a new crew on 544, Flight Lieutenant Pilcher and Flying Officer Robbins, were killed on their first op. – their plane crashed near the English coast on the outward trip, only thirty minutes after take-off. This was just the time when we would usually climb up to operational altitude. Fire did not destroy the Mosquito when it hit the ground, and the investigators found a simple explanation: the oxygen supply had not been turned on. Just too easy. . . . Regulations stipulated that oxygen should be turned on when an altitude of 10,000ft had been reached. Frank and I never relied on memory alone to follow that rule, but added the item to our cockpit check at the end of the runway before take-off; by that method we were always sucking oxygen for the whole period we were airborne. The supply was more than sufficient for our longest trips, with the exception of a return trip from Moscow.

My diary note that day says: 'Since August, from PRU, I've seen twelve good fellows "go west".'

		Single-Engine Aircraft				Multi-Engine Aircraft						PASSEN-GER	INSTR./CLOUD FLYING [Incl. in Cols. (1) to (10)]	
		DAY		NIGHT		DAY			NIGHT					
		Dual	Pilot	Dual	Pilot	Dual	1st Pilot	2nd Pilot	Dual	1st Pilot	2nd Pilot		Dual	Pilot
		(1)	(2)	(3)	(4)	(5)	(6)	(7)	(8)	(9)	(10)	(11)	(12)	(13)
Totals Brought Forward		37·05	39·55	2·40	·20	108·40	122·05	3·10	7·45	8·20	-	86·00	46·00	2·55
OCT. 9							1·45							
OCT. 16							1·30							
OCT. 23							·30							
(boxed)							3·45							
NOV. 10							3·00							
NOV. 24							2·00							
NOV. 25							1·00							
NOV. 26							2·55							
NOV. 26							1·30							
NOV. 29							5·25							
Totals Carried Forward		37·05	39·55	2·40	·20	108·40	141·40	3·10	7·45	8·20	-	86·00	46·00	2·55

| YEAR 1943 | | Aircraft | | Pilot, or 1st Pilot | 2nd Pilot, Pupil, or Passenger | DUTY (Including Results and Remarks) |
Month	Date	Type	No.			
						Totals Brought Forward
						NO. 544 (P.R.U.) SQUADRON - BENSON OXFORDSHIRE - ENGLAND.
OCT.	9.	MOSQUITO IX	423	SELF	SGT. MOSELEY.	CONSUMPTION TEST.
OCT.	16.	MOSQUITO IX	474	SELF	SGT. MOSELEY.	ALT. AND CAMERA TEST.
OCT.	19-NOV. 7.	ON LOAN TO NO 301 F.T.U. - LYNEHAM - WILTS.				
OCT.	23.	MOSQUITO XIII	400	SELF	SGT. MOSELEY.	FERRYING FROM FILTON.
		(PoW)				SUMMARY FOR MONTH OF OCTOBER. UNIT: 544 SQD. TYPE: MOSQUITO IX XIII DATE: 31.10.1943. SIGNATURE: _____
				B.G. _____ B.Flt.		
				O.C. B FLT. 644 SQD.		
				B.... C.... O/ w/cdr.		
				O.C. 544 SQUADRON.		
NOV.	10.	MOSQUITO IX	246	SELF	SGT. MOSELEY.	CROSS COUNTRY (34,000')
NOV.	24.	MOSQUITO IX	242	SELF	SGT. MOSELEY.	CROSS COUNTRY.
NOV.	25.	MOSQUITO IX	426	SELF	SGT. MOSELEY.	OPS. - D.N.I.O. TRIALS @ 2 WOOD.
NOV.	26.	MOSQUITO IX	426	SELF	SGT. MOSELEY.	X/C - LANDED AT LEUCHARS. MOVING
NOV.	26.	MOSQUITO IX	426	SELF	SGT. MOSELEY.	RETURN FROM LEUCHARS.
NOV.	29.	MOSQUITO IX	247	SELF	SGT. MOSELEY.	OPS - CANNES - 27000' - O.K.
						Totals Carried Forward

GRAND TOTAL [Cols. (1) to (10)] 849 Hrs. 55 Mins.

Logbook, November 1943: Ops Nos 1 and 2.

4

Target Europe – a Typical Sortie

Fierce fiery warriors fought upon the clouds.
William Shakespeare

Op. No. 6, 21 February 1944

Someone calculated that for crews on these tours of operations, the first three trips were five times as dangerous as the average of the later trips, but as skill and experience increased, so did the chances of survival for each trip. No one told me that at the time.

Frank and I duly completed our third, fourth and fifth ops. They were not long trips, about four hours each, though we experienced a few incidents. No. 3 involved a great amount of 10/10ths cloud; on No. 4, down the Rhone valley, we were intercepted by eight aircraft; and on No. 5 we were close to five trails, but surprisingly never saw the aircraft making the trails. On our return to base it was necessary to make a W/T descent through cloud.

Foster and Moseley were allocated the call sign 'Filter 77'; Benson's call sign was 'Gingerwine'. We maintained radio silence when setting out and while over enemy territory, but on return to the English coast – and what a great sight that was, when it was visible – we would call up an RAF base on the south coast and report an ETA at Benson. Often it was convenient to speak to 'Bluefrock', which was Manston on the east Kent coast. The main reason we liked using 'Bluefrock' was because the Waaf who answered us had a perfectly charming English voice, and her calm and efficient manner gave us a wave of confidence and relief. The battle to get home seemed all worthwhile. Small things can matter, and do linger.

Only once did we try to obtain a course to steer to reach England and Benson while we were still over Europe; we had been in and over cloud from mid-Europe onwards, having been chased about by fighters, and fuel was low. Even a good guess might not have told us which country we were over. I called up 'Gingerwine' and a man replied in good English, but he gave us a course, using all the proper procedures, that would have taken us down towards the Bay of Biscay and off to oblivion.

I ended that call swiftly: it was a German interception, and apart from the fact that I knew the course given to us was wildly incorrect, it was just as well that I knew all the men in our control tower, and their voices. But the episode gave us a strange feeling, and I lost the urge ever to try again. Our Intelligence told us that the Germans knew the names and ranks and some details of all Benson aircrew: they knew 'Filter 77', and in the event of us becoming POWs, would interrogate us accordingly. After that I made all the more effort in the training we were given that taught us how to avoid capture and the risk of being so interrogated.

During those early days on the squadron we attended lectures from Intelligence. We learned about escaping from Europe, and how to handle POW procedure. Down in the hangar, in the evenings, our wingco supervised a series of practice bale-outs. He had us strap ourselves into our seats in a Mosquito, then at a signal, navigator and pilot had to disentangle themselves from R/T cords, oxygen leads and seat harness, before undoing the exit flap on the floor of the cockpit, and hurling themselves in the approved technique down to the hangar floor. Frank and I threw ourselves into this exercise with total effort, shredding elbows of battledress jackets and various parts of our skin in the process. Our best time on the stopwatch was just under sixty seconds for these practice bale-outs, though it seemed an eternity to me.

Further skills to enhance our chances of surviving on ops were flying on instruments, and practising approaches to landings using R/T and W/T aids. Regular hours of 'link' trainer were mandatory.

My second Christmas away from New Zealand came and went. In my diary notes I had speculated 'whether the "Second Front" would shortly be opened', referring to the projected invasion of Europe by the Allies; and in a further entry at the end of 1943 I wondered 'whether the European war will be over in 1944, as most people seem to think'. Sadly the public, and us, were indulging in some wishful thinking!

The months of December, January and February were noted for their frequent and dense fogs. In my Austin 10 drophead coupé it took me four hours one evening to travel 36 miles; I never saw another vehicle on the road, and I couldn't see both edges of the narrow road at the same time. These conditions were reflected in the infrequency of flying. Many times trips were laid on, and then scrubbed. A Canadian crew on 544, Miles and Cawker, did not return from a trip one day, but the following day we heard they had landed OK at Gibraltar, which surprised us. Two more days and they were back in the fold in our crewroom. Frank flew an air-test with Steve, and it was a compliment to me that he confided he felt safer with me than with the wingco. Navigators never did know much about flying, as such.

On 21 February 1944 we flew our sixth op. After our early breakfast in the airmen's mess, the two of us went to the operations' room. This was a 'gen' place that basically we only visited on the occasions of being briefed prior to an op., and de-briefed after it; many of the staff here had held senior positions in their pre-war workplace, and there was an impressive nucleus of highly bright people, including many Waafs, all intelligent and pretty. It gave me a good feeling to be waited on for a short while by a sweet smiling girl. She was probably a sweet-smelling girl, too. I hope they did not keep diaries: how many items did they issue to young men who did not come back? Every trip we were entitled to a ration of boiled sweets and chocolate, and at times I could not resist handing mine back to the girl for the pleasure of seeing her smile. More to the point, we received emergency medical packs, and items to accompany a trip in a rubber dinghy – we were all kitted out with a one-man dinghy.

One day when Frank was feeling a bit bored, he undid one of these survival packs, and opened a packet marked to the effect that it should not be opened until one was in dire straits. It contained some Benzedrine tablets, and he swallowed a couple. For some hours he boasted they had no effect, but he could not get to sleep that night, and was a wreck the next day. We were never quite clear what the illicit experiment proved; nor could we agree on what was meant by 'dire straits'.

The Meteorological Section was quartered adjoining the ops room. The officer, a squadron leader, who was in charge of the Met. was a Czech known as 'Bouncer', which derived from 'a dud cheque (/Czech)' – one that 'bounced'.

To progress with our pre-op. briefing, our targets were detailed to us: they might be airfields, aircraft on the ground, factories, oil installations, railway junctions, ports, ships, secret depots, rocket launchers, dams, rivers, or fields of crops and forests: the list almost endless. Depending on many factors, we might be given ten different targets at various areas and locations en route.

Once we knew our targets, Frank obtained the relevant maps and these we spread out on the floor; they extended for several metres. With a long straight-edge ruler, Frank drew the track for our route, and then calculated the courses to steer, having obtained the met. forecasts for our areas of operations. For this sixth sortie we needed maps of France, Germany, Austria and Czechoslovakia. While Frank worked on the maps, I requested, from the pretty Waafs, packets of currency notes for the countries we would be flying over, plus those nearby such as Belgium and Holland for this particular trip. The money was not the wartime variety, but the pre-war authentic notes for use if one ended up on the ground somewhere in Europe. Needless to say it was signed for, and handed in again after an op.

The latest escape aids were also issued, together with silk maps relating to the territories covered; these maps crumpled up into a tiny space, and were invaluable when you were on the ground trying to escape from one country to the next, and planning the route of return to Britain. The escape aids

Date	Aircraft Type	No.	Pilot or 1st Pilot	2nd Pilot, Pupil or Passenger	Duty (Including Results and Remarks)	SE Day Dual (1)	SE Day Pilot (2)	SE Night Dual (3)	SE Night Pilot (4)	ME Day Dual (5)	ME Day 1st Pilot (6)	ME Day 2nd Pilot (7)	ME Night Dual (8)	ME Night 1st Pilot (9)	ME Night 2nd Pilot (10)	Passenger (11)	Instr/Cloud Dual (12)	Instr/Cloud Pilot (13)
					TOTALS BROUGHT FORWARD	37.05	39.55	2.40	.20	108.40	154.15	3.10	7.45	8.20		86.00	46.00	3.25
JAN 1.	MOSQUITO IX	432	SELF	F/S MOSELEY.	W/T RGH LOCAL.						1.00							
JAN 3.	MOSQUITO IX	432	SELF	F/S MOSELEY.	X/C 32,000'.						2.50							
JAN 10.	MOSQUITO IX	434	SELF	F/S MOSELEY.	AIR TEST. (MT)						1.00							
JAN 14.	MOSQUITO IX	432	SELF	F/S MOSELEY.	OPS - RHONE VALLEY. - INTERCEPTED. L.R.FRANK V/S.						3.40							
JAN 20.	MOSQUITO IX	434	SELF	F/S MOSELEY.	TEST - (I/E W/S).						.20							
JAN 20.	MOSQUITO IX	434	SELF	F/S MOSELEY.	CAMERA AND AIR TEST						1.05							
JAN 23.	MOSQUITO IX	247	SELF	F/S MOSELEY.	Q.G.H. BY W/T. LOCAL.						.55							
JAN 26.	MOSQUITO IX	231	SELF	F/S MOSELEY.	R.G.H. AND 2.2.						.50							
JAN 30.	MOSQUITO IX	247	SELF	F/S MOSELEY.	OPS - FRIEDRICHSHAFEN, RGH-WA (5 TIMES)						4.20							
					SUMMARY FOR MONTH OF JANUARY													
					UNIT: 544 SQD TYPE: MOSQUITO IX	OPER. TO/10 FLYING.					8.00							
					DATE: ...	NON. OPERATION-IN.					8.00							
					SIGNATURE: Ronald Lofthouse F/L.	TOTAL FOR MONTH.					16.00							
FEB 5.	MOSQUITO IX	231	SELF	F/S MOSELEY.	Q.G.H. BY W/T. LOCAL.						1.00							
FEB 15.	MOSQUITO IX	425	SELF	F/S MOSELEY.	TEST.						.50							
FEB 19.	MOSQUITO IX	231	SELF	F/S MOSELEY.	LOCAL - 2.2.						.50							
FEB 20.	MOSQUITO R	242	SELF	F/S MOSELEY.	TEST - HIGH LEVEL.						2.00							
FEB 21.	MOSQUITO IX	432	SELF	F/S MOSELEY.	OVS - REGENSBURG AREA. FLAK (ACCURATE FLAK SPENT SCARE).						5.00							
FEB 24.	MOSQUITO IX	434	SELF	F/S MOSELEY.	TEST - (AIR AND CAMERA).						1.20							
FEB 25.	MOSQUITO IX	231	SELF	F/S MOSELEY.	TEST.						.25							
					TOTALS CARRIED FORWARD	17.06	39.55	2.40	.20	108.40	181.40	3.10	7.46	8.20	–	95.00		

O.C. "B" FLIGHT.

O.C. 544 SQUADRON.

GRAND TOTAL [Cols. (1) to (10)]. 3.3.9 Hrs. 4 0 Mins.

Logbook 21 February 1944, the sixth op. Note that Frank is now a flight sergeant.

were being constantly updated. One was a knife that slipped down a flying boot, sharp enough to cut off the fleecy-lined tops or legs of the boots, leaving you wearing a normal-looking shoe instead of a flying boot. Another was a button containing a compass. As the Germans discovered our tricks, so did our people think up better modifications; it was a serious game of war, and I entered into it with enthusiasm.

While the aircrew were at their briefing, the aircraft allocated for that particular flight would be undergoing its last service checks, and having its cameras installed in its belly. Usually our Mosquitos carried two main cameras, 'F/36s', which took side-by-side photos with an adjustable overlap to obtain a stereo effect. On top of each camera a film magazine was clipped, each of which held 500 exposures. Another camera was also fitted, an 'F/6', that produced a larger print of about nine inches square, and covered a wide and extensive ground area surrounding the actual target. One Mosquito on 544, a fighter mark, had a forward-facing camera for use in very low-level flights; the pilot operated it from a button on the control column. We called this kite *The Dicer*. At times our usual aircraft were also fitted with an 'oblique'-facing camera, an 'F/14', operated by the pilot who sighted it along the port wing when flying close to the ground.

The locker room in our squadron crewroom was the last stop, where we put on our flying boots, and took off our ties and replaced them with a soft silk scarf so our necks did not chafe from the continual head-turning. Why did we turn our heads? A good question with a good answer: the Mosquito, like all aircraft, had a broad blankspot behind and under it, and a clever fighter pilot could sneak up unawares and be firing at you before you knew anyone was near. So every few seconds I swung the tail from side to side, and when he was not lying on his tummy taking photos, Frank knelt on his seat, with his head up in a perspex blister, and looked backwards for fighters. When over Europe it was my responsibility to cover the view to the front. Frank and I developed into such a skilled team that he would give me the course to steer and I would pick out the pinpoints on the ground until we reached the target area. As the months went by and we flew over every country in Europe except Portugal and Greece, we were able to recognize where we were to an astonishing degree of accuracy – provided we could see the ground. When going well into Europe for example, we would decide where we wanted to cross the River Rhine, and I would fly us there without needing to look at any maps before we tackled the next leg.

From our lockers in the crewroom we took our parachutes and inflatable dinghies, donned our Mae West life jackets, collected our helmets with their oxygen masks and microphones, and we were ready. If we were popular with the groundcrew, some fresh-faced erk would dash up and carry the heavy 'chutes and dinghies for us. At the aircraft, parked on the asphalt dispersal area bordered by the well-mown green grass outside our hangar, the flight sergeant in charge of the groundcrew would talk to me about the kite, and comment on its condition or its peculiarities. Our flight commander, and sometimes our wingco, would then say in their 'pukka', clipped English voices: 'Have a good trip, Kiwi!' Two or three close mates were always standing in the background to give a grin and a 'thumbs-up'. The same small, loyal and affectionate crowd would be there when we returned . . . and they would be there if you did not return . . . before they dispersed to their respective messes to have a drink, or two . . . or three.

So you were off: up the aluminium ladder, make yourself comfortable in the intimate cockpit, check the controls and engines after starting up, chocks away and taxi off. One last general wave, and apart from a short burst of chatter on the R/T to clear Gingerwine, nothing existed outside our tiny, crowded, but intense miniature world.

My goal, or a target in every sense, was to arrive at the area where we had to do our work, and my mind was shut off from the return trip, or what I hoped to be doing that evening. It required absolute concentration – no idle chatter with Frank; indeed, I never looked at him, but just spoke quietly – well, most of the time – through the intercom to ask a question or to make a suggestion. We became like two halves of the same robot.

Our ops room gave us the targets, but we had extraordinary latitude as regards making our own decisions as to how we tackled the trip. Thus we determined what altitude was best on the day, and we picked our route, and the order of covering the targets – if Berlin was a target, for example, maybe we aimed for another city not on the same direct route, and then made a sudden swing on to Berlin, possibly arriving there at the end of a long, gentle dive, the idea being to prevent the Germans from having too much notice of where we were aiming. Our job was completed satisfactorily if we returned with good photos of the targets, and how we achieved this didn't worry anyone else. Of course I also took a pride in returning the aircraft in one piece, with the engines not overworked. A vain habit of mine was to return to Benson without requesting any assistance in navigation or any gen on weather conditions. This was silly, no doubt, and risky, but a certain mischievous satisfaction was to be gained from abruptly zooming low, out of the frequent haze or mist, over the 544 hangar before landing.

Climbing to altitude with a full load of fuel took about thirty minutes, and a combination of nerves, the big early breakfast and the constantly changing air pressure caused a non-stop series of belches and other wind-releasing noises to be produced as we did so. At cruising altitude we were over the English coast, and set course towards the targets. We settled down to the job, comfortable enough in our own cramped little world – much the same as going to the office every day, and organizing oneself behind one's desk. The main difference, and the thought, fortunately, never entered my ordered mind at the time, was that there was a far better chance of returning home safely by road or train from the office to read the day's paper after work than there ever was of us getting back at all.

Sometimes the weather was clear, but usually it was hazy. At other times we climbed in thick, bumpy cloud to 30,000ft or higher, and then flew for a couple of hours over cloud. Our met. forecasts were sufficiently accurate nearly all the time that a break in the cloud layers often occurred just when the target area was reached. But there was the occasional trip where 'DNCO' applied, usually because cloud cover completely obscured what we wanted to photograph. Nevertheless, at times on those trips we had secondary targets in other areas that could be covered successfully.

I recall returning from one particular trip and flying through cloud for the best part of a couple of hours; this had necessitated flying on instruments, which takes concentration and energy (our Mosquitos had no 'George', or automatic pilot facilities, and 'hands-on' was the only practice). During this return trip much of the flight in cloud brought a fair amount of turbulence that bounced us about uncomfortably. For about ten minutes I wrestled inwardly with the strong feeling that we were definitely flying left wing low. Had the artificial horizon instrument packed up? Why was I leaning so hard to the left? Eventually the strain and uncertainty forced me to clear my throat and ask Frank as casually as I could: 'Franko, my friend, do you have any feeling we are flying one wing low?' I hated displaying my lack of confidence, and anxiously waited for his reply. 'Funny you should say that Fos, I was just thinking we were a bit right wing low!' Whew, what a relief! All at once I felt perfectly upright and on an even keel. I started humming to myself, and that in itself was abnormal!

A theory of mine concerns another abnormality. Lack of oxygen is a peculiar phenomenon, and signs and symptoms appear which resemble drunkenness. Experiments in the decompression chamber at Benson proved a number of funny things. One cocky Aussie considered he did not succumb to suffering too much from lack of oxygen – or 'lock of axygen', as we joked. The officer-in-charge of the chamber asked him to take off his oxygen mask for a few seconds, and in this process his intercom was disconnected. The rest of us were asked during those few seconds to take off the trousers of our over-confident friend, then his mask was slipped on again and his supply renewed. He did not realize anything was amiss until the instructor, through the intercom, told him his fly was undone, whereupon he looked down and was incredulous to find he was improperly dressed!

We enjoyed the joke, but there was a lot to learn. My theory was that we all suffered to some limited degree when we flew at altitude for hours on end, and were in reality then functioning at a level below par. The only consolation I drew from this was that the enemy fighter pilots were also hopefully not 100 per cent normal when we encountered them at altitude.

Often when Frank and I found ourselves in a mighty tight corner while flying high, I would dig him hard in the ribs with my elbow and shout at him what he should be doing. But this was not my nature, and I surely would not have dreamed of acting like that at a low altitude – so blame lack of oxygen. Every time Frank went down to the nose of the aircraft to operate the cameras, I formed the habit of turning up his oxygen supply to maximum on the gauge. This gave us both a shot of extra confidence, even if it may have been all in the mind.

This sixth trip covered targets mainly in the area of Regensburg, a city on the Danube, in Bavaria. It was winter, and everything was blanketed in snow. The conditions reminded me vaguely of Canada, but it all looked too cold and cheerless for me. Although *The Blue Danube* was one of my favourite pieces of music, the view from six miles above the romantic river showed me a twisty, black strip, accentuated by the stark white banks. Not one glimmer of enthusiasm or a single note of music could I raise.

During our first five trips we had negotiated attacks by fighters; on one early trip it had given us some confidence to outplay *eight* of them in one pack. Now, since the war, on the very few times that I have thought about our encounters with the fighters of the Luftwaffe, I am almost startled to find that I have no recollection of ever receiving any instruction or advice as to how we should deal with enemy Focke-Wulfs and Messerschmitts. Having received so much intensive training on a huge variety of subjects, it seemed to be left to us to figure out for ourselves the problem of facing armed fighters when we carried no weapons: '*Dulce bellum inexpertis.* War is pleasant to those who have not tried it.'

It was taken for granted that in the mess 'the hangar doors were closed', meaning that one did not talk 'shop'; therefore I never heard a conversation on the subject of fighter attacks. In our room, Joe and Vic and I talked about nearly everything under the sun, believe me, a very broad field – but never discussions about attacks, or flak, for that matter; and no lectures from the hierarchy at Benson, either.

In action, the situation and the plan always came to me very clearly; I never had to think it out. Our intention was not to be shot down, nor to be wounded, but at the same time to so manoeuvre ourselves that when the aircraft was not turning and twisting, we were heading somewhere near northwest because England, Home and Beauty were in that direction. The Germans, of course, always wanted to drive us further into Europe. In these circumstances it was pointless studying the instrument panel or the compass, which would have toppled, and be spinning wildly due to the continual severe tight turns – you had to rely on the sun to determine which was the direction for escape, thus also drawing the fighters further away from their bases. If they used up their fuel or their ammunition, then it was their turn for a not very successful sortie.

Up to the time of this sixth sortie we had not encountered heavy flak, but this day was to be our initiation. What a surprise it was, at 32,000ft and in the crisp, clear blue sky with a blinding white landscape below, to suddenly find ourselves enveloped in a large box of black puffs; as I jinked the aircraft away from the centre, my mathematical mind counted more than fifty bursts all close around us. The Mosquito rocked about all over the place. Then hey presto! It was all change, and the puffs turned into one black and bumpy cloud, and we were right in the middle of it before we staggered out and away. It was a surprise that we were not holed, and very pleasing that no more flak came up.

The procedure that Frank and I worked on for photographing the targets was based on close and practised teamwork, together with making sure that we covered each target perfectly on the first run. It was a dodgy-do if the navigator felt we had missed it, or only covered a part of it: if that were the case, then another run was necessary, and the flak guns had two chances at us in the same position, or if there was no flak, then the fighters had more time to climb up to us. For the best of reasons we became fairly expert at completing a quick job.

Ensuring that the target was well and truly covered was one thing; the other was to have a method that we were both confident was the least risky way of going about the job. It was a matter of minimizing the risk from anti-aircraft fire and fighters, and on occasions also taking into account factors such as the quantity of fuel left, with the time and distance to fly back to base. At least we knew that when flak was shot at us, no fighters were about to come on the scene; it was when the flak stopped for no apparent reason that we could then expect fighters to engage us.

The moment we were close to the target I swung the aircraft around so we both snatched one last good look all around us, and particularly below us: we had to be positive no fighters were near us. For my part, I would loosen my seatbelt so that I could stand up as much as the reduced headroom would allow. I stood with feet braced hard against the rudder pedals, and stretched my arms down so my right hand gripped the control column, and my left was handy to the throttles if we needed an extra burst if attacked. In that position, where my head reached halfway into the roof blister, I twisted the aircraft about until both of us were satisfied that we had no close company. I might say that wearing a tight leather helmet and an even tighter-fitting oxygen mask, I ended up limp and sweat sodden (and I now realize that I never, ever asked Frank how he felt!).

Frank was certainly an expert at his job. He would disconnect his oxygen tube, fling himself down on the floor in the nose of the aircraft, and quickly reconnect his oxygen supply into a different socket. In our training days we used a bombsight to line up the run towards and over the target, but on ops we had perfected a much simpler method: parallel white lines were ruled down the perspex panel in the very nose of the Mosquito, and Frank sighted the target between these lines. When he wished me to go left he simply called through the intercom 'Left! Left!', and when we needed to go right, he called 'Right!': like this there was never any doubt as to which way I had to manoeuvre.

The beauty of our system was that it didn't matter whether we were flying 'straight and level' or doing a turn, or even climbing or letting down: as long as Frank could sight the target at a certain angle through his clear panel, he could push the button activating the bank of cameras with confidence, and in this way our time over the targets was minimal. The printouts that were available for us to study the day after a trip showed the Foster-Moseley combination's efforts splattered about at varying angles to right and to left, but it is satisfactory to record that we never missed a target when it was visible – nor did we carry an unwieldy bombsight.

Flying along a straight line such as a railway yard or a dockside took several seconds, and this was long enough for a fighter to be in range. Our defence for that, while Frank was sprawling in the nose, was for me to again loosen my straps, levering my feet hard against the rudder pedals, and with my head halfway into the roof blister, and by screwing it nearly off, I could take a quick glance to each side. And in between photographing one target and then another close by, I would swing the tail about, and by dint of this painful and almost impossible stretching exercise, hope to snatch a glimpse below and behind us.

This taking of photos was a nervy, high-tension business, but by necessity and effort Frank and I became experts, and brought back first class results. I do not recollect ever being fearful: I was 'wound up' to such a degree that I never imagined *not* being able to extricate ourselves from any position in which we might find ourselves. But of course this is only another way of saying that 'it may happen to others, but it won't happen to me!'. Certainly from time to time after landing after a particularly close encounter, it did seem a good idea to hasten to the washroom for a quick shower.

Once our jobs were completed to our satisfaction, the big moment came when we turned for home; and from then on, all my interest and concentration was instantly centred on taking us and our photos back in one piece. This was not always easy, because the enemy knew exactly where we were, and more or less had a good idea of the route we would have to use to return; they could prepare fighters along the way and flak stations could be alerted. Within the bounds of fuel available we therefore had to try to fox them on the way out of the fortress of Europe.

Many times on ops trips we never spotted one aircraft, friend or foe, but several times we witnessed mass bombing by American Flying Fortresses and Liberators. On one occasion we saw 1,000 bombers escorted by hundreds of fighters, all formations being engaged by German fighters or by flak. Our task was to photograph the damage they had done without us becoming the target for fighters, both German and American. Some of these scenes stick in my mind like a nightmare: smoke coming up thousands of feet from the bombing, bombers shot into pieces falling out of the sky, and dozens of parachutes floating down of those who had escaped from their fiery tombs. Each bomber carried a crew of ten men, and they were each and all some mother's son. During Anglo-American 'Big Week' air raids from 20–26 February 1944, including the one on these Regensburg targets, the American losses were 2,600 crewmen either killed in action, seriously wounded, or taken prisoner.

When we leave the continental coast to head back across the Channel, we can afford to let the nose drop and start a gentle let-down towards the English coast; but we don't stop looking for enemy fighters until we have crossed into England. We make a short report on the R/T to a coastal RAF station, that Filter 77 expects to be over Gingerwine in twenty minutes – and then maybe the glimmer of a first smile appears. The pulse is racing a little with happy relief now; a shallow dive over our hangar so they know to have the men handy to unload the camera magazines, and we are down: five hours exactly since being airborne, and about 1,500 miles flown. It is good to see the small welcoming committee, and the personnel ready to transport the camera magazines to the First Phase Interpretation Section.

We report on the aircraft and return to the ops room, where we are debriefed. Here we return the emergency packs and the currency notes, and describe the targets, the enemy action, and anything else of interest. Then to the crewroom to unload our gear, and back to the mess for a special operational meal, and maybe a drink, probably a pint of real orange juice for me. On going to bed that evening, early, at eight o'clock, a slight feeling of satisfied happiness is still with me. Maybe it is predominantly one of pure contentment at simply still being there to climb into my snug little bed with its white sheets for another night. I sleep the clock round till breakfast lures me to the dining room, and get there at the last minute just before the doors are closed.

Two days later Flying Fortress bombers of the USAAF decimate the targets we have photographed: they had been classified as a 'first priority' job.

5
Crew-Room Capers

Some credit in being jolly.
Charles Dickens

Each of the four squadrons at Benson had its own hangar. The extraordinary individuality of the Benson environment is possibly illustrated by the fact that I do not recollect ever having the need or the desire to visit any other hangar than that of 544 Squadron. These large buildings accommodated more than just Mosquitos or Spitfires: workshops and recreational rooms for all the many trades involved in the servicing and maintenance of the aircraft occupied large areas; offices for the squadron CO and the adjutant, as well as store-rooms, were tucked away on mezzanine floors. Aircrew had their crew-room on the ground floor, from where windows looked out to the adjacent tarmac on which the aircraft were dispersed. A further vista brought a long view of take-offs and landings from the runways that were in constant use.

A section of the 544 crew-room was filled with metal cupboards in which pilots and navigators stored their flying gear: a parachute, inflatable dinghy and a Mae West lifejacket took up most of the space in these closets. Helmets fitted with microphones, earphones and oxygen masks hung from hooks. Another part of the set-up was a sparsely furnished lounge, perhaps more accurately described as a waiting room: on one wall a large blackboard listed the crews out on ops that day, with times of take-offs, and ETAs entered. Apart from tables and chairs and heaters, the rest of the space was filled with men – men waiting to fly: perhaps the weather had to clear, or they were waiting for those who were flying to return. I did my share of waiting, on both counts.

During inclement weather, no one ventured outside. On the sunny days, be they balmy or crisp, it was usually the Aussies and the Kiwi who cajoled the others to come outside, away from the smokers' fug, and who found some pretext to wrestle and romp on the grass. At times when the room was packed with fellows playing cards, maybe bridge, maybe poker, and most of them smoking like chimneys, Joe and Vic and I were soon bored and wanting some more strenuous activity. Our plan then was to start to push one another about as if we were arguing amongst the three of us, and more often than not we would pressurize our reluctant navigators to join our mischief – the Aussies would give them no peace until they agreed to join forces with us. As the three or, more probably, the six of us were pretending to wrestle on our feet, we would fall, accidentally on purpose, and tumble into the nearest table of card players, exclaiming 'Oops! Sorry chaps!' as the table, cards, chairs and their occupants crashed over. Naturally enough, this would infuriate the victims, but we were skilled in keeping up the momentum, and in the crash of the next table, we would manipulate things and bodies so that some from the first table were among those falling on to the second one.

From that stage it was only a matter of moments before the entire room was in an uproar, with at least half the company rolling about on the small amount of floor space. Tables and chairs were often broken, and we would then find an item added to our monthly mess bills for 'Damage to crew-room furniture'. It was a small price to pay for such merriment, however – or that's what we thought, anyway. This riotous confusion could well last until lunch- or tea-time, by which stage any number up to about a couple of dozen weary men staggered off to freshen up for the meal. Many had to change their clothes and present their batwomen with some repair-sewing to torn garments. Strangely enough, no higher authority ever appeared on the scene to demand peace and quiet; on the contrary, our self-generated bursts of activity probably dispensed with the need for organized 'physical training'.

Sometimes during these skilfully planned fracas, the adjutant, whose office was directly overhead, would stamp on his floor in an effort to restore law and order beneath. He was a decent fellow, rather elderly in our minds, but a gentle, nervous man who could make no impression on wild characters like big Joe. Yet it was amusing to see the good relationship that developed between these two unlikely types.

When tea-time came along in the mess we were often able to enjoy some surprise delicacies prepared by our attentive kitchen staff during the afternoon. One of my strongest memories of war-time Britain, in England more than Scotland, was of always being hungry. Our antipodean appetites were not easy to satisfy, and as a result of this fact of nature, Joe and Vic and I made no bones about making a reasonable effort on most days to be amongst the first ones to enter the dining room when one of the Waaf waitresses came from the kitchen to unlock the double swing doors.

Now our 'Adj', as the Aussies nicknamed him, was a big, slow-moving chap, but he had a desire for food that we could only admire and wonder at. But being such a polite gentleman, he was ill-equipped mentally to be in the forefront of the tea brigade. Joe, also a gentleman, but of a different ilk, and with the natural astuteness of the Australian bushman, took it upon himself to shepherd the Adj into the dining-room ahead of us – and no one got in front of Joe if he decided to stand firm. We therefore formed a quartet for tea, instead of a trio, and that became a regular habit. Joe made sure old Adj had the best of the goodies, and I'm sure Joe was Adj's hero. If Joe was outspokenly straightforward in style, Vic was adroit in turning situations to his benefit. He was taking out the prettiest Waaf in our kitchens, and he had her tipped off to let him know when some special tea-time treats were on the menu. It wasn't entirely selfish, because Adj participated in this inside intelligence information.

This innocent friendship paid some dividends at a later date when Joe badgered Adj to acquire three tickets to a grand birthday party at, and for, The Windmill Theatre. This Windmill became a famous institution in wartime London: one reason was the understandable attraction of its chorus of 'Windmill' girls attired in their very scanty costumes, and the other reason was its world-famed headline of publicity: 'We Never Closed', this referring to the fact that even at the heights of the blitz on London, never a show was cancelled.

Adj was well connected with the world of the London theatre, but he implored us not to divulge who we had got the tickets from. Moreover, he told the three of us in no uncertain terms that we were not to show that we knew him when we were at the party. We did not so embarrass him – but could not resist catching his eye from time to time as we happily glugged our free champagne, attacked the refreshments with our usual gusto, and joined in the dancing that followed the show itself.

At this notable event, we three flight lieutenants were the junior officers present. All the Benson senior officers were putting their best feet forward in their efforts to celebrate the birthday with due PRU élan. In addition to our small 'junior' group, there were twelve in our 'senior' party, and the members of the Benson contingent certainly added to the colour of the occasion with their abundance of medal ribbons. The fact that we had such a crowd there was not solely due to our Adj's connections: Flight Lieutenant Vandamm had completed a tour at Benson, and was a flight commander at the OTU at Dyce when we had done our training for Mosquitos. The Vandamm family, as it was understood at the time, controlled the Windmill enterprise; hence the favour to Benson personnel. Group Captain 'Sailor' Malan, the South African fighter ace, was one of the many other famous guests. Thus it would be fair to say that we Australasians were not out-ranked in the enthusiasm of the manner in which we toasted the success of The Windmill.

Not all the winter days were spent inside the crew-room. During the earlier months of our tours, when fog definitely spelled 'No flying!' someone, our wingco, I suppose, insisted on all his crews jogging round the perimeter track, making a circuit of the airfield; and you had to keep up with the bunch, or it was lost to sight in the zero visibility. The second time we had our foggy peace interrupted by a run, Vic arranged for the three of us to gradually fall back from the pack. This was timed so that we were by the break in the fence where we could branch off and call at the Riverside Café. Here we could relax and most times be rewarded with a fresh egg, boiled or poached. No one ever did notice that the cross-country running club was three less in numbers at the finish.

Vic's improvement to the running schedule did not surprise me. When we first met up at AFU at Grove, he had applied the same tactics when we were marshalled for church services. We three fell in at the rear of the marching formation, and as the column swung in to the doorway of the hall, we three marched on, round the corner of the hall, and back to our billets for another hour's Sunday rest: 'Hitting the pit', Joe called this preferred activity.

On another no-flying day, Group Captain Beamish, famous as an international rugby player, arranged for Benson station to play a game against a junior team from Oxford University. I did not know the big man, and I'm sure he did not know me, but the night before the game he came up to me in the mess and said, 'All Kiwis play rugby; you will be on the left wing tomorrow.' Joe was similarly commandeered, but Vic ran true to form by pleading his ankle was not in fit shape to play. This sudden injury, however, did not stop him from keeping his date with a Waaf transport driver that evening. The game was a success, and Joe and I stood up to the knocks well enough – our rough-and-tumbles had obviously set us up well as regards fitness.

Other activities that were provided for our voluntary use, and which appealed to me, included the squash and badminton courts, and the table-tennis tables. All these ball games well suited my New Zealand background. The medical officer considered that table tennis, in particular, kept our reflexes in good shape for flying. A few miles up the London Road, Lord Nuffield, the motor-car magnate who had started life as William Morris, allowed us to play on his nine-hole golf course; the two Aussies and I enjoyed this.

Except on the really bitter winter days, some of us were always tinkering about with our cars or bikes outside the crew-room. In war-time Britain, only a few cars were to be seen on the roads, apart from service vehicles. Doctors and some nurses drove cars, and aircrew while on an operational tour had the privilege of owning a car. Petrol was rationed; when granted leave, we could apply for sufficient petrol coupons to get us to our destination and back. Frank's wife's family lived in Torquay, Devon, and that was a good distance to quote when it was time for me to apply for coupons. The penalty for using service petrol was severe: it had a distinctive colour that readily identified it, and if caught using it, any of us could be court-martialled and discharged from the Air Force in disgrace. Despite the risks of using service petrol in one's car, several pilots that I knew did so, arranging elaborate contraptions to utilize hidden tanks and connections in the hope that if they were stopped for a vehicle check, there would be time to switch over and have the civilian petrol flowing through the system when the inspection was made. All that was too dodgy for me, and I stuck to low flying for my risks and thrills.

One of the 544 groundcrew sergeants, Costello, took an interest in me and my old cars, and in return for his assistance in matters of servicing and the odd supply, I lent him the car for the occasional evening out. He was able to top it up with oil and anti-freeze – both, surprisingly, of aviation quality. Even more helpfully, he returned my Riley-9 one morning shod with two nearly new 19in tyres. He was pleased with himself, but my feelings were of immediate guilt: where had these beauties sprung from? The answer was, that the car's tyres were identical in size to those on the battery carts that were wheeled out to the aircraft for starting. My sergeant friend refused to change the tyres back again, and that was that. For a while I used to inspect the tyres on every battery cart I saw, and wonder if anyone would recognize my worn old ones. My conscience was eased a bit by thinking that when our wingco borrowed the car from time to time, he would not be so likely to have his plans for the evening frustrated by punctures in my old tyres. In my turn, I went out in other people's cars. One Spit pilot with whom I struck up a short friendship was the son of a London West End dealer who specialized in Rolls-Royces and Bentleys. It was good fun when he took a few of us out to a pub in such a distinguished limousine.

During the war it seemed impossible to obtain new tyres or a decent battery, and trouble starting, and problems with punctures, were constant companions. These older cars had no heating systems, and most of us carried a raw potato with which to rub the windscreen in order to alleviate the freezing up that occurred throughout the winters. Headlights were blanked off to comply with blackout regulations, so attempting to see the road at night entailed winding down the side windows and leaning out and peering intently. A belief that as aircrew one's eyesight was better than average gave a little moral support – but maybe the intake of alcohol evened out this apparent advantage?

Early in our tour, Joe and Vic and I were fortunate to obtain a 'forty-eight', a forty-eight-hour leave pass; the fact that we were attached to different flights made it unusual for the three of us to often be on leave together. As I had recently bought the Austin-10 coupé it was agreed we should travel up to London in it. No road maps were available in those years, so we would use RAF flying maps – not quite the same thing. Road signs had all been removed so that the enemy, when they invaded, would become as lost as we often were on the rambling English lanes and roads. As the war continued, signs were gradually replaced. However, all we had to do was to head off on 'the London Road' and follow our noses to arrive at the capital of the empire that was awaiting us.

This expedition was a big adventure for a young Kiwi, but what I had not appreciated was that my two Aussie men-of-the-world intended to stop at every pub en route and have a quick beer. It was therefore a surprise for all of us when we eventually realized we were on the approaches to the metropolis. All of a sudden we were at Marble Arch with no idea where we were aiming for, and due to a complete lack of organization, the three of us desperately in need of toilet conveniences. By this time, in our confusion, we had resorted to driving slowly round and round Marble Arch, weighing up the options.

The little Austin was fitted with one seat across the car. It was narrow, and for three men, rather on the cramped side. Naturally enough, as owner I sat behind part of the wheel and steered it. Vic, as the smaller of the two Aussies, and as the car's previous owner, sat next to me, squashed in by big Joe who was bulging out the celluloid side windows on his side. I operated the accelerator and the brake; Vic operated the clutch and the long gear lever. Joe shouted instructions, criticisms and warnings to both of us.

The nervous excitement, combined with the results of the pub crawl, made it imperative for me to achieve some relief to the bladder. Vic, as chief mechanic, unearthed the old jam tin that was used to pour in oil and anti-freeze liquid. He passed it to me and said, 'Kiwi! You do as I say on the throttle and the brake; I'll steer, and you get on with your urgent job while we keep going round and round.' And that's how relief was obtained. Australians certainly have initiative, and Vic was not finished yet with demonstrating his: taking the tin from me, he neatly pulled up a floorboard from amongst all our feet, and through a space next to the area where the battery was stowed, duly emptied the can while we completed our last circuit around the roundabout.

With the pressure off, as it were, my brain cleared considerably and I suddenly got my bearings, exclaiming: 'That's Park Lane going down there; I know where we are!' And only too glad to abandon the continual circling before the Metropolitan Police Force investigated us, I steered down this famous thoroughfare with its row of internationally known hotels. As we slowly drove along, Joe suddenly commanded me to stop. We were outside the main entrance of the Dorchester Hotel. Immediately, the head doorman, an impressive figure indeed in his topcoat and top hat, sprang to the side of the car, opened Joe's door so that he half fell out, and whipped up a smart salute. 'Gentlemen! What can we do for you?' And Joe was equal to the reply: 'Be a good chap, George, and tell us where we can unload this car.' 'Certainly Sir. Take this ticket, and drive round the next corner, and you will find the hotel's garage.' Naturally, this grand major-domo looked at us as guests of his eminent hotel.

We found the garage, had our ticket inspected, and descended a steep slope to the underground carpark. Up we walked, said 'Thank you' to the man at the barrier, and walked briskly away. Vic hailed the first taxi, and off we went to where we had intended to spend the night, the Hotel Waldorf: never in a thousand years could we have paid the tariff at the Dorchester – though as Joe pointed out, they more or less gave us the invitation to shelter our car for the night.

The sequel the following morning was not so amusing, because the car decided it wasn't up to climbing the slope to street level. To improve the power/weight ratio, Joe and Vic got out to lighten the load, but I still could not get it up. Vic tersely told me to get out from behind the wheel while he had a go. But no better fortune. We had to enlist the aid of two hotel employees, and a team of four was then available to push the reluctant vehicle up to the daylight. We were thankful to make our escape without confronting George again.

* * *

On the many sunny and pleasant days we often just lay on the grass outside the crew-room, though that peace never lasted for long. One of our navigators was a Canadian keep-fit fiend, Hughie Cawker, and on one occasion he suggested to all and sundry that we should build a human pyramid: all the big, solid fellows at the bottom, the medium-sized on top of them, and the little ones at the very top – you know how it goes. It was energetic work, and took a long time to get everyone organized. Hughie said we needed more manpower, so we had to hold our positions while he rustled up some more unwilling volunteers from the groundcrew. The whole thing must have looked good, but we were getting shaky with the physical effort and the strain. Then round the corner of the hangar came the smallest member of 544, a little red-haired sergeant navigator known as Ginger Baylis, always a pleasant and obliging fellow, and Hughie grabbed him with glee: 'Come on Ginger! Be quick! Hop up on to the very top and we'll get a photo!' he cried. Ginger obediently scaled his way up to the peak.

A large aircraft hangar probably does not look very high, but the peak of the roof is a long way above the ground. Ginger was high enough that by raising his arms he could touch the ridge of the roof at its peak. For a second he held on – and at that very moment the whole pyramid collapsed because no one could last any longer. But where was little Ginger, the man of the moment? There he was! A forlorn figure facing the front like a figurehead and hanging on for dear life with both arms stretched above his head, and shouting fit to bust. It was hard to know whether to laugh or cry. He seemed to be miles above us, and had a precarious hold, and to rescue him the whole pyramid had to regroup with all speed, though this was made nearly impossible by our smothered hysterical laughter. But we got him down before collapsing again. This venture was definitely a 'oncer', and for some reason the desire to build another pyramid never did return to us. Hughie was unpopular for a while, and Ginger was scarcely on speaking terms with any of us, including his pilot.

In the summer we had the Thames just across the road to play in and on, and we swam, rowed, paddled, punted and sailed; pollution was a word unheard of in those halcyon days. I revelled in being brown from the sun, and 'ozone layer' was another term not then in the dictionary. I remember on one fine day Vic and I sharing a rowing skiff, when another chap, not controlling his boat too well, rammed us and we were pitchforked into the river. For some reason we both had on our tunic uniforms instead of casual clothes, and visibly dripping, we had to put up with the smirks of the guards at the entrance to the station. The corporal kept a straight face as he saluted, thereby forcing us to reply with salutes. He asked, 'Good day for a swim, gentlemen?' Even Vickers was at a loss for a reply, but he could produce a mean scowl.

On some perfect, never-to-be-forgotten days, a few of us went to Goring on the river, where we rowed and sailed dinghies before having high tea at the Swan Hotel, prior to hurrying back to the mess for dinner. Occasionally when we managed a day off, we drove through Reading and Maidenhead to Windsor and boated on the river there. Joe and I made one happy sortie by pushbike: we rode through Henley, Marlow and Maidenhead to Windsor, and then stayed the night at The Bull, where we met Frank and his wife Margaret, who had a couple of day's leave from the Wrens. After boating on Old Father Thames, we two shipped our bikes and ourselves on the river steamer up to Maidenhead, and completed the journey to Benson by pedal power.

It was an ideal and enchanting relaxation for me. Those idyllic English summers, watching the Etonians sculling their skiffs on the Thames with Windsor Castle as a backdrop, made me realize that I was a willing fighter for Britain and its freedom, and its resistance to a tyrannical Europe. Occasionally my mind wandered down a line of thought where it tried to visualize what sort of a mess Europe, in particular, would be in when the war ended – and I just could not see it at all clearly in my reckoning at that dramatic and uncertain stage of my life. Europe had lasted only twenty years after the conclusion of 'the war to end all wars' in 1918 before this confrontation had spread viciously around our planet. How would, or even could, a prosperous permanent peace be established? Winning the war did not seem to be the end of the saga.

6

Touch and Go
in the Baltic

Out of this nettle, danger,
we pluck this flower, safety.
William Shakespeare

Ops Nos 9 & 10, 16 & 17 March 1944

'B' Flight was detached from our squadron for two months in early 1944
under the command of David Douglas-Hamilton, our flight commander
after Bill Aston became a POW. We were to operate from RAF Leuchars, on
the east coast of Scotland, with the object of covering the Baltic area.

DDH accorded me a great deal of pleasure by sharing friendship with me.
David was the youngest brother of the premier duke of Scotland, and in a variety
of ways he fortified my morale, as he did for all in his flight, and indeed for all that
came under his influence. He did not have to try to be a leader: his leadership
qualities must have been born into him, and thus he carried the responsibility
effortlessly, or so it appeared. At times we enjoyed serious talks, and at other times
we had tremendous fun. On the squadron, David was of serious mien and kept a
low profile. He was thirty-two years of age while I was twenty-two.

His eldest brother, the Duke of Hamilton and Brandon, was a group
captain in the RAF, and in the pre-war years had been the first pilot to fly
over Mount Everest. As well as these two brothers, Malcolm was the CO of
Benson's other Mosquito squadron, No. 540, and a fourth brother, George
Nigel, the Earl of Selkirk, was also a Royal Air Force officer. In 1938 David
married Miss Prunella Stack, and theirs was undoubtedly the social wedding
of the year. Prunella was then leader of the Women's League of Health and
Beauty, and known as 'Britain's perfect girl'. They had two sons: Diarmaid
then aged four, and Iain aged two.

Enemy shipping convoys and German naval vessels were spread all over
the Baltic area, and knowledge of their movements was of prime importance. For instance, it was a 544 Mosquito that photographed the mighty
Tirpitz battleship when it was in hiding in a northernmost Norwegian fiord.
DDH was to be in his element, commanding and leading his own half

57

squadron on a beautifully sited Scottish airfield.

After taking off from Benson to fly up to Scotland, Frank and I beat up over the Riverside Café where, by arrangement, Joe and Vic were outside to appreciate our effort and to wave enthusiastic but temporary farewells. Most of the excitement for me was wondering if someone would report us for this blatant low flying, but it is my belief that the Benson villagers were on our side – the publicans and the owners of the Riverside should have been, in any case.

Snow lay on the ground up in the frozen north, but this was nothing compared with my Canadian prairie days, not to mention the near-arctic conditions of the Gulf of St Lawrence in wintertime. We all enjoyed the general atmosphere of Leuchars as a happy and compact unit, and the feeling of general comradeship flourished in a way that it had not at Benson. High-pressure tensions temporarily disappeared. When not flying we sat around the big stove in our crew-room and were content with each other's company. David was issued with a Humber Snipe shooting brake in which we enjoyed many exhilarating outings: as many of us as could be crammed into the vehicle found ourselves whirled round the countryside at 70mph. Life in Scotland was freer and more relaxed, and one felt that the war was not quite so close.

One afternoon after tea, Frank and I set off to go to St Andrews to the cinema. Probably due to a navigational error, we caught the wrong bus and finished up in Dundee after crossing the Tay in a ferry; we blamed each other and had a good laugh. Frank reckoned he was just testing me out to see if I was aware we were going in the wrong direction. Navigators don't have many opportunities to even the score with their pilots. . . .

Leuchars airfield was packed with big Liberators that flew anti-U-boat sorties for many hours at a stretch over the sea areas around Scotland. One of their pilots, an Englishman, told me how keen he was to have a ride in a Mosquito. Frank and I liked to fly air-tests at every opportunity, and David agreed for me to take the chap up one morning. The Mosquito cockpit is a squeeze for two people, and to cope with a third, as we did from time to time unofficially – and even a fourth at a real pinch – meant that Frank had to volunteer, at my request, to crouch down in the nose while our guest took his seat next to me; like this, Frank had a clear view of the passenger's face. . Once airborne, our new friend started telling me how very low they used to fly their big four-engined machines; these had a wingspan of 110ft, which meant, our friend explained, that to make a turn they had to be higher than 55ft to avoid a wing-tip dipping into the waves. In fact our extra pilot talked non-stop, and the thought came to me that it would be a good educational exercise to demonstrate to him how a Mossie flew at low level.

On one occasion a few weeks earlier, from Benson, when Joe and I knew we were both due to cross out over the Channel at the same time, each on a low-level op., we had quietly arranged to meet off Beachy Head at a precise time. Joe's navigator took a small camera in his hands, and we flew low alongside him while Alec photographed us. Joe had called out to me over the VHF, 'Kiwi! Get Frank to look behind you! You are making a wake like a speedboat!' That was exhilarating, even if unnecessarily dangerous. But now and then, when over a calm sea, I used to methodically try to fly as low as possible – though you couldn't stand the strain for too long before having to climb up to relax.

My method was to fly low, loosen the friction control knob holding the throttles tight, and hold both throttles firmly, in my left hand, ready for immediate action. The sea had to be dead calm, absolutely flat with no ripples or a swell. I concentrated on the surface of the water, and tenderly edged the kite lower until my judgement told me we were at the same altitude as when sitting on the ground with the undercarriage down. That was reasonably low. The final phase of the exercise was to ease us down a few more inches, at which level the propeller blades were close to skimming the surface. I considered *that* was low flying, though I never admitted it to a soul until my flying days were over – but the feeling of exquisite ecstasy I experienced each time gave me a satisfaction that lasted for a long while. I also believe that succumbing to this temptation from time to time provided relaxation from other stresses. But now, with decades of hindsight, I also see that my father's farewell advice to me on departing from New Zealand was well and truly broken. He had told me, and I really did not grasp the full import at the time: 'Never hesitate to take a risk, *but* never take an unnecessary risk.'

With our Liberator pilot passenger we spent a few minutes displaying to him our version of low flying. For once he did not talk or make a sound until we had landed, and when back on terra firma he never made a comment, but just stared at me. Frank said his face had been a picture. In truth it was never my intention to frighten the poor fellow, I really thought he would enjoy it. Several days later I found myself walking into the dining room alongside the same man; he gave me a short, severe look and whispered to me so no one else could hear: 'You're absolutely mad!'

Our next two ops were over southern Norway, and in the second we came up against some difficult opposition; these two were the first we had flown to Norway, and we chose to fly at 33,000ft. Op. No. 7 was successful, but on the second occasion the reception committee was waiting for us just off the coastline, and six fighters kept us occupied for thirty-five minutes of constant attack. We were intercepted in a clear and vivid blue sky over the southwest coast of Norway at an altitude of 32,000ft, and we manoeuvred and sweated for the whole of that time before they broke off the engagement (not all broken engagements are bad things).

The situation was not like our previous continental trips where, if necessary, we could scoot away to another area and cover secondary targets. Here, we were outside the front door, and we could not make an entrance; moreover we were mostly attacked by a pair of aircraft at a time, and this scenario was new to us. All we could do was try to avoid being shot down, and although a large number of shots were fired, we just managed this. After this second op., No. 8, we had clocked up 29hr 55min of operational flying.

It was not just enemy action that gave us difficulties: two other factors to consider were weather conditions, and navigational errors. An example of the latter occurred when, on one short trip from Leuchars to Norway, we were surprised to find that it took us much longer to get there than we had estimated, and to our cost, we did not give this fact sufficient emphasis when the time came to return to Scotland – it was just too easy to nip back across the North Sea. After clearing the Norwegian coast, and considering the risk of attacks negligible, we used to allow ourselves the indulgence of relaxing somewhat; at times I even used to stretch one leg at a time by placing them up over the control column.

On that particular trip, I soon eased the nose down in a long gentle dive to bring us back to our base on the east coast of Scotland. During the descent we entered cloud, and we remained in it right down to about 2,000ft before the cloud base permitted us to see the surface of the sea. We continued on our course waiting for the familiar coastline to appear ahead, and a ghastly and unusual feeling came over me as I calculated from the cockpit clock how far we had travelled since we had expected to reach base. The ETA given me by the navigator had come and gone, and Frank had now also become agitated. We agreed that this was a time to break radio silence, and for him to obtain a course to steer by means of our W/T set. Now Frank was a top-class operator, but just when we needed to make contact, he could not raise a response. That decided me: here we were at a low level over an angry grey sea with the daylight starting to diminish. A pain, like I imagine an ulcer produces when it bursts, pierced my stomach. I threw the aircraft around on to a reciprocal course and we flew back from whence we had come.

Sure enough, ten minutes flying brought us to the *west* coast of Scotland! We had completely overflown the country, plus a further sixty miles or so out into the Atlantic. How could that happen? The met. people at Leuchars told us later that after we were airborne a considerable aberration in the wind systems had occurred, and instead of the prevailing westerly at 30,000ft, the wind currents for a short period had faced opposing forces and had become more or less zero. That accounted for the longer time to reach Norway, and conversely, we had returned to the east coast in less than an hour in our shallow dive. Another twenty to twenty-five minutes to flash across Scotland, and we were on our way to oblivion . . . . Strange that such a strong feeling made me turn round when we did – but hooray for strong feelings.

YEAR 1944		AIRCRAFT		PILOT, OR 1ST PILOT	2ND PILOT, PUPIL, OR PASSENGER	DUTY (INCLUDING RESULTS AND REMARKS)	SINGLE-ENGINE AIRCRAFT				MULTI-ENGINE AIRCRAFT					PASSEN-GER	INSTR/CLOUD FLYING (Incl. in Cols. (1) to (10))	
MONTH, DATE		Type	No.				DAY Dual	DAY Pilot	NIGHT Dual	NIGHT Pilot	DAY Dual	DAY 1st Pilot	DAY 2nd Pilot	NIGHT Dual	NIGHT 1st Pilot	NIGHT 2nd Pilot		Dual	Pilot
						TOTALS BROUGHT FORWARD	37·05	29·55	2·40	·20	108·40	181·40	3·10	7·45	8·20	—	85·00	46·00	3·25
FEB.	29	MOSQUITO XII	274	SELF	F/S MOSELEY	BENSON TO LEUCHARS.						1·50							
						SUMMARY FOR MONTH OF FEBRUARY					OPERATIONAL	5·00							
						UNIT: 544 SQDN. TYPES: MOSQUITOS IX & XII					NON-OPERATIONAL	8·16							
						DATE: 29 FEB 1944.					MONTHLY TOTAL	13·15							
				SIGN'TURE															
OC C FLIGHT																		
		8 PIT 544 SQDN		DETACHED TO RAF EVANTON SCOTLAND —															
MAR.	3.	MOSQUITO IX	·31	SELF	P/S MOSELEY	OPS – SOUTH NORWAY (3300').						3·45							
MAR.	7.	MOSQUITO XVI	240	SELF	F/S MOSELEY	OPS – STH. NORWAY: 32000 OVERS...						2·50							
MAR.	10	MOSQUITO IX	·13	SELF	P/S MOSELEY	TEST – (OBLIQUE PHOTOS).						1·30							
MAR.	16	MOSQUITO IX	·47	SELF	P/S MOSELEY	OPS – DANLO – STBD ENGINE FEATHERED.						1·20							
MAR.	17	MOSQUITO IX	247	SELF	P/S MOSELEY	OPS – MILAN, HEL...						6·05							
MAR.	17	MCGRIM ...	431	w/c STEVENTON, DEC.	F/S MOSELEY	...														
MAR.	18	MOSQUITO XVI	233	D HAMILTON	P/S MOSELEY	SERVON TO LEUCHARS —												·40		
MAR.	30	MOSQUITO IX	231	SELF	F/S MOSELEY	OPS – BERGEN FJORD. REC'D – FLAK.						3·15						1·20		
MAR.	31	MOSQUITO IX	327	SELF (P.M.)	P/S KENNEDY	LEUCHARS – COLTISHALL.						1·20							
MAR.	31	MOSQUITO IX	3·17	SELF	P/S MOSELEY	COLTISHALL – LE SON.						·45							
MAR.	31	MOSQUITO XVI	283	SELF	P/S MOSELEY	BENSON – LEUCHARS						1·30							
				SUMMARY	CURR PAGE	AID SUCCESSFULLY "MONTE ROSA" 34,000 FLAK	37·05	39·55	2·40	·20	108·40	206·50	3·10	7·46	8·20	—	97·05	46·00	3·25
				GRAND TOTAL [Cols. (1) to (10)] 413 Hrs. 44·5 Mins.		TOTALS CARRIED FORWARD													

On 16 March 1944 we were airborne on the most ambitious trip of our short career: it would take us about 900 miles to the east, and first priority targets were our goal. David allocated us my favourite aircraft at that time, No. 247. But well on the way at operational altitude, we had ominous signs of engine failure: how disheartening. The propeller had to be feathered, and then the engine stopped, so back we flew for forty minutes and made our first single-engine landing. DNCO is hard to take. The kite was repaired, and we took off the next morning at 11am to try and cover the same targets. These lay in an area at the eastern end of the Baltic Sea. The most easterly was then called Königsberg, the commercial and industrial centre of East Prussia, and an important military and naval fortress. Russians changed the city's name to Kaliningrad, and it now lies in the western region of European Russia. So the wheel of history moves round. A little to the west other targets were around Pillau and the Hel Peninsula, close by Gdynia in Poland, and facing the Gulf of Danzig; this latter city, a fortified seaport town and naval station, was the capital of West Prussia. But a sensational aspect of the sortie, and one that overshadowed the risk of trying to fly so far east, was that reports had come in that the entire German navy, at least all that was left of it, was out on exercises in the Gulf. Probably they thought they were too far east for any Allied aircraft to spot them. We believed that at the time we flew there, no other Allied aircraft had flown a sortie so far east, and returned direct to Britain.

What I did not know at the time was that 'Hel' is an adaption of the name 'Hela', the goddess of death in Scandinavian mythology, and who reputedly lived in a place of eternal snow and darkness. And on that 17 March 1944, Frank and I had a face-to-face encounter with death. Although that date held no particular interest for me at the time, I was vaguely aware it was observed by many as St Patrick's Day, and because I then remembered the date for its Irish associations, it remains a fact that for many years after 1944, every successive 17 March brought me bad news and some danger. However, all that is well gone now.

At eleven o'clock in the morning we were airborne, again in Mosquito No. 247. Two main factors decided the time: the need for the sun and light to be the most favourable for our cameras, and secondly, the met. officer's forecast of weather conditions over the targets. The actual route was left to our judgement and discretion. In fact we did not have many options, because to fly 1,800 miles meant that conserving petrol was the vital ingredient to survival, let alone success, and so it was too risky to deviate far from a straight line. Our route therefore took us across the North Sea, Denmark, just south of Copenhagen, over the southern tip of Sweden and the Danish island of Bornholm, and then along the eastern Baltic.

It was also up to us to decide what altitude we would fly at. We had to be above about 22,000ft in order to take advantage of the second-stage 'blowers' that increased engine boost; then we had to consider the estimated wind speed and direction, and whether it was more of a headwind or a tailwind. Another variable was how low an rpm we should risk flying at, in order to reduce fuel consumption: fly at too low a setting of the engine revolutions, and the kite lost speed and took up an uneconomical flying position by increasing the drag. A further anxiety was that reducing the revs tended to cause the spark plugs to lead up, and subsequent engine failure.

A prime factor was the matter of condensation trails, the thinking in PRU when my ops tour commenced being for us to definitely not go high enough to make trails. (Remember that my instructions for my first op. made us return because trails were being made at too low a height to be able to fly at an economical altitude.) During those earlier ops we quickly lost a little height if we saw we were leaving trails, since they were vivid 'tell-tales' for the enemy world beneath. Even though we knew the German radar followed us all the time we were over enemy territory, it was a negative feeling knowing we were leaving two dazzling white streaks behind us, inviting both flak and fighters to come and make contact with us. However, during these earlier months of 1944 the thinking changed, and this change was confirmed from D-Day onwards, when obtaining results at any cost became the order of the day.

The new theory – and we at PRU were the pioneers and guinea-pigs in this high-flying game – was that we should fly as high as possible when we could. Sometimes it was possible to fly through the trail layer: thus if trails appeared at, say, 24,000ft, maybe they disappeared again at, say, 32,000ft, the advantage of this being that we would be able to spot fighters coming up to us as they flew through the trail layer. This layer varied from season to season, and from one set of weather conditions to another set on another day. There were many variables. With the newer theory, even if you did have to fly within the trail layer, you still had the advantage of seeing any other aircraft climbing up. But if you chose to fly above vapour trails, you had to make sure that you *did* see the enemy on his way up, otherwise he would be in range of your Mosquito having shown no tell-tale trails as he manoeuvred into his attacking position.

In tackling this ultra-long trip, whereas our previous trips over Norway had been at 33,000ft, we decided the optimum altitude to give us the necessary range was around 30,000ft, and not to worry whether we were making trails or not. On most flights these con-trails billowed out behind our two engines and blocked some of our view when trying to see fighters climbing up on our tail, though in usual conditions the trails disappeared once they had streamed behind for about a mile. However, on one peculiar day some weeks later, again in the Baltic, our trails remained continuous for such a long period that after we had photographed our targets and turned for home, the trails from our inward track were still in position. This was most uncanny. They had fluffed out a bit, but were still remarkably virgin-looking, and for a while we actually flew back along them even though they must have blown away from their original positions. In normal conditions our Mosquitos, in their PRU light blue colour at, say, 30,000ft and against a bright blue sky, were not visible from the ground with the naked eye. But imagine our feelings when we realized we were up there, nearly a thousand miles from home, streaming two brilliant banners behind us for all the enemy world to see.

Half an hour after take-off we were at our selected altitude, flying the course to make good our chosen track over the ground, and the engines set at revs and boost for maximum fuel economy. Our ground speed was about 360mph (580km/h) before applying the effect of the wind. Every thirty or forty minutes I opened up the throttles and gave the engines a burst in the hope of preventing the plugs leading up. Frank knelt on his uncomfortable seat with his head up in the cabin blister and scanned for fighters. I searched ahead for any moving object, and that included quick glances at the instruments. Sudden movements on the instruments, especially downwards, were not good for morale.

Both at Benson and at Leuchars my pet foible before becoming airborne on a sortie was to insist that the windscreen be immaculately clean and free from insect marks, because the time for us to spot another aircraft was when it looked the same size as a fly spot on the windscreen. The best grade of sunglasses available at the time was issued to aircrew because we experienced continual near-blinding glare from the sun for hours on end, especially when it reflected off snow-white clouds. But whenever we did see a fighter, my compulsive reaction was to throw the sun-specs on to the floor and leave them there: self-preservation, rightly or wrongly, told me my natural eyes could see best. The legacy has been an overdose of crow's-feet at the corner of my eyes, but that has been a tiny price to pay.

Pilot and navigator (if he was *my* navigator) were uncomfortable, cramped and stiff, their neck especially. Actually I should say *my* neck, because I never had any idea what Frank's neck, or any other part of him, felt like – it was not a point of conversation. Frank never complained to me: what an ideal companion. Indeed, conversation was not a feature of our flights, and silence prevailed except when instructions and observations had to be made to progress the trip. My thoughts on these trips towards the targets never contemplated anything in the future beyond arriving at the said targets and photographing them. Keeping alert for any change in the sound or feel of the engines occupied a great deal of my time and nervous energy; at times I tortured myself with anxieties, some real and some imaginary.

As the Rolls-Royce Merlin engines roared on and time ticked by on the cockpit clock, the flight seemed never-ending. I felt in my bones that we were a long way from home, and every minute saw us, with the usual westerly tailwind, a further eight miles into enemy territory. Our job was still ahead of us.

Neither of us, however, was mentally prepared for the sight that opened out ahead after flying for more than two and a half hours. The Germans had suffered many losses to their navy up until this stage of the war, but a still considerable number of naval ships were now sailing in formation from one side of our vision to the other. I remember thinking, let's hope their surprise is greater than ours, and at the same time my ship-recognition courses in Canada leapt up in my mind. Every type and size of vessel was on display, including two-men midget submarines that proved to be a new variety. I wondered how we would ever cover them all with our cameras, and what sort of opposition they would provide.

Frank quickly disconnected his oxygen tube and his intercom plug. Dropping to his knees, he took up position lying face down with his head over the clear panel in the nose, and once there he had to promptly plug in again to the two vital connections. When I had loosened my straps and levered myself up against the rudder pedals, it was just possible for me to reach him with my right leg and kick his lower left leg. If my shouting at him over the intercom did not produce the result I wanted, then the message by a kick was usually effective.

Our briefing had not given us any idea as to the sort of reception we were likely to receive over the German fleet. In my own thoughts, the most optimistic conclusion I had reached was that no Allied aircraft would be expected so far east, and therefore the defences would not include top-line fighters such as Bf 109s and Fw 190s that could reach our altitude and speed. A second hopeful thought was that the available anti-aircraft guns, although being formidable at lower levels from both warships and shore batteries, might not be able to reach our height.

A surprise third factor came into play, however, something we had never experienced and never thought about. While we commenced our first run over the nearest line of ships, and I stretched and strained to see fighters, at the same time as instinctively obeying Frank's calls to go 'Riiiight!' or 'Left-left!', countless smoke-screens started to appear. What a to-do for one little Mosquito that had no bombs and no guns. Most of the smoke screens had been lit round the perimeters of airfields immediately adjacent to the coast; others came from ships, because the entire fleet was close in to the shore. The interesting thing was that the surface wind was a normal sea breeze – that is, the wind blew towards the land from the sea, and the result was much in our favour. This benefit, combined with our ability to snap photos at all angles and on the oblique, enabled us to complete a comprehensive coverage.

No flak or fighters interrupted us, but that did not lessen our growing tension as we completed run after run over the fleet. We still had other targets in the general area, over ports, factories and airfields. Of all places to be, and of all days to feel like it, Frank was in tremendous form. As the minutes ticked by, my nerves could scarcely stand, 'Just another run, Fos – I don't think we've got this one yet!' as Frank became absorbed in his task over the ships. One part of my brain cleared enough for me to be constantly monitoring the many fuel gauges. Mental arithmetic calculated how many gallons had been used to get us here, then how many gallons left, and how many hours to return against the average headwind of 100mph (160km/h). My head spun when my answers told me we had already used more than half the fuel supply . . . therefore in theory, we could not fly back to Britain.

It was high time for a message to be transmitted to Frank by the kick method. I swung away at the same moment to go that little bit further eastward to cover the remaining targets. Still no opposition, but a sinking feeling of having a three-hour struggle to escape from this fringe of Europe back to my clean and tidy room at Benson, surrounded by my few personal possessions. No thoughts of family or New Zealand entered my mind. The big attraction was to hide myself in my own little hiding place with its neat bed and white sheets, and to be able to think of anything else but the present situation. It was clear we should have to fly back in the most economical manner that we had ever accomplished. No spare fuel to enable us to open up the throttles to escape from attacks by fighters, nor to do a dog-leg to avoid heavy concentrations of flak. It did feel a lot better, though, when we were heading west, instead of that daunting east.

We crawled our way back across the map of northern Europe: from more than 20° East longitude, our objective, Leuchars, was close to 3° West longitude – and when you are more than six miles up in the sky the ground does not appear to be moving past. Expecting to be intercepted by fighters as we slowly approached the more heavily defended war zones gradually raised the adrenalin level. I flew the Mosquito with my fingertips, trying my hardest to fly with the utmost precision. The ideal was to incur the least drag, and no deviation from the course that Frank had calculated in the ops room before being airborne.

Once on a trip we had no means of determining wind changes apart from a seat-of-the-pants feeling, and maybe some clear observations from the outward trip if that course or ETA had needed much amendment. Another reason why we did not play about with navigational exercises was my demand for Frank to look out continually. We had proved many times that the eyes-out procedure was a vital ingredient of survival. My mind, and surely Frank's as well, never ceased from churning over all the ingredients and options that could affect our heading when we were flying ops.

About half way back from our naval targets, towards Leuchars, the starboard engine started to lose its oil pressure. This was grim. It was the same engine that had failed the day before, but what a difference in location for this to happen: here we were still to the east of Denmark, not too far from Kiel. We struggled on as the engine lost power and the oil-pressure gauge showed me for the second time in two days that again, a well-judged decision had to be made, namely the exact moment to press the button to feather the failing engine. To feather the propeller prior to switching off the engine depends on a certain minimum of oil pressure: leave the feathering a few seconds too long, and it is not possible to avoid having a burnt-out engine at the same time as having a runaway propeller. I watched in fascination as the pressure dropped. *The Pilot's Handbook* states that normal pressure is 60–80lb/sq in and minimum is 45. Maybe it would pick up again? Stupid thought – just a daydream. Feather the wretched thing and take the consequences while you can. I pushed the button to feather it when the gauge showed 30lb: the propeller stopped, and thankfully turned its angle into one of streamlining with the flight of the aircraft.

Frank announced we were near Kolding in eastern Denmark. The aircraft commenced losing altitude: we were like a duck that had been wounded in one wing. Where should we head for? What a prime, valuable cargo of photographs we carried; the information we had gleaned was of unmistakable worth to the Allied war machine, and so our effort from this moment on had to exceed the best we had ever made previously.

Frank and I agreed we had to aim for the nearest part of Britain; that was East Anglia, where the land bulges out to the east just south of the Wash. Estimating a course took about five seconds, and we turned on to it, still descending, in cloud now. Frank projected our new track on to a small map that covered all Europe, but it was a handy size to hold in one hand, and we often used that scale for our return trips. The track showed us to be going perilously close to the Frisian Islands, some of which lie off the German coast, and others off the coast of the Netherlands.

It was a nightmare area to be in, on one engine: bumping about in dark cloud, having to lose altitude because the single engine would not support us any higher, and probably within twenty miles of the enemy coast. We could not divert to put more distance between the coast and us, because being limited to one engine meant that a certain quantity of fuel was isolated – that is, we could not draw on all the fuel we had on board because the whole supply could not be transferred to one engine.

While I was furiously busy in my mind figuring out the options and calculating in my head how many hours the available fuel would keep us in the air, if we were left in peace, another blow struck us: the port engine began to stutter and falter. Flying on instruments in the cloud now became more difficult. To ensure adequate air speed I increased the rate of descent. It was also important to try and find out the height of the cloud base while we knew for sure we were over the sea, and not faced with the possibility of being over land with its attendant hills and obstructions. To a large extent an aircraft is like a ship or a boat, in that the greatest danger is when it is too close to a landmass, be it a reef for a ship, or a mountain top for an aircraft. The further away from land, in many instances, the better the chances of having more time to overcome any other difficulties.

At the same time that everything else was going on, I asked Frank to call up an S-O-S on his W/T – the first time we had been obliged to take this drastic action. Many, many attempts were made, but just the luck of the draw, he could not obtain the slightest response. This was somewhat demoralizing. All the lessons and experience that had been hammered into turning out Frank as a 'gen' wireless operator seemed to be worthless at that moment. What we did *not* know until later was that his message *was* picked up by a station right up in the north of Scotland, and it was relayed to Leuchars where David Douglas-Hamilton and our friends were waiting for us.

Dismayed at the apparent failure of the W/T, I tried continuously to call up on all channels of the VHF where our S-O-S became 'MAYDAY'. All the chances were that we were far out of range, but it helped my morale to continue calling: channel A, channel B, channel C, channel D and channel E; then start at 'A' again.

The port-engine trouble was a mystery. It sprang from oil pressure, but was a different fault from what had happened to the starboard engine on both days; in this one the pressure surged wildly, up and down. And then something triggered in my memory, and I suddenly remembered reading about an emergency oil system in our Mosquitos that I had never dreamt would be of use. It consisted of the navigator having to reach awkwardly up to a connection behind the pilot's head, fitting in a handle, and manually pumping oil from a reserve tank to the port engine. We did this, though the pump was hard to activate. Each time the pressure dropped on the gauge, I yelled at Frank (no excuse of lack of oxygen at this low altitude!) to 'Pump!' and he did. So he was occupied and so was I, and on we staggered.

We prepared the aircraft for us to bale out if the worst occurred and we were left with no engines. *The Handbook* did not have to emphasize that baling out was to be much preferred to attempting to ditch a Mosquito in the drink. It would dive like a brick; I knew that.

The minutes ticked by slowly as I let the aircraft continue its slow descent. Seeing the air speed read a shade more than that of level flight made me feel that we were approaching England a little more quickly – then all at once we broke cloud and were over the North Sea in stormy weather and still in turbulence. The wind-lanes on the surface of the sea reminded me of the flying and navigating I had done over the Gulf of St Lawrence, and there was certainly some similarity: violent rain and hail squalls and temporary periods of nil visibility, and the kite bucketing about in a sluggish fashion, all its normal admirable Mosquito qualities gone; more like a bucking bronco at times, or even a half-dead blowfly at others. Frank, with his sea-twitch operating full blast, said: 'It's not a suitable day to bale out!' and that reminded me of how Joe had pushed his young Alec out.

At least we must now be well away from German interference. More and more, my concern was the importance of landing our prize photos safely; to put it mildly, how galling to be so close and then miss reaching dry land. 'Filter 77' continued its MAYDAY bleats; I could not bring myself to stop calling. Frank had to continually pump the squirts of oil with all his strength, and he didn't have to wait for me to tell him; it was apparent to both of us without looking at the pressure gauge when the engine revs tailed away to a whisper and I had to push the nose down to maintain air-speed. Then he would pump, and after a few seconds the engine picked up a little and in those short intervals I was able to gain a shade more altitude up again to the cloud base. This base was gradually lowering, and experience told me that the coastal weather would see the cloud and mist close down to the deck. That possibility did not bother me – just let us get over l-a-n-d, and I would drop the kite down somewhere and somehow.

We had battled our way back for about 400 miles when both of us nearly sprang up from our seats: a loud, clear Englishman's voice answered cheerfully on the VHF and gave us a QDM to steer to the nearest suitable airfield. Call it coincidence if you will, but I prefer to admire Frank's handiwork, because the course was precisely the one we had been trying to fly for the last hour and a half. An encouraging sign. I informed the station we had a valuable cargo, my thinking being that even if we crashed, they had to do their best to find and protect that cargo. The RAF station to which we were directed was Coltishall, a name that forever rings out a most pleasant and welcome signal to my mind. It lies less than ten miles inland from the coast, in the area of the Broads, and is not far from Norwich. The controller further advised us that three 'friends' were on their way to locate us and lead us in.

By this stage of events the pulse was ever quickening, principally because the fuel gauges that related to the tanks we could use were all showing 'empty' – so it was going to be 'touch and go' all right. After what seemed a long period, and one in which the cloud base had lowered so much I felt it safer to climb up a few hundred feet into cloud again, the voices of the three pilots called to me. I talked to their leader, and we agreed that I would have to descend again until the three friends, that were Spitfires, had found us. This we did successfully, but the pressure for me to be on terra firma was intense. The three Spits took up close formation on us, one ahead, and one on each side. Their close formation round us made me nervous, especially as I could not fly the aircraft with any precision, so we agreed the side supports should break off and I would attempt to follow the leader only.

He told me he had to climb up into the cloud in order to lead us over the airfield; we had to follow in his slipstream. What a good Mossie to still be able to make these gentle climbs on its one failing engine – I doubt if any other make of aircraft could have performed as willingly on one 'missing' engine. The Spit pilot told me that Coltishall was a big grassy airfield where damaged bombers used to land or crash when they returned knocked about from night raids. 'Close up!' he said, 'I'm taking you over the airfield; I'll waggle my wings and then you are on your own. The fire-engines and crash-tenders are waiting for you. Good luck!'

Following this helpful and calm guide took every tiny piece of my remaining strength, in and out of turbulent cloud, with rain swept by strong winds, and darkening visibility. He waggled his wings. We had set our altimeter from an air pressure given us from Control: we were just below 600ft. The port engine was more intermittent. There is a laid-down procedure as to which way a twin-engined aircraft should make turns when flying on one engine, but I ignored it; although the instruction entered my mind clearly enough, my decision was dictated by our lack of fuel and the resulting imminence of having no engine power at all.

Through the rain I saw the black-and-white chequered caravan that marked the edge of the field for the touch-down, and once I had spotted it, I could not bring myself to do any turns or manoeuvres that would take me out of sight of that marker; nor did I dare re-enter cloud in order to be in position for any part of a circuit or proper approach: I yanked back the one port throttle, shoved the kite down on its nose, and we dropped like a stone. I felt myself come forward on my straps. The two men manning the signal caravan darted out from it and ran for their lives across the field – they were not waiting to be hit by a suicidal Mosquito, and I don't blame them; I thought how sensible they were.

As we dropped, with no power on, I pulled back hard on the control column and at the same moment lowered the undercart. My eyes glanced at the airspeed – 180mph (290km/h). We were in the approach position, but going half as fast again as we should have been. The landing field was grass, and a part of my mind flashed back to Tiger Moth flying days in New Zealand. We had flown on grass there, and my instructor was puzzled as to how I could land in a small circle more accurately than he could. We had talked it over, and I said my eyes told me the moment when the grass changed from coming up to me, to flashing past me: that was the moment I pulled back on the stick and the kite landed, close to stalling speed. I had also explained in a boyish way how the instant the grass went past, it reminded me of a rugby field.

Well, on this helter-skelter, mad, semi-controlled approach at Coltishall, the same phenomenon occurred: I saw the grass flashing past – the rugby field came to mind – I pulled hard back on the control column, and there

70

we were doing a fine wheeler landing. The only snag was that our speed was still miles too fast, and the length of ground available ahead was rapidly diminishing.

A row of pine trees marked the far end of the airfield, and I braked as hard as I dared, several times. We had no control from the engines to change direction. The kite rose up with its tail in the air and the three-bladed propellers tipped the ground in front. Down went the tail, *bang!* and I repeated the process. When the trees became a definite hazard, I risked a last burst of throttle from the poor old port engine, and it responded enough to enable me with a last touch of brake to slew sideways to the right – and we stopped with the port wing-tip about six feet from the tree branches. Both propeller tips were turned in for about three inches. That was the only damage I recall ever doing to any beautiful Mosquito, apart from bringing from Moscow a length of aerial wire jammed round our wing-tip. I felt sorry for hurting it.

The first vehicle to dash up to us at a furious pace was an army jeep manned by a sergeant and three airfield defence soldiers, all carrying small arms. The sergeant leaped out before his vehicle stopped, and met me as I slid stiffly down our little boarding ladder. I was exploded out of my daze by his springing to attention in front of me while he simultaneously snapped up a parade-ground salute and in stentorian tone shouted: '*Sir!*' It was a bewildering but comforting welcome after more than six hours in the air.

The smartness and efficiency of this quartet transmitted some of its spirit to me. My principal thought was for the cameras not to be touched. I requested the sergeant to remain with two of his men and guard the aircraft, and Frank also remained to see fair play. The fourth man drove me to the control tower, and in response to my question, led me up the stairs at a run to the operations room. Breathless, I rushed in, and asked for the officer-in-charge.

We PRU pilots, in recognition of the urgency to obtain the results of our sorties, were authorized to use an extremely high-priority telephone link with Benson; we understood it was the second highest level available in the UK. No previous situation had occurred for me to request this service, and nor was this the last time Foster and Moseley had to use it. On each occasion my request was queried, but when I insisted that our instructions were valid and quoted the code word, it was interesting to observe their subsequent alacrity to make the necessary contact.

In a few seconds my call went through to the ops room at Benson. As the telephone receiver was passed to me and I put it to my ear, a conversation was in progress between two men. The first voice I heard was Douglas-Hamilton's, from Leuchars, saying in a deliberate and solemn voice: 'Well, Steve, I'm afraid poor old Kiwi has had it.' Obviously, since the time in which we could still have been airborne had long passed, David had had no

71

option but to assume that the Foster-Moseley combination had fallen to the cursed law of averages, particularly since the sortie involved trying to reach so far to the east. He was also aware of our S-O-S from the Baltic. So there he was, in the process of reporting our fate to our wingco, who was waiting in the Benson ops room to see if this important bag of targets had been covered satisfactorily.

The moment David finished his sad sentence to Steve, I broke into their conversation and piped up: 'No I haven't! Here I am! and so is Frank!' This is the *pièce de résistance* of my surprise telephone calls – and I mean for all my lifetime.

I told both men the results should be good, and worth waiting for, even though one should never expect too much, too soon – occasionally engine oil sprayed over the camera lenses and spoilt the prints. Wingco then asked that Frank should remove the magazines from our cameras, and that we should take them to a position on the airfield from which a Mosquito could take off. We were to wait on that spot, and Steve would fly over and collect us and our cargo as urgently as possible. The CO at Coltishall paid us a visit in the ops room, and he and his staff could not do enough for us. This station commander, a group captain, was one of the famous Donaldson brothers – three brothers, all of whom were awarded the DSO for gallantry in the air. A few days later, at David's suggestion, I wrote him a sincere letter of thanks for his Spitfires and all the superb services that had been laid on to look after us.

We found out later that our 544 members at Benson, as well as our detachment at Leuchars, had been following our sortie with some interest. When Steve had completed his telephone calls to David and to me, he drove up to the mess and put a message over the tannoy telling all 544 aircrew to go down to the hangar immediately. The normal hours of duty for the groundcrew were well finished for the day, so Steve press-ganged our flying friends into dashing down and pushing out a serviceable aircraft so that he could nip over to Coltishall.

Frank and I soon spotted the Benson Mossie in its distinctive sky-blue colours, and we were glad to see it, as both of us were tired and cold. All our gear was loaded in holus-bolus; I sat in the navigator's seat, and Frank curled himself up, down in the nose. Steve was an RAF Cranwell man, and knew every square mile of the countryside. He flew low, just skimming the tree tops – though we nearly did not get up to tree-top level! A Mosquito uses its outer fuel tanks during take-off, and then the navigator awaits the pilot's command to switch the fuel cocks over to the mains; these cocks lie behind the pilot, who never sees them. As soon as we had left the deck, Steve said to me: 'Change over to mains, Kiwi.' I put my hand back and turned the two cocks, but I did not turn them on to mains – I turned them *off*! The engines coughed and missed a beat by the time it dawned on me just what I had done. Too much flying for me that day. Even the birds had gone to ground, or to bed, by the time we landed at Benson.

Steve shepherded us around like a cat with its prize kittens. No doubt he saw our weariness, but I also believe he was pleased for his squadron that we had pulled off this sortie, hazardous as it had been. The de-briefing took much longer than usual because the wingco also wanted to know in detail how I had balanced the revs and the boost and the altitude – in other words, how we had managed to stay in the air. We answered the questions about our findings for forty minutes. All targets were covered, and the prints were good. The smoke screens attracted plenty of attention as something of a novelty.

Following this period at the ops room, Steve drove both of us to the officers' mess. The cooks were off duty, but Steve chased round and found one to cook both of us an ops meal of whatever we fancied; and understandingly he allowed Frank, who at that time was an NCO, to have his meal with me in the kitchen. When he asked if he could get me a beer, I recall saying I would prefer an orange juice – and in two ticks he was back with a pint handle brimming with real orange juice. That was a real favour! And all the while he continued to ply us with questions.

Frank departed for the sergeants' mess, and I headed for my room. It so happened that both Joe and Vic were off on leave, so I had the room to myself. After a soak in the bath I snuggled into my pleasant bed, with no desire to do anything except fall asleep. But what a peculiar night it was to be. My brain raced faster than I could cope with, and every tiny detail of the trip continued to roll before me. Interspersed with this, I started laughing, sometimes a chuckle, and sometimes a good, loud, uproarious guffaw. I was powerless to stop, and at times the tears rolled down my face, not from crying, but from near-hysterical laughter. I reminded myself of the old gramophone record with Cicely Courtenage and the laughing gas. So what was so funny?

Sleep was impossible. How pleased I was that Vic and Joe were not present. Half-pint screamer, indeed; one pint – of orange juice! When I wasn't laughing, my mind was itemizing the details of the whole trip, and eventually I hopped out of bed and, taking some sheets of paper, wrote down a more or less blow-by-blow description of every incident. It took a long time, but it absorbed me completely: I jotted down the exact times we were here or there, the revs of the engine, the state of the fuel tanks, the descriptions of the ships, the time and details of feathering the engine, and every other minute detail. How had my mind chronicled these 365 minutes so precisely, and why?

When I had written down the whole experience, although I would still succumb to the odd fit of giggling, I did at last get a little sleep. In the morning I handed my sheets of records to the ops room, thinking they might help clarify the de-briefing – though in reality, for some reason or another, it had also been necessary for me to get the whole story out of my system.

Later on in the morning I went looking for Frank, and we met as he was coming to find me: good teamwork! We were both most surprised to learn from each other that in fact *both* of us had succumbed to this laughing business. It is probably something secret that we have not wanted to divulge to many people – it seems so absurd. All I think now, when the remembrance comes to me, is that I was laughing for sheer joy at being alive for one more day.

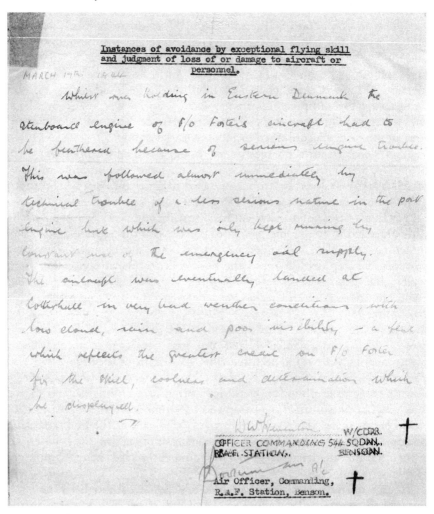

A 'green endorsement relative' to Op. No. 10.

Air Commodore Boothman interviewed us, and offered his congratulations on the successful sortie. Reading between the lines, I had the idea that the results had not done the whole Benson set-up any harm at all. David flew down from Leuchars in a Mosquito and, squeezing the two of us in, gave Frank and me a joyride back up to Leuchars. This was no trouble for him: he had already told me that he had once given his wife a flight in a Spitfire, sitting on his knees! That evening in the mess, 'B' Flight celebrated our return, and the next day we went off on seven days' leave. Frank travelled to be with Margaret, his dear wife, and my glorious week was spent out of uniform with my Scottish friends: we walked around the exquisite Trossach countryside on many days, and the laughter this time sprang from joyous companionship and gratitude at the arrival of each fresh day. . . . Not an aircraft to be seen, no engines to be heard, not even any trails high in the sky. . . . Bliss!

* * *

Two postscripts round off this chapter: the first was that both Frank and I received a 'Green Endorsement' for insertion in our logbooks, Frank's suitably worded for his sterling contribution to the success of sortie No. 10. Most endorsements in flying logbooks are 'red' ones and record some fault or misjudgement, such as failing to lower the undercarriage before landing. For myself, it was a pleasant surprise to receive a 'green' one, written in Wing Commander Steventon's handwriting, and signed by Air Commodore Boothman. These were two remarkably fine men, though sadly both were to live until only a few years after the end of the war, having made such a distinguished contribution to its victorious outcome.

The second comment on this Baltic sortie concerns my personal reaction to our predicament as we came in to land, an exhortation that occurred only this once while Frank and I were partners, and which evidently sprang involuntarily from deep inside my inner self. As the grass flashed past and I pulled back on the control column for the landing, noting the nearness of the trees at the perimeter ahead, I was heard to shout

'Please help us, God!'

How do I know that this is so? Frank has told me, several times since, over the years. Who heard me? . . . Well Frank, for one, certainly did.

7

My Life in Benson Mess

Let us eat and drink;
for tomorrow we shall die.
Isaiah 22:13

RAF Station at Benson, Oxfordshire, was my home from October 1943 until April 1945. During that period, a pleasant fifty-mile drive along the Thames valley via Nettlebed, Henley and Maidenhead took me to London, the capital of the empire. Benson provided a well-ordered life of comfort and good company in the officers' mess.

I never had to get my hands dirty unless I was playing around trying to start my car, or jacking it up after the twentieth puncture in old worn tyres. A batman or a batwoman polished my brass buttons, darned my socks, washed my clothes and pressed my uniforms. My batwoman for most of the time at Benson had the lovely English name of Rose, and I never told her how much I enjoyed saying her name. My bed was made for me, the linen changed, and the room always kept scrupulously clean, tidy and welcoming. Meals were served in a splendid dining room, and I never had to wash a dirty dish. The mess was complete with a spacious and handsome ante-room furnished with an ample number of armchairs and settees; a wide range of current papers and magazines was laid out neatly on occasional tables. At one end of this room was a large open fireplace and mantelpiece, and a radio and record-player with a fine selection of records were available at the other end. A billiard room and bar, together with a ladies' room and piano, ensured the service and ease of a first-rate club – though not a gentlemen's club, because several ladies filled responsible positions on the station as Waaf officers.

The operating costs of these facilities were charged to us by means of monthly mess bills, and it was a simple matter for any extraordinary items to be added, as required. Thus if you had the misfortune to break an item of furniture, the cost of the repairs was added to your bill, and if it was not clear who had caused the damage, the cost was shared by all. As regards the paying of these bills, my bank account never blinked. My salary was paid into it regularly, and now and again when in London I called to find out what the balance was. In fact it continued to mount up slowly, but never since in my life have matters financial taken so little of my time or thoughts; at that period, what level of salary was my due never concerned me in the slightest.

Now one can say 'How our circumstances have changed over the years!' – but in reality, it is not so much the circumstances as a drastic change in the major anxieties and priorities of life itself. The old Latin tag *'Dum spiro, spero'* sums it up well, meaning 'While I breathe, I hope', or 'While there is life, there is hope'. For my sojourn at Benson, the 'next breath' held a vastly higher priority for me than anything so trivial as money.

The mess building itself, in which my bedroom was located, was, and is, attractive and inviting. Substantial, and covered in Virginia creeper, it is surrounded by colourful flowerbeds and tree-filled lawns. RAF Station Benson was constructed in the late 1930s, and the first squadron moved into residence early in 1939. The station now boasts a crest, approved by HM The Queen in 1955, depicting a red lion rampant on a gold scallop. The lion signifies that the station is built on land once known as the Manor of Bensington, and belonging to the Royal Duchy of Cornwall. The ancient village of Benson, derived from Bensington, adjoins the perimeter track on one side of the airfield. Another gem of a village, Ewelme, is also a near neighbour. The scallop on the crest, which is the traditional emblem of pilgrims, signifies the mobility of the many units that have been stationed there over the years. It carries the motto: *'Spectemur Agendo'*, meaning 'Let us be known by our actions'. RAF Benson is privileged to hold the honorary freedom of the historic local town of Wallingford, a Thames-side market town only one and a half miles distant.

So what was the price that my companions-in-arms and I had to pay, to allow us to enjoy these first-class facilities? The average cost, spread over the ever-changing flow of aircrew personnel who manned the four squadrons during the war, was quite simple to assess: we placed our lives on the line. In my case this was every few days, for a period of eighteen months.

For the years 1939 to 1941 the King's Flight was based at Benson. When the Photographic Reconnaissance Unit commenced its operations from Benson with Spitfires in 1941, the King's Flight was disbanded until after the war; the PRU activity grew rapidly in size and importance as the war progressed. After the formation of the second Mosquito Squadron, No. 544, the flying strength remained at four squadrons. In 1946 the flight took up residence again at Benson, and on the accession of Queen Elizabeth II, its name became the Queen's Flight.

When Joe and Vic and I, together with our navigators, had completed our operational training at Dyce and were posted to Benson, it was not then clear to us whether we would remain at Benson, or be posted out to India for long-range PR operations. My diary notes remind me that I was '. . . in the dark, and very restless'. A following entry records: 'I will be one of the first from our original New Zealand course to be flying on ops.' But we did not have long to wait, and the next day we became the nucleus of 544 Squadron, based at Benson.

Living in this mess was a big change from all our previous training residences, where mostly we had lived in Nissen huts and eaten in temporary wartime messes. On those training airfields were two distinct groups, the instructors and the pupils; whereas now, all aircrew were operational except for some older men, many of whom wore wings from the 1914–18 war, and who were serving in various support sections such as transport, the control tower, and other activities. But amongst those more experienced men, many wearing decorations, we felt ourselves to be what in truth we were – the new boys.

But those natural feelings did not last long, for the sound reason that life on the squadron, and the station, moved on apace. Casualties occurred; men completed tours and were posted away for a rest; others moved on for medical reasons, so replacement crews – or in the case of Spitfires, pilots – were continually arriving, and thus it was not long before it was *us* who felt old hands. Frank, then being a sergeant, was not in our mess, and although he and I were the best of friends and companions from the beginning, we only met while flying, or in the crew-room. After one of the early days spent wholly in our crew-room, I noted: 'Am glad of Frank's company – he's a good egg!' (– because eggs were in such short supply then, and therefore a valuable commodity, to be compared to one was indeed a high compliment). Without Frank as a companion in the mess, it gave me constant pleasure and merriment to have Vic and Joe as such stalwart and reliable henchmen; every day they made me laugh.

We gravitated together as a comradely trio, making our own fun, not really disturbing anyone, but livening up the proceedings in general. The constant parcels of foodstuffs we all received from our families back home, and from many patriotic funds in our own countries, certainly attracted a flow of visitors to our room: many a feed of tinned fruit salad and cream and rich fruitcake cemented jovial relationships. Joe especially liked tinned sausages from Australia, and he rigged up a little electric cooker in our room which, although against all the regulations, always remained in action. The appetizing odours from his 'cooking' were like a smoke signal to the Indians, and fellows used to pour into our hospitable quarters as the smells wafted along the corridors. Steve, our wingco, had the room directly opposite our door, and he was the main visitor.

In addition to the basic personnel at Benson, we had a constant stream of visitors passing through. One reason for this was that we had a decompression chamber on the station, and aircrew would come for a couple of days for tests. At one time an Indian Air Force officer occupied a room opposite ours and a few doors along – next to the bathroom, as a matter of interest. This impressive-looking gentleman was dark and tall, and wore an eye-catching big turban; he also wore an equally eye-catching big bushy moustache and beard. Joe, in his never-changing egalitarian style, christened him 'Soya Bean', but only divulged this to us in a whisper.

One evening when Joe had taken in a large quantity of beer, he needed to arise during the night and set off up the passage to find the 'little room'; but unfortunately he didn't take a navigator, and turned into the wrong one. Back in our room I was awakened (Vic was absent on leave) by a loud scream, followed by yells and oaths (these last noises, as I recognized all too well, coming from Joe's Aussie-bush-trained vocal chords). I dashed out to see what the uproar was about. There was Joe, stumbling about somewhat. After making sure he completed what he had set out to do, I manoeuvred him back to his bed. 'What's up, Burfield, you old menace?' I scowled at him. Eventually the story was told.

Joe had opened the door to the single room temporarily occupied by the formidable Soya Bean. He had just grasped the rail at the foot of the bed for support, still thinking he was in the smaller room next door, when Soya Bean sat upright in a most sudden movement, at the same time flashing the light from a big torch straight at Joe, and screaming something in his own language. The surprise and fright that Joe received when this beturbaned and bewhiskered monster confronted him caused our usually unflinching Aussie to let forth with some words in *his* own language, before he managed to beat a retreat out the door.

Joe was a subdued version of himself in the morning, and told me in a quiet voice that he didn't fancy any breakfast. It was clear to me that he had no desire to clap eyes again on the visitor from India. We shall never know how that same story sounded when the Indian told it to his mates, and perhaps that is just as well. And that is how links were forged in the British Commonwealth.

A few weeks after D-Day, a grand mess party was laid on to bid farewell to the air commodore who, after receiving a DFC for his Spitfire sorties, was promoted and posted away for higher duties. This was the only time I recall such a party having official sanction, and it was also the only time when all four squadrons combined at one party. For all those reasons, it was bound to be a humdinger – and so it was. Our 544 put its collective self well and truly on the map. The diary says, 'We all rather enjoyed ourselves': was I beginning to suffer from the English understatement syndrome?

'John', as the air comm. was irreverently referred to, pushed off to his home and wife at quite an early hour. So what should we do to pass the time? Some bright sparks made a marvellous suggestion: make a circuit of the huge ante-room, around the four walls, without putting a foot on the floor. Fellows swung from the curtains, walked on their hands – which are not feet, you see – and made record-breaking leaps from chairs to settees, utilizing every sort of ingenuity to abide by the rules. Furthermore it took several beers to replace the sweat lost from these exertions.

The second and more brilliant idea initially provoked a lengthy argument as to who was most suitable to take the central role. Eventually one such was chosen. (It reminded me of how Ginger Baylis ended up as the lucky one having to scale our human pyramid). Then there was another delay while a fire was lit in the big fireplace; by the time it had produced the substantial heap of ashes needed for this escapade, the preliminaries had been completed. This long period provided useful refreshment time; besides, it was after midnight before the ashes were deemed to have cooled down sufficiently for the major operation to be started.

All hands united now in a task reminiscent of the construction of the pyramids. Bodies bent to the job of supporting the appointed one in one corner of the room until he was able to touch the ceiling, a pure white plaster one – and a long way above the floor at that. Once the supporters knew the exact positions they had to maintain in order to perform this, the chief climber then had to come back to earth. His shoes and socks were removed, his trousers well rolled up, and his feet buried in the warm ashes. The difficulty now was for another team of supporters to manhandle this poor volunteer up so that the principal supporters could turn him upside down. Once this stage was reached, all present who were not out of puff by being members of one or the other supporting groups, let out wild cheers. The final manoeuvre was for the upside-down one to firmly plant the blackened soles of his feet on the ceiling. And then the whole human edifice came tumbling down, only to be repeated in identical fashion about six feet further away in a line that traversed the ceiling diagonally from one corner to the opposite corner.

By sheer will-power and perseverance this complicated procedure was repeated and the whole diagonal line had an impeccable set of footprints implanted along it. Imagine how many times the constructors had to construct and dismantle their supports! And imagine how many times the appointed one had to be manhandled and turned upside down! But Robinson Crusoe himself never set eyes on a better example of mysterious footprints, and we were all thoroughly pleased with our efforts . . . It was late into the night before the occupants of the mess retired to their well earned rest.

The next morning the effect was startling, even to us. But that was nothing compared to the effect the new ceiling decorations had on the air commodore on the very morning of his departure – and if we are to believe rumours, the effect on his wife was so great that it could not be put into words. One funny thing was, that until this day, nobody ever figured out how those footprints appeared like magic. Our mess bills showed an unhealthy rise that month, reflecting the heavy cost of the redecorating. We also all suffered a dreadful amount of inconvenience from not being able to use the ante-room for several days because the decorators took an inordinate length of time completing their handiwork; we reckoned we could have shown them a far quicker method of doing the job.

Another effective way of creating interest for the people in the mess was discovered one other suitable night – again this was a situation where an earlier prank led to a better one. Outside the front doors of the mess, beyond the driveway and parking space, was a semi-underground air-raid shelter, never in use in my time. The whole exterior had been cleverly grassed over so it was not too noticeable either from the air or from ground level. The four walls sloped up at an acute angle, with the result that there was a small top to it. One evening a gang of wags, by sheer musclepower and weight of numbers – probably working along the lines of the builders of the Great Wall of China – parked the Baby Austin car belonging to the Wing Commander Flying on the top of the shelter. It looked great in the morning, perched up on its own special little parking lot.

Then one evening some time after that, some industrious and cheerful types measured the same car with a tape measure, and then measured the double doors at the end of the main passageway of the mess. By pure mathematics, clearly one into one would not go, and it was too wide; but determination and ingenuity were the qualities that brought fellows to Benson in the first place, and their idea was not to be so easily stifled. Further precise measurements proved that if the wheels and their hubs came off the car, there was room to burn, as they say. So no sooner said than done: the wheels were put on again once the car had been lifted inside, and then it was driven and pushed right along until it was outside the dining-room doors. And there it stayed until everyone turned up on the dot for breakfast. Once again, no one could believe their eyes.

In theory we were all due to have one day off duty every week, but often this was not possible. The allocation of days off, forty-eight-hour passes and seven-day leaves was all decided by the squadron COs, as circumstances permitted. I don't remember thinking about it at the time, even though Frank was married to his Margaret all the period we were together, but the crews who lived in the UK at least had *some* opportunities to visit their homes and families from time to time. Accommodation was at a premium in the neighbouring towns and villages, but those who were able rented a cottage for a spell, and brought their wives and kiddies to be near Benson. That must have been a mixed blessing, and have required strong nerves. Who wanted, as a wife, to hear a Mossie take off, and then have to wait five or six hours to see if it returned or not with her husband? That ordeal was hard enough for me to endure as a mere friend, or even just a short-term acquaintance, of any of the squadron crews.

For those of us whose homes and families were not in Britain – a comparative handful – it was natural that we spent more of our time on the station, and inevitably that meant more time in our rooms. I was happy to have peaceful times when it was good just to read or write, or lie on the bed and listen to the radio. My correspondence was considerable, and grew as my postings moved from country to country, and area to area. My parents wrote regularly; they numbered their letters and parcels to me, and by the war end, the numbers had mounted to well over the hundred. It is a quirk of those war years that every single item sent to me from New Zealand reached me eventually, U-boats and various post offices notwithstanding.

During my tour at Benson I spent some gloriously happy and carefree leaves, sometimes with my Scottish friends in Stirling, sometimes in London, and often in Wiltshire with a dear old country lady who had other members of her family living with her from time to time. Her married son and family lived nearby. When relaxing there, eating good country fare, and dressed in civilian clothes, the war did not exist for me.

One day Joe, who over a long period had wormed the address out of me, shot over in his Mosquito and 'beat up' the house and the village until I was alarmed that someone would report his daring antics. I was also fearful because I had never seen Joe displaying his flying abilities like this, and I was scared he might crash; he just wouldn't go away – it was a relief when he waggled his wings and disappeared over the trees and hedges. But of course later on, back in our room in the mess, it was good for a laugh.

On these welcome interludes in Wiltshire I had the added pleasure of the company of one of the pretty granddaughters, and we enjoyed many fine outings together. The kindness and the solace proffered to me during this hectic period undoubtedly helped me to keep my nerves under control, and to maintain excellent health. These were two prime factors that helped to keep me alive.

Visiting London was always an adventure. Usually Joe and Vic were my companions, because wingco obliged us – without us requesting the favour – by occasionally arranging for us three to be on leave at the same time, even though we were on different flights and schedules. On the visits when I was on my own I tried to stay at Kiwi House, where it was fun to find who else was there at the time. Coincidences often occurred: on two occasions I found myself sharing a room with a friend who had been in the same form as myself at Wellington College.

From Kiwi House we used to congregate at the NZ Forces Club in Charing Cross Road, and there it was equal fun to catch up with fellows who had been in the same Air Force training courses. We visited most of the leading theatre shows during the war; Ivor Novello's *The Dancing Years* was a favourite, and we revelled in the humour and sentimentality of Flannagan and Allan. We lunched and dined at the best restaurants we could find, even if we had to eat a horse steak – by mistake. We supported the RNZAF rugby team at Richmond rugby ground when it played the Welsh Guards, and of course as typical Kiwis, whether in peace-time or war-time, we saw the sights of London as hard as we could.

After a leave, your mind clicked back into the Benson mode without even trying, and by the time you entered the mess and eagerly collected the mail from the mail rack, someone familiar would be bound to casually pass on the latest 'score' relating to casualties. By this time my stomach would be starting to regain its hard knot, and I would have to lick my lips to neutralize the dryness in my mouth. Everything was back to normal again. Heigh-ho! Let's put on a bright smile and get on with the job.

8

D-Day – Invasion of Europe

Boast not thyself of to-morrow;
for thou knowest not what a day may bring forth.

Proverbs 27:1

Op. No. 18, 6 June 1944

Our tour of operations moved on steadily, trip by trip, and we learned from experience. My logbook reminds me that during our first seventeen trips we were attacked either by fighters or flak, or both, on ten occasions, and we twice returned on a single engine. Our learning curve was reaching upwards sharply. Of more concern to us was that we were still *on* the graph: it was common knowledge that the war could not be won until the Continent was invaded, and the question was 'When?'. Notes in my diary indicate that many observers had thought the year 1943 would see the big event, and as the months of 1944 came and went, rumours were rife concerning the impending invasion.

During our first detachment to Leuchars during March and April, Frank and I flew Op. No. 11 before we were recalled to Benson, a high priority trip to urgently locate a German ship, the *Monte Rosa*. A heavy naval escort protected it, and although we photographed it from a height of 34,000ft (10,300m) in Bergen fiord, we still received a large amount of accurate flak. It was well protected all right: on our return, a raid was made on the ship and its escorts by a Mosquito torpedo-bomber squadron, and though the attack was successful, losses and casualties occurred, the leader of the squadron being one of those killed. The crews who returned were not pleased with PRU locating the targets in such a difficult and heavily defended area, and one or two personal comments were aimed in the direction of Frank and myself. War being what it is, a copy of a signal was given to me from 18 Group that reads: 'The first class reconnaissance you did today resulted in a really successful attack. Well done.' Yes, if you survived it was 'well done'; but if you didn't, you became a casualty, and it was 'a poor show'.

Later the *Monte Rosa* was revived; she passed to Britain as a prize ship at the end of the war, and joined the New Zealand Shipping Company. Ten years to the day after the attack, the ship, now renamed the *Empire Windrush*, caught fire off Algiers with about 1,500 people on board, and was abandoned.

We were recalled to Benson because extra manpower was needed to cover targets in Germany, and we wondered if this extra activity at Benson pointed towards invasion plans. There was no trip for us the following day, and we sat in the crew-room and fraternized with our friends on 'A' Flight. We played darts for hours at a stretch, then Joe and I enjoyed each other's company on a long brisk walk, finishing off our day with a game of snooker in the mess. While we were playing, someone told us that one 'B' Flight crew flying from Leuchars, Howarth and Kelley, had failed to return this same day – and they never did return to anywhere. It was immediately in our minds that Foster and Moseley could well have been detailed for that trip; and Joe had come back from his trip with his kite 'looking like a sieve', I was told by someone else.

The next day, 8 April 1944, we appreciated why we had been hurried back to Benson because we were briefed for an arduous trip into the mid-Reich. The target area covered Leipzig and Magdeburg that, with Berlin, formed a triangle with sides of about eighty miles. It was necessary to cross the Ruhr region to reach these targets, and the Ruhr, as the powerhouse of German industry, bristled with defences; but to avoid the whole area by skirting right round it took too much of a dog-leg.

This op. was our twelfth, but our 'experience account' was not yet sufficient to help us avoid making a basic error in our execution of this sortie. The day was typical for the region and the season of the year: there was no cloud, but a thick haze made visibility most tiresome. When approaching the prime target near Magdeburg we had climbed to 35,500ft (10,750m) in the belief that this altitude would be high enough to reduce the possibility of accurate flak, and at that height I did not expect to be jumped by fighters. In the hazy atmosphere, and with the previous target not very far distant from this next one, neither Frank nor I had been able to pinpoint what we were looking for. Conditions were unfavourable, and we had not allowed sufficient time. This was unusual for us, as we were normally fortunate in spotting targets in ample time to be organized and to choose our run-ins.

Here we were then, over the area, but with no target identified through the smoggy air. The basic error was already perpetrated, and I became furious at our lack of expertise; the risks and the danger increased second by second. We both searched frantically. I had a map in my hands, Frank had another, and I was decidedly unreasonable in my remarks. With each exclamation made regarding our unsatisfactory and negative situation, I dug my right elbow into Frank's ribs for emphasis. For sure, that proved my theory about lack of oxygen – or at least, that is what I wanted to believe.

Straps undone, feet braced on the rudder pedals, and legs stretched to their limit to give me more height in the tiny cockpit to look out and downwards, I somehow managed to execute a continuous steep turn. It was not easy, technically, and I knew in my heart we were taking far too much of a risk cavorting about in one spot, slap-bang over the heartland of the enemy. Our method had always been to decisively swoop over a target, photograph it expertly, and then just as smartly disappear from view. Now we were breaking all our own hard-learned rules.

Out of the blue a dart of steel went through my body. That's how it felt, and what we saw was an Fw 190 going up close behind us. He was shooting up nearly vertically, to be in the classic position of about 500 feet above our tail. Shooting up? Yes, like a *rocket*! This was a 190 equipped with a tail-booster rocket probably fired by some derivative of nitrous oxide: this is the gas described as 'laughing gas', and therefore known to pilots as 'ha-ha' gas. I had never met anyone who had encountered this invention, but had read about it in Air Ministry circulars. Basically, the application of it enabled a fighter to obtain a super burst of power sufficient to gain ascendancy over an adversary, including our peerless Mosquito. Our opponent had utilized his advantage perfectly, and the sight of the Focke-Wulf's thick black plume of fumes pouring out behind him reminded me of the Devil's tail.

He turned and dived to the attack, and I screamed into the tightest turn I could produce: my fingers, hands, arms, shoulders, back, stomach, legs and feet all combined to pull the control column hard back into my waist. The docile, easy Mosquito that I normally flew with the fingertips of one hand, wound up to such a degree of tightness that my mental strength was barely sufficient to force my physical strength to maintain this hold on the controls. The aircraft became a juddering monster, challenging me to see who was master – but man and machine had to unite for us to win this duel for survival.

The Fw 190 holed us through one wing at his first pass. Luckily he had not been able to follow our manoeuvre closely enough to sight us in the vital areas of the cockpit or the engines, and neither the fuel tanks nor any controls were damaged. For five to ten long minutes we tangled with him as he loosed off his ammunition at us, his attack fast and furious. It took us all our time to avoid his succession of passes, and there was no opportunity to think about trying to fly off in a direction of home. We wondered if his mates were coming up to join him. At the back of my mind I was unreasonably determined to still find and cover our last target, so I had to be content to remain in the area. The fuel supply was ample – and we also had unfinished business, because we had to get even with the man for the frightful shock his devilish equipment had given us.

My body was as wet as when I was tipped out with Vickers into the

Thames, but my throat so dry that talk was impossible. Frank did a mighty task in informing me exactly where the fighter was when he was behind us, and in estimating when the exact second had arrived for another wrenchingly tight turn. We varied these turns – sometimes going left and at other times to the right. Finally he broke away, either out of ammo, or fuel, or both. Apparently the rocket only had one burst in it.

We then found the elusive target, and covered it in one scorching shallow dive . . . . That was more like it!

Not many minutes later, on the homeward way, heavy flak from over the Ruhr engaged us: the poor Mossie was having to take more than its share on this day, and explosions rocked us about in all directions. It never came clearly to me at those times whether it was preferable to keep flying in a straight line and hope to get out of range as quickly as possible, or whether to throw the aircraft about and change directions. On this particular day the flak threw us about so much it wasn't possible to fly in a straight line anyway, so no decision had to be made on that score. The aircraft was hit and holed again.

On the way home, and letting down over the Channel, Frank must have felt an itch, and unbuckled his harness in order to have a scratch. He withdrew his hand from his chest and shouted through the intercom: 'I've been wounded!' This really did unnerve me – all I wanted at that stage was a bit of peace and quiet. Maybe the oxygen was not flowing too freely that day, but Frank's shout, for some reason, startled and surprised me so much that my response was to yell back at him: 'You can't be! What makes you think you are?' His reply was conclusive enough: 'Well, what's this blood then?'

Sure enough, his forefinger did show a trace of blood. After groping about under his singlet he proudly displayed a tiny sliver of shrapnel. What a smile he gave! It registered with me as, 'Who do you think you are, Fos, trying to tell me I'm not wounded?'

Our trip No. 12 therefore indeed had its moments, though my diary merely records: 'Glad to get back OK' and, 'A Mossie crew and a Spit missing on ops.' That evening we enjoyed a visit to a station show. Many well known artists came to provide entertainment at Benson, and if the general idea was to relax aircrew, it was a good one and effective; but not enough to prevent me waking during the night with what we called 'the screaming hab-dabs'. All too realistically I saw the Focke-Wulf again, in vivid and terrifying detail, flashing upwards like a meteor, propelled by its devilish, black smoky tail. It was a good thing I did not know then that this nightmare would recur at varying intervals over a period of many years – even when camping in the beautiful and tranquil New Zealand bush, this instant but unwelcome recollection continued to haunt me. Complete with its swastika, black cross and black plume, the enemy zoomed upwards and swooped down like an eagle, ready to devour its prey; and that was always the moment I woke up.

After this Magdeburg incident I made a private pact with myself, that if ever we found ourselves shot down by a fighter and did not have the time or conditions to bale out, then I would use my last seconds in this life to do my best to ram the enemy aircraft. In my heart I did not believe we would *ever* come off second best, but even so, at that time this decision gave me a good feeling. It has been a secret until now.

Prior to 1 May 1944, when 'B' Flight returned to Benson, a crew from our flight, Kennedy and Chambers, failed to return from a trip; but in three days' time we had the happy news that both men were safe in neutral Sweden. This was encouraging for all of us, particularly as after a few weeks the pilot was flown back to Scotland in the bomb bay of a Mosquito, and resumed his activities with us. These aircraft and their crews had the markings and the plain clothes of civilians, and were a great help to the Allies: if the Spaniards were supposedly neutral but had a strong bias towards a German victory, the Swedes leaned heavily in our direction, and a regular service, flown at night, came into operation between Sweden and Scotland for VIPs – and PRU pilots came under that classification. The navigator arrived back via the same channels shortly afterwards.

Our next op., No. 13, turned out to be a rare flop. We were out of bed at 4:30am, had breakfast at 4:45am, and were briefed for another Far Eastern Baltic experience. We took off at 7am, and refuelled further up the coast. We duly stooged around the track, in or over cloud for more than five hours, but there wasn't a sign of life, in the air or on the ground; I think the effort took more out of us than a normal clear-air trip. However, I never bothered to complain to the met. officer.

That was Op. No. 13; No. 14 was our last Norway trip for a while. It was successful, but again we had to evade attacks from a pair of fighters. During May we completed Ops Nos 15, 16 and 17, the targets in Denmark, Kiel and Dresden, and there was heavy flak from all parties.

As the weeks in May passed by, it was clear that a massive build-up towards an invasion was under way: you had only to drive along the secondary roads and country lanes to see the piles of army stores and equipment that lined the sides of these byways for mile upon mile. From the air, spread over southern England particularly, you couldn't fail to see airfield after airfield stacked with rows of camouflaged gliders, and all sorts of ordinary fields, not formal airfields, were also pressed into service to park these huge fleets.

Near the end of May we commenced an intensive but short course in low flying. Please don't think that any instruction was offered! This 'course' was self-taught: you either learned well, or not. We flew at an altitude just high enough to miss the higher obstacles attached to the ground, such as trees and wires, before dropping down again to skim the buildings and hedges. For certain agreed periods of the day it was open slather along the Great Western Railway lines around the area of Didcot, and it took great efforts of concentration to make a good and safe job of it. Once we whipped over a haystack that was being built by two Italian POWs; Frank, looking back, said one of them chucked his pitchfork in our direction, so we made a turn and passed over them once more. This time the feedback was more satisfactory, and he reported that they had both been blown off their stack, and were lying on the ground shaking their fists at us. With the determined mood I was in, and as a relief from the tension, it was good for a grin.

Our Mosquitos had been modified to have optimum performance at high altitude, and did not have an outstanding speed at low level, and we wondered just what it would be like, whizzing over enemy territory in an unarmed kite at speeds which did not have the advantage over the best German fighters. It could be said that things were beginning to move – fast. During the first week in June all aircrew were summoned to their respective hangars, and were detailed to assist groundcrews in an important and urgent job. The order was to paint three white and two black stripes around the fuselage and each wing of all operational aircraft: these were referred to as D-Day 'recognition stripes'. The idea was to identify every Allied aircraft that could appear in the skies over Britain and the Continent – British, American, Free French, Czech, Polish, and all the rest. I was only too pleased to wield my paintbrush. Already Frank and I had once skirmished for more than twenty minutes with a dozen USAAF Mustangs that had unwittingly attacked us while we were over Germany. These Yanks were brought up no doubt on the legends of their Wild West grand-daddies that shot first, and asked any questions later: if they saw one lonely kite up high over Europe their immediate reaction was that 'it must be an enemy and must be attacked'. Our private battle, before we could proceed further into Germany and get on with our job, had steamed me up considerably on that occasion. Yes, these stripes would make our reconnaissance planes more visible to all and sundry, but on balance the idea gave me a feeling of greater safety, rather than less.

Everyone was guessing that the invasion would take place the following day, but as is generally known, the weather conditions for the landings were not favourable. General Eisenhower, the commander-in-chief of the Allied Expeditionary Forces, had to make the momentous decision to postpone the day. No aircraft could fly in the interim because of the painted stripes, and tight security was enforced on all personnel regarding the stripes and what they signified.

On Monday 5 June I made the most of the no-flying day, and spent the afternoon sailing on the river at Goring, in a stiff breeze, and having a superb time – the same wind, doubtless, that across the Channel was delaying the biggest invasion in history. After our sail we had tea at the White Swan, and returned to Benson for an evening at the station cinema. That was my preparation for D-Day, 6 June 1944: I felt on top form and ready to go.

A vast number of other people had done a great deal more preparation. On the eve of D-Day 1.5 million US servicemen were stationed in Britain; another two million had already passed through en route to North Africa and Italy. By a quirk of timing, American troops entered Rome late on 4 June, after Allied armies had slogged their way up Italy during the previous nine months. On 5 June more than a thousand British bombers struck at the ten most important German gun batteries in the invasion assault area, dropping 5,000 tons of bombs. That night, a fleet of more than 3,000 ships was on its way across the Channel, and over the period of the invasion a total of 6,500 vessels was utilized; this included 4,000 landing craft. The RAF and the USAAF put a combined total of 12,000 aircraft into the air.

The BBC sent a coded message to leaders of the French Resistance, instructing them to sever railway lines throughout France. From a planned total of 1,050 breaches, 950 were cut. For three months prior to D-Day, more than 8,000 British bombers had dropped 42,000 tons of bombs on railway marshalling yards in France and Belgium. In the single month of May, American bombers had dropped an additional 11,000 tons of bombs on the same targets. As well as bombers, ground-attack fighters destroyed 500 locomotives between 20 and 28 May. The down side was that during April and May the air forces between them lost 2,000 aircraft and 12,000 aircrew.

While the Allies were bringing their preparations to a climax to launch the invasion of Europe, referred to as the 'Second Front' and codenamed Operation *Overlord*, the Russian armies were advancing against the Germans on the Eastern Front. As one Red Army advanced towards the Hungarian border, the Nazis speeded up their transportation of three-quarters of a million Jews from Hungary to the concentration camp at Auschwitz in Poland. Thousands were deported every day. From amongst this number, the SS camp administration records show that 40kg of gold was taken from the teeth of the corpses in a period of fifteen days . . . . And people still ask me at times: 'What was the point of your going to war? Especially bothering to volunteer.'

On the morning of 6 June, thousands of British and American troops landed by parachute in Normandy, closely followed by others who went ashore in amphibious tanks. By midnight, 155,000 invaders were successfully holding their beach-heads. The German High Command, including Hitler himself, was not yet sure if these landings were the real thing, or just a diversion to cover a major landing somewhere else on the European coast.

At RAF Station Benson, the overall pulse quickened considerably: it was the day of 'all change'. No longer, on 544 Squadron, was 'A' Flight on duty one day, and 'B' Flight the next – all serviceable aircraft were pressed into action, and that involved all fit crews to be on call. All leave off the station was cancelled.

No longer was high altitude our defence, and our normal 'comfortable' place in the sky: now, any altitude was to be used to ensure photo coverage, and low-level oblique-facing cameras were now fitted in addition to the battery of vertical ones. No longer were trips and take-offs cancelled because of fog: we took off regardless, obtained photos of targets, and paid any price to do so.

This increase in the tempo of our operations was reflected in our squadron losses. For the 100 days following D-Day, ten Mossies from 544 failed to return from trips. Of the twenty men missing, five eventually turned up alive. Three out of the five were prisoners of war until the war's end. At the time, none of us gave much priority to trying to keep statistics. For sure nobody talked about them, and in all probability most of us never thought about them; it was best not to.

In this period of pressure and increased danger, DDH came into his own as a quiet and gentle man of steel. He allocated himself trips as frequently as for anyone else. His navigator, Phil Gatehouse, already wearing the DFM, was a cheery, competent man about the same age as David.

Two days after D-Day, and following an op. that Frank and I had flown, David drove me up to Oxford, his student stamping ground, where we enjoyed a fine meal and companionship. About three weeks later Frank and I had a day off, and David stretched it to make it two days, and drove me to his home, eighty miles away in Dorset. He and his wife, Lady Prunella, and their two boys lived in an attractive house that had been the head gardener's cottage in earlier days. David's mother, the dowager duchess, lived in the main house. Pouring rain stopped us from going riding, but we enjoyed what was a memorable time for me. It was strawberry-picking time, and regardless of the teeming rain we collected a big quantity of the luscious berries. My hosts gave me a huge bag of them to take back to camp, together with a container of real cream – ideal gifts to a hungry Kiwi. All of this family came to hold a place in my heart, not because of their exalted position in the scheme of things worldly, but purely because of their striking qualities of character and example.

That eventful morning of 6 June, Frank and I were airborne amongst the throng. No need to climb to the usual high altitude: surely all the German fighters would be more than engaged at lower levels. Another reason not to climb too high was my personal desire to fly low enough to obtain the closest possible view of the immense armada that stretched across our horizon from one side to the other. What a unique spectacle! A once-in-a-lifetime experience.

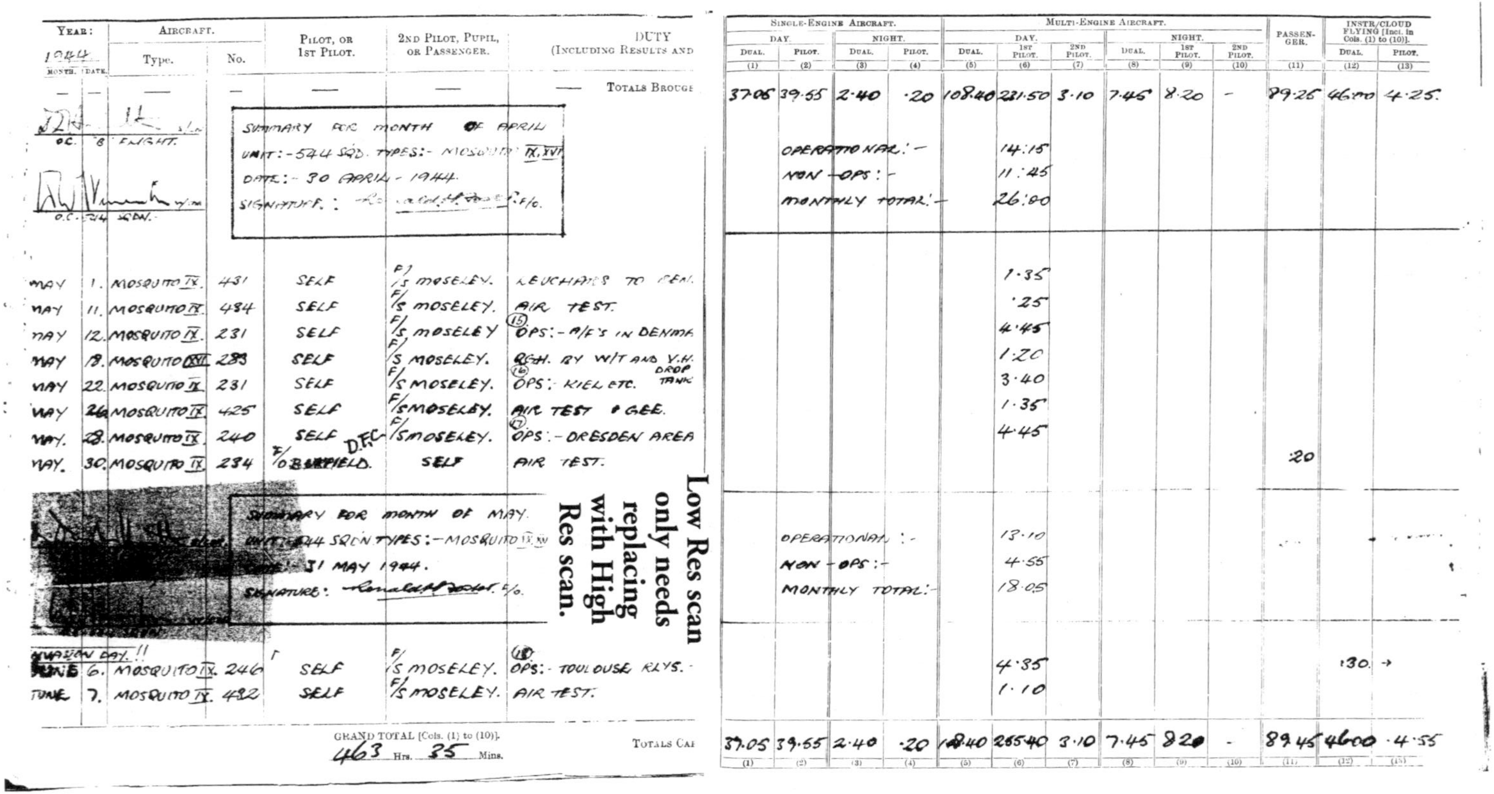

(flight logbook page — handwritten entries)

Duty (Including Results of Bookings):

SUMMARY FOR MONTH OF APRIL
UNIT:- 544 SQD. TYPES:- MOSQUITO IX IV
DATE:- 30 APRIL 1944
SIGNATURE:-

Date	Aircraft Type	No.	Pilot	2nd Pilot	Duty
MAY 1.	MOSQUITO IX	431	SELF	P/ MOSELEY.	LEUCHARS TO BEN.
MAY 11.	MOSQUITO IX	494	SELF	F/ MOSELEY.	AIR TEST.
MAY 12.	MOSQUITO IX	231	SELF	F/ MOSELEY	OPS:- M/S IN DENMARK
MAY 12.	MOSQUITO XVI	293	SELF	F/ MOSELEY.	RETN. BY WIT AND VIK
MAY 22.	MOSQUITO IX	231	SELF	F/ MOSELEY.	OPS:- KIEL ETC.
MAY 24.	MOSQUITO IV	425	SELF	F/ MOSELEY	AIR TEST & GEE.
MAY 28.	MOSQUITO IX	240	SELF DFC	F/ MOSELEY.	OPS:- DRESDEN AREA
MAY 30.	MOSQUITO IX	234	W/O BURFIELD.	SELF	AIR TEST.

SUMMARY FOR MONTH OF MAY.

| JUNE 6. | MOSQUITO IX | 246 | SELF | F/ MOSELEY. | OPS:- TOULOUSE RLYS. |
| JUNE 7. | MOSQUITO IX | 482 | SELF | F/ MOSELEY. | AIR TEST. |

**Low Res scan
only needs
replacing
with High
Res scan.**

Logbook: 6 June 1944 = D-Day: the Invasion of Europe. Op. No. 18: note Joe Burfield's name, and the signatures of Sqn Ldr David Douglas-Hamilton and Wg Cdr D. W. Steventon.

Across the Channel conditions were cloudy. Our targets were railyards and installations at various places, extending as far south as Toulouse. Aircraft from our squadron were deployed to cover all areas from which reinforcements of troops and their equipment and supplies were expected to be drawn, to defend the landing zones.

We climbed and set course when nearing the beach-head areas, and on dead-reckoning, let down in a long glide towards our first target. Our met. advice predicted a cloud base over France of about 3–4,000ft, and to let down through cloud, not being sure of where we were, was all against recommended practice: it was, and still is, a leading recipe for suicide. But caught up in the mood of the day, I steeled myself to do it, trusting that Frank's calculations would see us avoid the high ground that France has in plenty. Leaning forward hard in my seat against my straps, I peered down to glimpse the ground, holding the throttles in my left hand, ready to open up if potential disaster was the first thing we saw. We spotted the ground all right, about circuit height below us, say from 1,000ft. And where were we? No, not spot on over the target, in the way of a fairytale, but smack over a German Luftwaffe airfield with fighters parked all around the perimeter, the largest number of German fighters I ever saw at one time. It was handy I was holding the throttles: open they went, and up we went, back into the clouds to regain breath and consider where and how we should attempt to have another go, hopefully encountering some less hostile ground.

Suffice it to say we located ourselves, and moved from one target to another. At our briefing we knew which crew from our flight was now adjacent to our target territory, and in a moment of bravado I called them up over the R/T. We made brief contact, and it gave me a boyish thrill to exchange reports; Simonson, with his Canadian accent and vocabulary, sounded as highly strung and skittish as I did. What was not so enjoyable was to hear a conversation in German, too, and that finished my desire to play about with the VHF. Our last target was Toulouse, where the marshalling yards were extensive and took several runs to cover. We made some runs at 4,000ft, and received some flak. We came lower and lower – on some of our evasion manoeuvres to avoid the thick flak we flew at less than the height of the flak towers on which some anti-aircraft guns were stationed.

On some of the runs, while Frank was operating the cameras, I dully wondered what the unusual noise was below us on the main body of the kite. Of all things, under those circumstances, the thought sprung into my mind that the sound was like being drubbed with many cricket bats. A weird line of thought to be sure, which I cannot explain. In fact it was the plane being hit, splintered and marked by shots and shrapnel that sprayed us from many directions.

The Mosquito was still flying well as we departed the arena; all targets were covered. As we flew north, inevitably along the railway line, we caught up with an unbelievably long train. It carried tanks and armoured vehicles, and also operated some anti-aircraft guns, and looked a formidable consignment. In a flash we were nearly up to the engine. I clearly saw the driver and the terrified face of the fireman as he looked over his shoulder at us; if our wheels had been lowered we would have been running along the roof of his cab. It was the nearest I ever saw a German during the war except for the Fw 190 pilot over Berlin. The fireman for a certainty thought his last day had come. Without thinking it out, I instinctively wheeled the Mossie round in a circle, came up over the train again and, trying to time it accurately, pressed the button that released the two drop-tanks of extra fuel, fixed under the wings. Due to a fault, only one came unstuck and left us flying one wing low, and anyway my attempt at bombing did nothing spectacular to the train – it is a mystery why all the flak at Toulouse didn't explode those tanks of ours.

Post-war records now disclose that on the afternoon of 6 June, the 2nd Panzer Division, equipped with the latest German heavy tanks, had been ordered to move from Toulouse, where it was based, to Normandy. This journey should have taken three days, but because all the bridges over the Loire had been destroyed by the Allies, and also due to sabotage efforts en route, the trip took seventeen days. The delays to this veteran division from the Russian front spared the forces landing in Normandy a major headache. It cannot be proved, but this was probably the train we encountered. Maybe the nerves of its crew were somewhat shattered by the swift-moving Mosquito that didn't bomb them or shoot at them, but did look in closely on them.

After leaving the train, we climbed up to a respectable height in order to relax a trifle, and to make sure we did not become mixed up with the air traffic over the fighting zone. What a free hand we had in handling our trips – all we had to do was to deliver the goods.

Back on the deck at Benson the scene was like some sort of picnic on the dispersal area in front of our hangar, with many kites parked up close together and their crews chatting excitedly over the highlights of their day. Several aircraft were holed, and the groundcrew boys started counting aloud as they ran their fingers over the fuselage of our kite. It was like a sieve! An accurate count was never arrived at, but it reached the hundreds; we would have won the jackpot for that day. Late in the evening, after dinner, the mess was crowded; everyone seemed to have congregated there, and the air buzzed with animation and satisfaction at the outcome of such a momentous day. The Allied Expeditionary Air Force had clocked up 14,674 sorties on this D-Day, as we were later to learn.

The next day Frank and I did nothing more than fly an air-test. In the evening we were briefed for our targets for the following day, a new procedure introduced to reduce the congestion in the ops. room the next morning. 'All leave off the station is cancelled indefinitely': I remembered this as I climbed wearily into bed at 8pm.

We were up at 4am the next day, and airborne at 6am, which because of double summer time was really four o'clock in the morning. A new routine was introduced for these 'railway' sorties, as they came to be known to us: instead of landing at Benson on our return, we landed at Farnborough, a fifteen-minute hop away. It usually seemed to me not worthwhile to waste time and fuel by climbing too high for that short trip, so we often enjoyed an illicit low-level whizz over the tree tops back to base. SHAEF had set up a specialized Army Photo-Interpretation Unit at Farnborough in order to obtain the latest proof of the movements of German forces at the earliest possible moment. As we landed there, an army despatch rider on his motorcycle with sidecar would pull up alongside the Mossie, the magazines were unloaded from the cameras, and then whisked away with maximum efficiency to be developed.

Our squadron continued with every available aircraft covering the railway networks for the next month. In June, we flew Ops Nos 19 to 23, all on railway targets. Frank and I confided to each other that we were very tired, with so many early rises, and sometimes not called for briefing till 5pm. One of these trips took us well to the south, where we suffered the worst turbulence I have experienced; the Pyrenees caused this, the towering cumulo-nimbus clouds reaching to more than 40,000ft. For July, we were then switched back to the usual targets in Germany and eastern Europe, while 540 Squadron, the other Mosquito squadron, took over our duties over France, Belgium and western Germany. After one month of that regime, we were to swop over again.

Seven days after D-Day one of Hitler's 'secret weapons' was launched against England: the 'V-1', a pilotless flying bomb that became known as the 'doodlebug', a jet-propelled plane carrying a ton of explosives that detonated on impact. By a coincidence of timing, the first of the 'V-2s' to fall into Allied hands chanced to land in Sweden by mistake on the same day; the British were later given the opportunity to examine it. In the first three days of attacks by the V-ls, casualties included 250 people killed indiscriminately around London.

By 28 June, more than three-quarters of a million British and American troops had been landed in Europe. In England, flying bombs had killed 1,935 civilians in the course of sixteen days of attack. To show the rate of the build-up of Allied troops in Normandy, by 2 July the Allied armies on French soil numbered more than one million.

Frank and I, together with everyone else, were kept busy flying. Although we had no leave for several weeks, we did have odd days off duty. On those days, probably due to increased pressure while on the station, I frequently spent time in Wallingford or Oxford, occasionally going by car with David for a fine meal and to talk of peaceful pursuits. Often I chose to ride my pushbike on those glorious summer evenings, for the sheer pleasure of the exercise and the enjoyment of the countryside. Life tasted better than ever in that summer of 1944, and there was all the more relish in still being around to savour it.

At one stage during these days of heavy drama, when I was alone in my room late in the evening, I was glancing through my diary for the previous year, 1943, looking for an address. The following lines happened to catch my eye, lines I had penned on 19 April 1943 when travelling on my own by train from Montreal to Halifax prior to embarking for England:

> My wander-thirst must be quenched again,
> I am restless and longing to go,
> Adventure and action must I taste
> 'Fore life slides by too slow.
> It's all very pleasant to sit and to dream
> Just letting the world slip by
> Much better to reach out, undismayed,
> – To live before we die.
> Our world is full of peoples and places
> Calling out to be met, to be seen;
> Baghdad and Beirut, Colombo and Cairo,
> Tropic isles, arctic seas, valleys green.
> So let us be off, for England and Empire,
> Proving ourselves in the test.
> We are too young to sit back and linger,
> Let us live to the full, with zest!

Well, that's how I felt fifteen months earlier: eager enough to reach England, to do my bit – I even had anxieties that the war might be over before I ever arrived near Europe! Now here I was, working hard at the job I had been taught, and doing many things I had not been taught; attending the funerals of the best of friends, packing up their belongings and writing to mothers and wives and sweethearts while the tears dropped on to the paper. I picked up my pen, and this is what I scribbled, on 13 July 1944. It is my reply to myself:

> . . . Oh yes I agree, that is all very fine,
> A spirit which must be admired,
> But for how long does one wander and thirst
> 'Fore body and soul become tired?
> To roam and to drift would doubtless be grand

But it all must end some day;
If life now runs both hectic and grim,
What gain to continue that way?
It seems a few years can pass by so fast,
Be filled with events that thrill,
That one could easily be content
To settle, and rest, and be still.
We're doing our duty and taking the risks,
They are worth it for the Evil we fight,
But when this war is over and won,
Which way of life will be right?
I want to try both, but that can't be so,
It must be to wander or rest,
Will I feel like roughing and risking again,
Or find peace, and quiet, the best?

Some random diary excerpts from these hectic wartime days help to illustrate this trying period:

- Our losses are pretty sticky.
- Tired and ready for leave, but satisfied with the job we're doing.
- With the changes in personnel, feel a bit of a veteran on the squadron these days.
- We are really earning our crusts (pay) this month!
- 540 had two crews go missing this week. One crew were on the last trip of their tour.

On all fronts, the war was hotting up – including the 'Benson front'.

On 20 July a number of German army officers attempted to blow up Hitler: they failed, and he survived. One conspirator, Field-Marshal Erwin Rommel, committed suicide. During August the Allies landed on the French Mediterranean coast, and a French force re-entered Paris, with General de Gaulle making a triumphant entry two days later.

In a period of four weeks Frank and I flew thirteen ops totalling more than forty-nine hours, and to the groundcrew, at least, we were beginning to stand out as survivors. This was a subject I never let myself dwell on, and one that others had never brought up. The squadron flight sergeant and his two sergeants, one a fitter and the other a rigger, had a good view of the air-crews: fitters attend to engines, and riggers to airframes. These senior NCOs observed the pilots and navigators coming and going, and waiting around, and one sergeant, from Northern Ireland, had shown me a particularly friendly and helpful attitude; it was he who borrowed my car occasionally.

One morning we were preparing to fly an air-test and I was sitting at the controls. Frank had not yet climbed up into the little cockpit when this friend mounted the ladder and talked quietly to me: 'We blokes think you have done more than your share of ops trips, Kiwi; you are pushing your luck too far.' This blunt opinion astounded me. Quite apart from the taboo subject matter, NCOs did not talk to officers in that vein. But before I could expostulate on the topic, he continued:

> Yes, we say it's time some of the others pulled their weight a bit more. Do you know that some of them declare the kite to be U/S when it's not? Now, we know that you do the opposite, and when the engine does have too big a magneto drop, you flick the switches too quickly for the drop to register on the gauge, and off you go on your trip. Now you listen, Kiwi: any day you do not feel like going through with a trip, just indicate to me or to So-and-So, and your kite will be U/S for flying that day.

He lectured me like a kindly father. I was shocked and shaken. All I said was: 'Look here, Serg, you mustn't say things like that. I do appreciate what you are saying, but both of us must forget this conversation ever took place. Please hop down now, and ask Frank to come up.' I never shared that conversation with Frank or anyone else, but it made a profound impression on me.

Surely this was not a reason why pilots kept to themselves on this lonely and dangerous job? Did all of us fail at times, in morale and effort? Logically enough, everyone was not over-brave all the time. In hindsight, I was a good investment from the point of view of those 'running' the war: I was young, fit, capable and obedient to carry out my instructions. My mother had been right: all the mothers should have vetoed their sons from going to war. Operational aircrew were sometimes removed from their tour of duty with no open reason; maybe their files were marked 'LOMF'. As has been observed already, this could happen to fellows who imposed too much restraint on themselves when they were off duty – they failed to 'let themselves go' when the right opportunity offered itself. Perhaps they held back at squadron aircrew parties, and never released the tensions.

We did enjoy those hilarious parties. The command would come from the wingco: 'Everyone to attend!' All our gatherings were held at the *White Hart* at Nettlebed, along the London Road. This is a first-class and well known hostelry, which in those years and for long afterwards was owned and managed by Mrs Clements, dear 'Clemmie'. Visiting that pub, with the understanding and love that emanated from this home away from home, was undoubtedly a big factor in keeping up my spirits and morale for that long eighteen months.

For some obscure reason I was never released from my duties as squadron entertainment officer, and as such it was my pleasant responsibility to purchase suitable gifts for engagements and weddings and other worthy causes; an engraved pewter tankard was often chosen. These presentations were made at our parties, for which occasions, in defiance of the restrictions rationing foodstuffs, Clemmie and her faithful staff scoured the adjacent countryside with such prolific success that we were able to indulge in meals of a first-rate standard and including fresh fruit and vegetables, eggs and cream. Roast meats made a magical appearance. All men present on these grand occasions were dressed in their number one uniforms, and the commencement of proceedings was delightfully formal and correct: a cheery but respectful 'Good evening, Sir!', a firm clasp of the hand with the wing commander, and a restrained round of pre-dinner drinks. Then the toasts to 'the king' and to 'absent friends', the repast, and any presentation accompanied by a few words and polite applause.

The formalities completed, the evening proper began. As the diners left the dining room for the main lounge bar, staff scurried to roll up the main carpet and rugs before the windows over the bar counter were raised, and action commenced. Pints of best beer were the main choice, and down they went; and as if at a pre-arranged signal, the singing began. After one or two preliminary efforts, the repertoire was deemed unsuitable for Clemmie and the staff, and this was acknowledged by Clemmie who pulled down the shutters each time the song started – and then strangely enough, pulled them up again ready to take orders, the moment it finished! The songs all had good tunes, and the words are known to a wide fraternity amongst Britons who served in the armed forces. By means of the local grapevine, other clients discreetly left us so we could have the big room to ourselves.

The next item on the programme was usually an uproarious rendition of 'The Muffin Man'. This old song has to be accompanied by the sport of singing at the same time as balancing a half-full pint handle of beer on one's head. It became my privilege to accompany this song by playing the mouth-organ, and the instrument player was also expected to perform while balancing his handle on his head. After a few occasions when my uniform had to be cleaned, I became remarkably adept at tilting my head slightly to one side, playing with gusto, and tapping my foot in time: all simul-taneously, and not too many drops spilt. Now you can see the wisdom, and the rush, to have the carpets out of the way. The floor underneath was slates, and over the centuries had probably benefited countless times from the effects of surplus beer.

The last item was in wingco's hands, and it was the only concession to his rank, once the dinner had come to an end. He it was who, after a surreptitious glance at his watch, and calculating how much time was left before the bar in our mess closed for the night, suddenly made a beeline for the entrance door and shouted, 'Last one home's a cissy!'

This was a challenge indeed. It was also one that Steve could hardly fail to win, as he was invariably the first one to collect his passengers and roar off down the hill back to base. This was a stern race, with no handicaps and no rules except the last arrival had to shout a large round of drinks.

Once when I had the Austin Coupé, Joe sat next to me with Vic the third one in the narrow seat; the dickey-seat held Frank and another navigator. As we descended the main hill, car lights partially blacked out, David managed to come alongside in his Baby Austin Tourer; he had the hood down, and his three passengers waved and yahooed at us. The road was not wide, and the hill became steeper. Neither car could get ahead of the other – indeed, Mr Austin would have been proud of his productions. Both were going as fast as possible – in fact those little cars never went any faster than on that night. The two vehicles inched closer and closer together – our outside passengers started grappling with those who could reach from David's chariot, and wild shrieks rent the quiet country air. I was putting as much effort into the encounter as if the cheeky little tourer had been an Fw 190!

Gradually I was aware that Joe was shouting at me, in all the din, and also trying to pull the steering-wheel. This was no good to me; I had to give him my attention. 'Let him go Kiwi! Your car will get hurt! He can afford the damage better than you can – he's a lord! And he only paid five quid for the so-and-so Australian thing!'

Having descended this hill, you had to reduce speed considerably in order to negotiate the entrance to the station. Generally, by the time we arrived during these races, the guards were well alerted to what was going on, and had the good sense to leave the barrier arm up, and to make sure they themselves were well out of the line of fire of the flying cavalcade of vehicles. Inevitably, one or more cars failed to make the turn into the entrance, with the result they ended up in the hedge. So well organized was Benson station that by morning these bent cars had been extracted from where they had stopped, towed round behind the mess, and the hedges and flowerbeds made tidy again.

But that was not the end of the night's festivities, not by a long way. Steve's timing was immaculate. He ran into the mess just in time to catch the sergeant-in-charge, and ordered many large enamel jugs of beer to be filled and taken to the ladies' room. This was a small, intimate room, tastefully decorated, with a piano standing in one corner. We all piled in, arguing cheerfully the rights and wrongs of the race, and hooting at the misfortunates who had failed to finish the course proper.

After a few more drinks, the usual pastime was to play 'saddle the nag' and have cockfights, and needless to say, the activities became fairly hectic; for those who had not learnt how to look after themselves in the crew-room brawls, the proceedings possibly reached the alarming stage. By the time the beer and the energy ran out, several hours later, everyone was exhausted, pulled about, sore, and probably soaked in beer. Just before the party broke up, I always did my best to encourage a finale by having everyone join in singing 'The Maori Farewell', referred to as 'Now is the Hour'. It made me feel good and homesick, which at the time seemed the right mood in which to finish the night.

During the next few days the piano, for reasons I cannot recall, invariably had to be dried out, cleaned and retuned. Frequently the room had to be redecorated. But that was the least of our worries: it merely meant that an item appeared on our monthly mess bills called 'Contribution to mess decorations'.

The net result for our small band and me was to feel rejuvenated until the next party, several months away. In between these minor orgies my inclination was to enjoy drinking orange juice, and build up the anticipation towards the next squadron aircrew party, 544 style. I might just keep my hand in, from time to time, practising 'The Muffin Man' on the harmonica in the privacy of our room.

The five July trips, Ops Nos 24 to 28, were hard going; some were to the Prague-Dresden areas, others to Munich-Salzburg – those names can still give me a shiver. A combination of difficult weather and flak called for plenty of concentration and effort.

Whatever July was like, with Si and Jack's funeral included, it was just as well that we didn't know what August had in store for us. . . . We flew forty-five operational hours, for twenty-seven sorties over twelve days – ops trips Nos 29 to 40 – involving a variety of jobs scattered over France and Germany, with a transit-trip landing in Italy for one night, just for good measure. And to keep the ball rolling, we had our third single-engine landing – and not forgetting our quota of fighters and flak.

During September 1944 our 544 casualties continued. A flight commander of 540 Squadron, Squadron Leader Fleming, already with a DSO, went missing over that horrible place Magdeburg: a Me 262 shot him down. The same day our wingco received a bar to his DFC: such were the contrary fortunes of war. A new crew pranged on its first take-off at Benson – the fire was terrifying, but the two men were all right.

Frank and I flew our No. 41 trip to Norway from Benson, but we experienced an anxious time because of cuts in the fuel supply, and opted to return to familiar Leuchars as it was nearer to our targets. While we were just over the coast of southern Norway, the red warning light had come on for one engine, indicating a shortage of fuel. This was followed immediately by that engine cutting out and then spluttering a bit before running more strongly again. Next, the other engine performed the same tricks. The aircraft was losing altitude while this was going on, and I was in a fix wondering, if we had to bale out, whether it was worse to be over the cruel sea, or over the more cruel snow and ice of the rugged Norwegian coast. If

Frank had a sea twitch, I suppose I had an aversion to coming down over jagged icy-cold areas. To compromise, I kept reducing height, but remaining just off the coast. Many times in the past we had been intercepted by enemy aircraft in this exact area (the 'front door', as it were), but thankfully this time no one came up to look at us. During a few seconds when both red lights were shining brightly, and neither engine was functioning, Frank volunteered the opinion that Jock Kennedy had been overjoyed to be in Sweden after he had been shot down. He reckoned the Swedes ran a most hospitable camp for Allied aircrew, and supplied lovely Swedish girls for company.

In a perverse way, this line of thought really decided me. An instant and clear picture sprang into my mind: do you think it was of my family, or some delightful snap of New Zealand's scenic beauty? No: what I visualized was my room in the Benson mess, its bed with the snow-white coverings, my clock and radio beside it, and all the neatness and familiarity of my wartime home. That was where I wanted to be, and intended to be. 'No, Frank, we're going home,' was all I said, and as if in agreement, the engines recovered their poise. We aimed for Leuchars instead of Benson, and continued to limp our way back.

The second time my diary has a remark to the effect that 'It's good to be back' was after the second of two trips, Nos. 42 and 43, over the 'Big Smoke', as PRU referred to Berlin. We flew two trips there in three days, each time being attacked by flak and fighters. These sorties to the 'Big City', as the German capital was also referred to, took place a couple of days after the Norway trip. 'Hotly chased' was one of my few descriptive entries from the logbook. (It may seem out of context, but my diary reminds me that after the second Berlin trip, just for a change, I went to the Wallingford fair the same evening and enjoyed the dodgems, the big swing, and hurling coconuts.) Two days after our last Berlin trip, one of our 'B' Flight crews, Jones and Parry, went missing on a transit flight down to San Severo in Italy. Parry remained alive. This was a period when another of our crews, Woods and Bullimore, did not return.

The next day I went to have a look at our Berlin photos, and it was interesting, to put it mildly, when the Waaf interpreter pointed out an Me 163 lined up on the tarmac of the airfield we had photographed. The following day Frank Dodd was intercepted in the same area by two of this new breed of German fighters, though happily he and Eric Hill came back safely. Both the Me 163 and the 262 were called 'jet fighters', though the 163 was actually rocket-propelled. Two days later again, our most experienced crew on 544, Hunter and Fielden, both received DFCs, the first such crew to receive gongs. But on their very next trip they were both killed: this was proving a hard game to win.

Our September was completed with Ops Nos 44 and 45 to Holland and

138A

S.NGLE-ENGINE AIRCRAFT. / MULTI-ENGINE AIRCRAFT.

Year 1944 Month Date	Aircraft Type	No.	Pilot, or 1st Pilot	2nd Pilot, Pupil, or Passenger	Duty (Including Results and Remarks)	DAY DUAL	DAY 1ST PILOT	NIGHT DUAL	NIGHT PILOT	DUAL	DAY 1ST PILOT	2ND PILOT	DUAL	NIGHT 1ST PILOT	2ND PILOT	PASS'GR	INSTR/CLOUD Incl. in Cols (1) to (10)
					TOTALS BROUGHT FORWARD	37.05	39.55	2.40	.20	108.40	3735	3.10	7.45	8.20	—	2.36 46.00	6.55
			D.S.O - D.F.C. A.F.C.	SUMMARY FOR MONTH OF AUGUST													
	"B" FLIGHT			UNIT:- 544 SQN. TYPES:- MOSQUITO	OPERATIONAL:-					45.00							
44	SQUADRON			DATE:- 31 AUGUST 1944.	NON-OPS :-					3.10							
				SIGNATURE:- [signature] P/o.	MONTHLY TOTAL:-					48.10							
					W/COMMDR												
SEPT. 8.	MOSQUITO XVI	652	SELF	W/O MOSELEY	CAMERA AND AIR TEST					1.15							
SEPT. 9.	MOSQUITO XVI	639	SELF	W/O MOSELEY	OPS:- OSLO-BERGEN. ½					4.40							
SEPT. 9.	MOSQUITO XVI	639	SELF	W/O MOSELEY	LEUCHARS TO BASE					1.25							
SEPT. 11.	MOSQUITO XVI	505	SELF	W/O MOSELEY	OPS:- BERLIN. 24000.					4.55							
SEPT. 12.	MOSQUITO XVI	502	SELF	W/O MOSELEY	AIR TEST.					1.00							
SEPT. 13.	MOSQUITO XVI	288	SELF	W/O MOSELEY	OPS:- BERLIN 28000.					4.25							
SEPT. 15.	MOSQUITO IX	231	SELF	W/O MOSELEY	AIR TEST.					.30							
SEPT. 16.	MOSQUITO XVI	288	SELF	W/O MOSELEY	AIR TEST.					1.15							
SEPT. 17.	MOSQUITO XVI	396	SELF	W/O MOSELEY	CAMERA TEST.					1.15							
SEPT. 19.	MOSQUITO XVI	502	SELF	W/O MOSELEY	OPS:- HOLLAND AREA					2.55							
SEPT. 25.	MOSQUITO IX	242	SELF	W/O MOSELEY	OPS:- GIRONDE PORTS & P.R.					4.35							
SEPT. 29.	MOSQUITO IX	276	SELF	W/O MOSELEY	THE LOIRE - COURSES -					4.10							
				SUMMARY FOR MONTH OF SEPTEMBER													
				UNIT:- 544 SQD. TYPES:- MOSQUITO	OPERATIONAL :-					22.55							
				DATE:- 30 SEPT. 1944.	NON-OPS :-					9.25.							
				SIGNATURE:- [signature] P/o.	MONTHLY TOTAL:-					32.20							
O.C. "B" FLIGHT																	
C.O. 544 SQDN.					TOTALS CARRIED	37.05	39.55	2.40	.20	108.40	389.55	3.10	7.45	8.20	—	96.35 46.00	7.32.

GRAND TOTAL [Cols. (1) to (10)]. 597 Hrs. 50 Min.

France respectively. In early October we flew Ops Nos 46 and 47; the first was to the Ruhr, yet we were not molested, which was a surprise and a relief. But in the middle of the second German trip, we were both interrupted and intercepted in a big way. By the time we eventually got ourselves clear, fifteen aircraft had opposed us, including one pass from an Me 163.

The momentum generated from D-Day by the invasion of Europe and all its ramifications never lessened after that, certainly from my point of view as a pilot on 544 Squadron. For instance, the months following 6 June had developed into a new pattern of increased pressure and increased activity: more high priority targets to cover; a constant drive to have more aircraft serviceable and available for ops; an obvious shortage of pilots and navigators – we never reached our quota of twenty crews. The total maximum number of our crews at any one time never exceeded sixteen or seventeen. Standards of personnel coming to Benson did not appear to lower, but my conclusion that 'There is no short-cut to experience' became more and more confirmed to me. Many of the pilots being posted to 544 had thousands of flying hours, and had completed a tour or more of operations in some other command. That background, however, did not take the place of flying our sorties in unarmed Mosquitos at altitudes anywhere between just off the deck, and up to 40,000ft. That hard taskmaster, 'experience', had to be bought.

It was clear to all at Benson that the Allies were winning the war. Reports from all sectors of the worldwide battlefronts spelled out that fact, and the public read and heard about it every day. Nevertheless, neither Germany nor Japan gave any indication of considering surrender; indeed, as the Germans were slowly but surely pressed back into their homeland, they had smaller perimeters to defend, and they fought even more tenaciously – 'with ferocity' is in fact a better description. Assuredly there was no lessening of effort. We at Benson felt the effects of this phase of the war by meeting more fighter aircraft, as well as having to avoid, or at least out-manoeuvre, the new German jet fighters. It is well in my mind that when the war in Europe did finally end, my sentiments were that it was just as well, from the Allied air forces' point of view, that it concluded when it did.

No wonder that on the occasional evenings when any sort of a serious discussion did take place in the mess, we used to ponder what our war would be like when the job in Europe was finished. Our PRU long-range Mosquitos would then be substantially reinforcing the reconnaissance units in the Far East, and I think we felt it might be a bit like hopping out of the frying pan into the fire.

9

Rupert, Milton, Francis and Company

We few, we happy few, we band of brothers.
William Shakespeare

No one doubts that aircrew needed to relax in the interludes between operational flights, but with such a collection of individualists at Benson, it was never obvious how most men did manage to relax. As long as we were available and fit when required to fly on operations, any other responsibilities were almost nil, and most pilots kept their non-flying times to themselves. My memory does not recollect having to attend any sort of parade during the eighteen months I was stationed at Benson; we had the task of duty officer from time to time, and on 544 I was the entertainment officer. One week's leave after every six weeks on duty, with permission to leave the station, was the quota. That, at least, was the theory, although in practice that privilege was often amended. Apart from the nights of organized squadron parties, our little band did not drink overmuch; but time and again, we always relished the carefree fun we had together.

Joe and Vic were cobbers before being chosen for PRU, and because I was a Kiwi also a long way from home, it was natural they added me to their friendship to make a trio. This was endorsed by one memorable evening in the lounge bar of the Royal Hotel in Bath. Since our navigators were our only crew, we became 'six musketeers', even though during our earlier days together it wasn't easy for the six of us to become close friends until Frank and Alec and Malcolm obtained their commissions and we were all accommodated in the same mess.

As Vic, amongst his many accomplishments, had experience as a motor mechanic, he quickly took advantage of the fact that operational aircrew could use a car and obtain a ration of petrol coupons. His first purchase was the Austin 10 that he soon sold to me for the princely sum of £30 because he had located a smart little red MG two-seater. Vic had a good eye for the girls as well as for motor cars, and he quite rightly figured he would attract better girls with a better car. He wanted to sell the 1934 Austin to Joe, but

Joe reckoned he could not be bothered with a car, and suggested young Kiwi should buy it. I pointed out that although my father had let me try out the family car once or twice, I had no driving licence; but the two Aussies had their usual swift answer: 'Let's all go up to Oxford and get you one, Kiwi.' So being the boy, I went along.

At the local council offices, Vic explained to the young lady clerk that this New Zealander was 'a famous Mosquito pilot' who had forgotten to bring his driver's licence to Britain. So the obliging young lady wrote me out a licence, and in fact did me a really good turn because years later, when back in New Zealand, the authorities there issued me with a licence on the strength of the English one. . . . Now I was the owner of a car, and Joe declared he had two chauffeurs to drive him wherever he wanted to go.

Being a conscientious young man I insured the vehicle. In about a week's time, when my little roadster was behaving itself parked round at the back of the officers' mess amongst its peers, an incident occurred. The kitchen was having a new boiler installed and it exploded; it was a bad accident, with people more than hurt. Bricks went up all over the block, and on their downward path fell on many of the cars parked in that area. Joe and Vic and I ruefully surveyed the scene. One of the Aussies confirmed with me that the car was insured, and then, picking up a broken brick, said: 'Look, Kiwi, this side window is broken, but the other one is only scratched. Best to have two new windows. . . .' Crash! and the piece of brick goes through the scratched window. This sudden initiative shocked me, but the car finished up from its visit to the insurance company and the panelbeaters looking almost good enough to take its place at the front of the mess. Joe summed it up: 'Sorry for the poor so-and-sos who got hurt, Kiwi, but all things considered it was a so-and-so useful explosion.'

Joe used to stutter a little, and we would laugh at this most times – and of course it was no use him getting excited about that. Our trio ruled by the voice of the majority, and any two could overcome the one left; often these 'votes' were finally decided by rough-and-tumbles, and from time to time one or other of us would sport a black eye or some other minor wound. The end result of these exercises was that we kept fit and in great shape. When he had had two or three pints of beer, Joe often had the fancy to imitate the pukka English accent, and the funny thing was that he then became much more fluent and his stutter scarcely noticeable.

One typical day in a stylish pub crowded with patrons, we three were enjoying our beer and the agreeable scene. The company consisted of a few local farmers with their wives or girl friends, some air force aircrew, maybe three or four with ladies, perhaps a couple of naval types, and generally a preponderance of army officers, nearly all of whom had female companions. A small number of well dressed civilians who could have been anybody completed the crowd: a genteel gathering escaping for an hour or two from the rigours of war.

After about three pints each, all members of our trio were in fine fettle and at peace with the world about them. It was at this stage, many times to be repeated in many varied locations, that either Vic or Joe raised their voices slightly. At the same moment the affected English accent came into play, but instead of addressing one another as 'Vic' and 'Joe' and 'Kiwi', we became 'Rupert' and 'Milton' and 'Henry', all our own names. Well, experience had shown us that this was guaranteed to attract attention: no matter what the subject matter of our conversation – though it was usually something of an ear-catching nature – this strange trio intrigued all listeners, and the general buzz of conversation gradually dropped away as the stares in our direction intensified. When this state of affairs was reached, we drank up, said 'Good-day' or 'Good-night' in the grand manner, and took our leave.

It all sounds rather daft now, but at the time, in that atmosphere, and in the company of those understanding, polite people, who never interrupted our bit of fun – incredulous and mystified as they were – these were hilarious escapades. Once outside and in the car, one of the Aussies used to say, 'Right-oh Kiwi, you can laugh now.' By such ridiculous pranks did we remain relaxed and balanced, with our comradeship strengthened, and our morale fortified.

The word 'balanced' might be an extremely suitable word, but not everyone was of that opinion. The senior medical officer at Benson was a well-known individual, Doctor Hussey. This gentleman had had a remarkable career, and was one of the few men to be wearing a white polar medal ribbon, awarded to him when serving with the Shackleton Expedition to the Antarctic. One evening in the mess several of us were having a few drinks; Doc Hussey had been sitting quietly on his own, also having a drink or two. He was studying us. He rose from his armchair and came over to us, saying: 'I've been diagnosing you pilots, and all of you are at least half potty!' Much laughter greeted this source of medical wisdom, but the memory has stayed with me.

Frank, later on during our tour of ops, felt ill and off colour, and reported to the medical officer – at least, that is what he told me. This made me anxious, and I made it my business to find the patient as soon as possible after his visit. Our worthy Francis was thoroughly put out: Doc Hussey had told him to keep flying, but to reduce his smoking, cut out all alcohol, do more exercise, and to go to bed earlier. A pity more doctors do not give the same prescription these days. Dear Francis seemed much fitter the next day. The only other comment relating to the medical profession at that period was the oft-quoted opinion at Benson that all us high-flying aircrews would probably find we were impotent. We were guinea-pigs as regards the effects of flying at such altitudes for hundreds of hours, and this prognosis definitely did nothing to improve morale. It is excellent to record that all the men I knew who later married – and I am delighted to include myself – fathered fine children. My understanding is that this misguided opinion did not emanate from the estimable Doc Hussey.

One of the founder crews on 544 was Downie and Ross. 'Duke' Downie probably acquired his nickname because he unequivocally had the appearance and manners of a duke: although short in stature, he looked the part, and spoke with a polished and pleasant English accent. He had been to Oxford or Cambridge university, and was a thoroughly likeable and most interesting person. When we first met him he was a warrant officer, but he soon obtained a commission as a pilot officer. He and I enjoyed each other's company, and had many a deep and sometimes confidential conversation. Duke knew so much more than I on many subjects, and was a romantic at heart. He used to softly sing the song *Pale Hands I Love*, and quoted many of the poets.

Before coming to PRU, Duke had flown Spitfires; he was a great pilot, and a daredevil. He beat up the centre of Benson airfield one day, and a few of us who should not have been walking there literally had to fling ourselves down on the grass for fear of being hit by his Mosquito's propellers. On 19 May 1944 I felt most honoured when Duke asked me to transport him and his Waaf fiancée, one of the ops room staff, to the railway station. They crammed themselves happily in the dicky seat of my little Austin, and the next day they were married. She was a beautiful girl, and they were an outstanding couple. And then on 9 June, just twenty days later, Duke and his navigator, Ross, were killed over France.

One didn't dare to dwell on these unhappy incidents. You could have a few melancholy beers in memory, then concentrate on today – find some enjoyment in the day – have a bit of harmless fun – cry on your own, but laugh hugely with your mates.

During our 'Baltic' detachment to Leuchars, although the strong influences of the Scottish way of life and the personality of Douglas-Hamilton offered us many agreeable advantages, our ops trips brought just as much difficulty and danger as operating from Benson. In addition, the North Sea crossing itself presented a hazard. Personally, as a swimmer and a yachtsman, my mind never envisaged anything worse than ending up in the drink, paddling my tiny rubber dinghy, complete with emergency rations, and awaiting rescue. But Frank was not so accustomed to things nautical, and dreaded the sea crossings: the jargon for this apprehension, which was commonplace, was 'having a sea-twitch'. This was not my particular problem: what I disliked intensely was flying over the icy peaks and valleys of snow-white Norway, including its fiords – the idea of baling out over *that* terrain gave me the shudders.

When we were not flying ops or air-tests, we enjoyed some fine excursions. Mostly we walked: we walked for hours and hours, and talked for hours and hours, going cross-country whenever the opportunity occurred. Leuchars lies between Dundee and St Andrews, and sometimes we walked to St Andrews, and sometimes to Newport-on-Tay, from where we caught a ferry to Dundee. A nearby nine-hole golf course provided some fun and exercise. DDH led us on several good outings, pointing out landmarks and monuments that related to his ancient and fierce forebears.

One evening about eight of us visited a pub not far from the station. It was dark and cold when, huddled in our greatcoats, we left the warmth of the bar and commenced the walk back. DDH had spent some time in Germany just before the war, and he had us turn up our collars, change our caps round back-to-front, and then instructed us to march the goose step, which he ably demonstrated. He also rehearsed us in some German salutes and cries. By the time we were approaching the Leuchars guardhouse, we were well into our stride. Hearing our feet stamping down in the frosty air, the corporal of the guard came rushing out. DDH was shouting orders in German, we 'Heiled Hitler', and marched on regardless – until the barrier broke up our formation. It was probably surprising we did not have shots fired at us! But we thoroughly enjoyed the boyish escapade.

Another evening our detachment laid on a party in the mess. The principal use of this station was as a base for Coastal Command Liberators that searched for German U-boats and surface vessels. A large number of personnel were stationed there, and we were the small minority, but with our sleek Mosquitos from PRU we had an image and a reputation to uphold. At the conclusion of the party, DDH organized us to form one long line, hanging on to the shoulder of the chap in front; for some forgotten reason we had to pull out our shirt-tails. David then played a martial tune on his bagpipes and led the merry procession like a pied piper. We methodically went along all the corridors of bedrooms, and tipped all the sleepers out of their beds. PRU popularity dropped, but with such a prominent Scot as our leader we felt impregnable.

Still later that night, for some reason that has escaped me, I decided to round off my evening by tipping David out of his bed. Possibly a Kiwi sense of justice and fair play for all. Just when I had tiptoed to his bedside he suddenly turned on the lamp and produced a service revolver from under his pillow and placed it against my ear. This was not very funny. David growled in his deep voice: 'And what do you want, Kiwi? – You don't think this is loaded, do you?' And to clarify the matter he spun the chamber, and sure enough it was loaded with six cartridges. We were both sober by now. 'Let's go and make some coffee in the kitchen,' continued David, and that's what we did. While having the coffee he outlined to me the story of Rudolf Hess's visit by parachute to his brother's estate when this deputy of Adolf Hitler made his mysterious flight from Germany in a German Messerschmitt Bf 110.

Simonson and Reid were both good friends of mine. They were characters, and top value at aircrew parties. Vic's navigator was Malcolm Moseley – no relation to Frank, but they had joined up together and were best friends. Malcolm played the piano for us, and he was also quite a poet. One of his more colourful sagas was about the aircrew of 544, of which this is the opening line:

> I'll tell you a tale of spirits and ale, consumed with lightning speed; of the dash-dash crew on PRU – of Simonson and Reid.

Their crash occurred on the northern coast of Scotland on 11 July 1944, and it is necessary to outline what a Benson Mossie was doing up there.

The German battleship *Tirpitz* was reported to be in one of the northernmost Norwegian fjords, together with its supply ship, at a tremendous distance from Britain. Probably the major difficulty for PRU was in keeping a Mosquito airborne in the ultra-cold arctic air, with its engines going for a sufficient time to last the distance to reach the *Tirpitz*, and to return with the evidence. Any defence fire from the target was probably of slightly less concern. Navigation had to be visual, and the pilot needed all his knowledge and flair to produce a successful sortie and to obtain the required photos. Si and Jock did the trip. Maybe they obtained perfect results, but at the limit of their fuel endurance they crashed near Banff, on the north Scottish coast, on their return, and were both killed.

Two days after that abortive attempt, Frank Dodd and his navigator Eric Hill, a Somerset cricket player, did complete an outstanding trip in which they brought back detailed photos of the targets. Admiralty was sufficiently satisfied that Frank immediately received a DSO and Eric a DFM. That evening, David and I and Lofty decided that we wanted to escape from the mess atmosphere, and we spent a memorable little session at the East Arms. We remembered our comrades, and were thankful we were alive – but it was well on our minds that we would be attending their funerals up in north Scotland the following day.

The next day Frank, and two other navigators from our flight, flew up North, with me as pilot, in an Oxford; it took us three and a half hours to fly each half of the trip. My piloting was responsible for an unnerving experience on the way north. The three passengers were busy playing cards, sitting somewhere behind me. As we plugged along at about 130mph over the north of England towards Scotland, I was relaxed and serious, probably day-dreaming and thinking how Frank and I could have been in the shoes of Si and Jock. The height of the land we were passing over gradually increased. Cruising at this unaccustomed slow speed, this fact did not register with me as soon as it should have – until all at once I realized we were far too low, and the slight slope ahead was bringing us into a dangerous situation. The

Oxford with four on board would not climb with any urgency – nothing like the Mossie that I could flick up a few hundred feet in next to no time. Judgement told me to turn quickly on to a reciprocal course and gain altitude before resuming the flight north. But something stupid in my attitude made me hold on and try to climb sufficiently to avoid hitting the heather-filled fields just below. Now why did I do that? Pride, in its ugly form, ruled my decision. We were in a classic situation prior to a crash.

My companions had faith in me as a pilot, and they were not looking out of the windows in any case. For me to turn round and admit I had half gone to sleep and made a botch of things was something my mood would not allow. In the event, with much sweating from the pilot and the kite scarcely above stalling speed, we just cleared the gentle brow of the uplands. At this precise moment one of the navigators glanced out a window and remarked in all innocence, 'Oh, I didn't know you were going to low-fly us up, Kiwi.' Such was the blind confidence of a navigator in a pilot! Hopefully I learnt a lesson from this bad example of my own selfish human nature.

Our small group was standing at the graveside later, under a crisp blue Scottish sky patched with a few heaps of white cumulus clouds, when David Douglas-Hamilton, who had flown up in a Mosquito, slowly gave all of us, one by one, a steady look, and enquired, 'Well chaps, who'll be next?'

I could not have voiced a similar thought for all the tea in China. Goose-pimples sprang out all over me while I stood to attention with tears trickling down my cheeks. Little did I know that some of the tears were for David and Phil.

On the return of our detachment to Benson, we learned that Air Commodore John Boothman had received his posting away from Benson; this coincided with his award of a DFC. During the invasion period he had been flying sorties in a Spitfire. A mess party celebrated these events. Air Commodore D. J. Waghorn, a brother of the Schneider Trophy winner of 1929, took over as air officer commanding at Benson; sadly he was killed in a flying accident a month before the war ended.

Four days after the funeral at Banff, another of our crews, Hampson and Newby, failed to return; happily they eventually turned up as POWs, although at the time, of course, one only thought of them as probable casualties. Frank and I had flown a sortie the day before, another one on the same day, and we were to go out on a third one the day following. Busy days.

On one of these trips, Op. No. 26, eleven targets in the south of Germany and Austria were successfully covered. It looked to be a dicey-do when we were briefed, and the usual apprehensions bounced about in my stomach before take-off. On most occasions one's flight commander strolled out to the kite as the crew mounted the ladder to the cockpit, and the usual farewell to me as the pilot was 'Have a good trip, Kiwi!'. But on this particular morning in high summer, David spoke quietly to me as I had one hand on the ladder and said, 'This one will keep you busy, Kiwi.' My impromptu reaction was to say, 'Ours not to reason why.' David was a straight shooter, and never minced words; he was also a patriot of patriots, and now he jabbed his hand hard into my ribs, looked me squarely in the eyes and whispered, 'No, Kiwi, yours but to do or die!'. Once again the chill shot up my spine. Yes, I thought to myself, he means all that – absolutely literally.

After a ten-week period, seven glorious days of leave were granted. My tell-tale diary reminds me: 'Not too keen to go back to camp.' Back at Benson a lot had happened. One of our flight crews had been intercepted in a particularly vigorous manner, another aircraft had returned badly shot up through the cabin blister, while a third, new crew had baled out safely. Joe and Vic and I drove to Oxford for the best meal and wine we could find, and saw Noel Coward's *This Happy Breed*.

Frank and I flew an op. on 31 July 1944, to the Dijon-Lyons area in France. Next day we flew a fifty-minute air-test. Frank and I used to volunteer for these relaxing local flights, and I fell more and more in love with the English countryside, especially the area where we were based: the Thames Valley, the Berkshire and Wiltshire downs, and the Chilterns. In poor visibility the Wittenham Clumps were a grand pinpoint when trying to find Benson airfield – how many thankful times have I wooshed between them. On the next day we flew another op. down south that included the Spanish border area; after debriefing, Frank and I went to the river where we swam and rowed. Then we heard the familiar roar of a Mosquito, but far too close, and sensed a crash. And now we knew which crew was to be 'next', after Si and Jock. David and Phil were dead.

They crashed on their Op. No. 31. At the time of the crash the aircraft was flying on one engine, having been shot up by anti-aircraft fire, and Phil Gatehouse was believed to be seriously wounded and probably dead. When right on the outskirts of Benson the other engine stopped, the Mosquito hit some trees, and crashed at the South Moreton Poultry Farm. The aircraft David was flying was not popular with me – I never did like its feel or performance, and it was heavy on fuel. Because of the irregular times of maintenance, it was never possible for our crews to be allocated any particular aircraft, so we flew any one that was serviceable. But David knew my preferences, and as far as was in his control, he always allotted me one of my favourites. It was a topic we never discussed, but on this 2 August, David had chosen to take the unpopular aircraft for his own sortie.

No flying for us the next day, and in the evening I went to the station theatre and listened to the station orchestra. Then it was up early the following morning for another op., and after that another afternoon on, and in, Old Father Thames, my playground during that summer. On 5 August we went to Oxford by special bus to the funeral of Phil Gatehouse.

AC pilot under training at EFTS New Plymouth, New Zealand, in May 1942.

Winter-time rig at EFTS in May 1942.

Crane twin-engine trainer at No. 12, SFTS Brandon, Canada, in January 1943.

Newly commissioned pilot officers, Ron and Ralf Bratton, at No. 31 GRS Prince Edward Island, Canada, in March 1943.

Ron at Grove No. 15 (P) AFU England, June 1943.

The budding pilot, in appearance at least! Grove, July 1943.

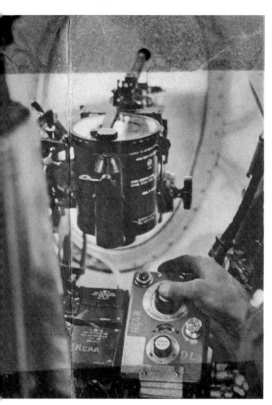

Frank Moseley wearing his 'O' for 'observer' wing, August 1943.

bombsight in the nose of a Mosquito, to line up the *hoto. We only used this when we were training; it was *o cumbersome, slow and unnecessary when in action. *3y courtesy of* Sphere *magazine, 11 September 1943)*

Installing cameras into a Mosquito. (By courtesy of Sphere *magazine, 11 September 1943)*

Ron and his 1933 Riley-9 Monaco saloon.

*Official squadron photo
(the Rogues' Gallery!).*

Early days at Benson.

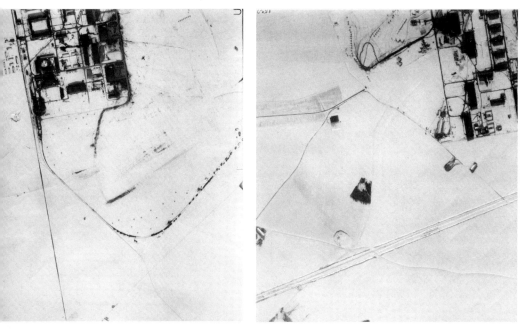

r-Trauling airfield near Regensburg, Germany; 106 fighters scattered about.

Op. No. 7, 3 March 1944: Kristiansand, South Norway.

Op. No. 10, the German fleet, with smokescreens, but the wind on our *side!*

As above, but off Gdynia.

German battleships including Nurnberg *and* Schelsien *off Hel Peninsula.*

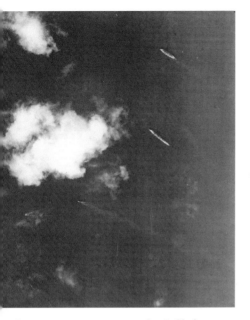

*e German navy exercising in the Gulf of
nzig area.*

Op. No. 10: the Baltic port of Pillau.

*b. No. 11: 30 March 1944, Grimstadt Fiord,
rway; the ship* Monte Rosa *and its support
sel.*

*Op. No. 11: Bergen, Norway, from 34,000ft:
flak. . .*

*Op. No. 11: Bergen port
note the considerable
shipping activity, hence t
priority given to these ph
and to the defences.*

No. 18: Tours, France, the remains of the railyards.

Op. No. 18: Toulouse, France, the railyards. Note: Our understanding was that by D-Day, throughout France there would be no major road or rail bridges left undamaged by RAF and USAF attacks. However, the Germans were adept at repairing them.

Op. No. 24, 7 June 1944: Leipzig, Saxony, Germany. Note the height of the black smoke, from oil.

Op. No. 42:
Johanisthall airfield,
Berlin, from 24,000ft.
An Fw 190 and flak.

Op. No. 42: more
details than the
previous photo. The
same airfield as
above, but taken by
a different camera.

Op. No. 43: another Berlin airfield. Intercepted again.

Op. No. 43: Doberitz airfield, Berlin, taken from 28,000ft.

Mosquito NS502 with D-Day recognition stripes. The author flew this aircraft on five sorties and two air tests between 28 June and 19 September 1944. These included sortie No. 31 on 6 August, to Paris, which gets a mention in the SHAEF letter illustrated on page 115.

Op. No. 31: Part of the huge Paris railway system.

HOW A *WOMAN* DISCOVERED ONE OF
THE TOP SECRETS OF THE WAR

HERE YOU SEE A W.R.A.F. PHOTOGRAP
Interpreter at work. She is usin
stereoscopic viewer to study aerial ph
graphs, which she will interpret and ch
marking down unusual features and p
ing together an intimate picture of
landscape. It's a fascinating job and
wartime, it played a big part in Brita
defence.

In 1943, Section Officer Consta
Babington-Smith was a photographic
terpreter in the Women's Auxiliary
Force at R.A.F. Medmenham. After months of careful study, she
covered a tiny speck on aerial pictures of Peenemunde airfield on
German Baltic coast. This speck appeared to be a small aircraft
type never seen before. Meanwhile, R.A.F. reconnaissance, of Pee
munde and the French coast had led to the discovery of the
concrete 'Ski site' installations. The mystery of the aircraft and
concrete sites was solved in December when R.A.F. pictures revea
a new pilotless aircraft on a launching ramp. *Flying Bombs!* More t
100 launching sites were destroyed by bombing. Thus, the skill
accuracy of a W.A.A.F. officer helped to delay the German fly
bomb attack until after D-Day, and precious time was gained.

In peacetime too, the Women's Royal Air Force (formerly W.A.A
offers you a career that is exciting and different.

You'll enjoy a full social life and you may get the chance to tra
abroad. Would you like to know more about this rewarding way
life? Write to: The Under Secretary of State for Air, Air Minis
(T.I.286), A.R.1, Adastral House, London, W.C.1.

Flight Officer Constance Babington Smith, an outstanding photographic interpreter.

*Wg Cdr Steven
and S/Ldr
Hampson
receiving
USA DFCs.*

...etachment at Leuchars (the Black
...roops) February–March 1945.
...ote: Frank was absent, being
...mmissioned as 'Pilot Officer
...oseley'. Front row: a sergeant,
...alcolm Moseley was Vic's navigator,
...ec Barron was Joe's navigator,
...ndreas, our Norwegian captain, Sue
...idner who married Vic, and finally
...e, Vic, Kiwi and Sgt Costello.

Foster and Moseley at Leuchars,
Scotland, March 1945. Our cheerful
faces may be due to the fact that we had
just landed from an op!

Op. No. 66, 5 March 1945, Kristiansand, Norway; this one was thirteen days before my last op., No. 69, which was flown without Frank. A dicey-do, the spark plugs oiled up, and DNCO! But we did land on two engines.

'Kiwi', or 'Fos', at the conclusion of his tour of ops.

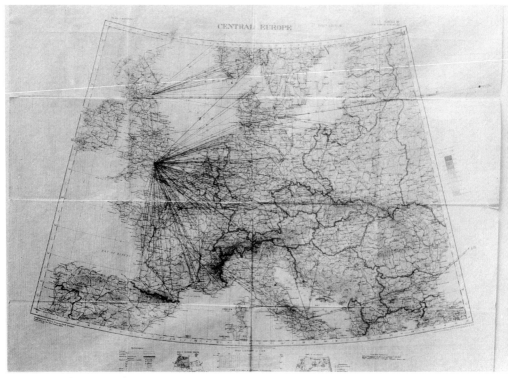

'Line map', drawn up after every sortie.

YEAR 1944		Aircraft		Pilot, or 1st Pilot	2nd Pilot, Pupil, or Passenger	(1st...)												
Month	Date	Type	No.				Dual	Pilot	Dual	Pilot	Dual	1st Pilot	2nd Pilot	Night 1st Pilot	2nd Pilot	Total	Passr	Instr/Cloud Dual / Pilot
							37.05	59.55	2.40	.20	18.40	215.20	3.10	7.45	8.20	–	7.45	96.50 46.50 5.55
Aug.	4	MOSQUITO XVI	500	SELF	F/S MOSELEY	OPS.						4.30			8.20			
Aug.	4	MOSQUITO IX	580	SELF	F/S MOSELEY	EARN						.16						
Aug.	6	MOSQUITO XVI	502	SELF	F/S MOSELEY	OPS.						2.45						
Aug.	6	HUDSON	9349	D/H.../AIR	SQUADRON MEMBERS	BENSON												
Aug.	6	HUDSON	9214	CMDR....		SEALS												
Aug.	8	MOSQUITO XVI	283	SELF	S/ MOSELEY	OPS.						4.00						
Aug.	8	MOSQUITO XVI	282	SELF	P/ MOSELEY	EARN						.15						
Aug.	9	MOSQUITO IX	432	SELF	P/S MOSELEY	CAME						.15						
Aug.	10	MOSQUITO IV	432	SELF	S/ MOSELEY	OPS.						4.10						
Aug.	10	HUDSON	432	SELF	P/ MOSELEY	EARN						.15						
Aug.	11	MOSQUITO	502	SELF	C/ RUSSELL	AIR						.40						
Aug.	12	MOSQUITO XVI	276	SELF	F/O SOUTH	OPS.						3.05						
Aug.	13	MOSQUITO IX	276	SELF	F/O SOUTH	OPS.						.50						
Aug.	13	MOSQUITO IX	417	SELF	F/O SOUTH	V.TRY						3.25						
Aug.	14	MOSQUITO XVI	502	SELF	F/ MOSELEY	OPS.						3.00						
Aug.	21	MOSQUITO IX	28	SELF	F/ MOSELEY	AIR						.55						
Aug.	21	MOSQUITO XVI	502	SELF	F/ MOSELEY	OPS. NOR						4.50						
Aug.	28	MOSQUITO IX	580	SELF	F/ MOSELEY	OPS. S						3.45						
Aug.	28	MOSQUITO IV	396	SELF	F/S MOSELEY	OPS. A						1.50						
Aug.	28	MOSSELEY IV	396	SELF	F/ MOSELEY	EARN						.15						
Aug.	28	MOSQUITO IV	396	SELF	F/ MOSELEY	OPS. A						2.30						
Aug.	28	MOSQUITO XVI	396	SELF	F/ MOSELEY	FORM						.16						
				[SUMMARY OVER PAGE]														
							37.05	39.55	2.40	.20	10.040	35.25	3.10	7.45	8.20	–	7.635 46.50	6.55

GRAND TOTAL [Cols. (1) to (10)] 585 Hrs. 80 Mins.

Logbook: 6 August 1944, Op. No. 31. Eleven ops in twenty-five days. Paris railways; five fighters and flak.

Our Op. No. 31 the next day, on 6 August 1944, was an interesting one. We were airborne for a mere two hours and forty-five minutes, but we were working extremely hard for most of the time. All we were asked to do was to cover a section of the railway system in Paris. Already we could fly ourselves to anywhere in Europe without a map, so Paris was a piece of cake! – Surely? SHAEF needed to keep a close eye on the entire railway system that the Germans were using to supply their forces opposing the Allied armies, and PRU kept our squadron at its busiest during August. It was also the worst month for casualties. As we have mentioned already, a specialized photo-interpretation unit had been installed at Farnborough, and on return from these railway sorties we used to land at Farnborough, before hopping back to Benson. The camera magazines were unloaded, and the photos sped on their way to the eyes of the experts in the shortest possible space of time.

Frank and I had the interest of seeing our trip to Paris obtain a mention from SHAEF. We were fortunate on three counts: first, Paris was half blanketed by an enormous cumulo-nimbus cloud, the dangerous anvil-topped one that can build up to 40,000ft. Its deceptively handsome white edges contain vertical upcurrents exceeding 100mph (160km/h), and big balls of frozen precipitation circulate downwards and upwards, propelled by these ferocious currents – any aircraft hit by these just breaks into pieces, and many a bomber was lost from such weather conditions, as distinct from enemy action or engine failure. Freddy Ball, one of the much-decorated wingcos leading a Spitfire squadron at Benson told a good tale: apparently he was in a Spitfire over North Africa and became embroiled with a cu-nim, and the kite broke up so that Freddy found himself still sitting strapped into his seat but nothing round him. He pulled his ripcord and landed by parachute, while bits and pieces of the Spit were strewn over a large area.

This cloud over Paris did not stop us from ducking and diving round it and obtaining photos; in fact all this suited our technique of taking shots at any angle, whether climbing or diving or turning to left or to right. Flak came up for a while, but the cloud at least obscured us from the ground most of the time. Parts of the cloud were fluffy enough for us to duck in and out of it without the turbulence damaging us.

The cloud was also fortunate for us, in that it provided cover against fighters: there was always an ominous interval of relative quiet that occurred when anti-aircraft fire ceased, and before the first fighters appeared, and we could recognize this interval, and were able to disengage and hop into the more friendly parts of the cloud. By this time I had a fair idea as to which parts could be entered with impunity, so in we shot, counted a few seconds, did a turn on instruments, and from memory sneaked out again to be in position to snap a few more photos before the fighters found us once more. They were not keen to tackle the cloud, but waited around for us outside.

Message of Congratulation.

A letter has been received from Supreme
Headquarters, Allied Expeditionary Force, concerning railway sorties
undertaken by aircraft under the operational control of 106 Group.

2.   It is stated that reconnaissances flown of
railways have been of the utmost value, and the unbounded admiration and
gratitude for work done by all pilots is most strongly expressed. S.H.A.E.F.
state that each of the reconnaissances carried out for them has, in its
own way, been "something to write home about! They appreciate that on the
very few occasions when sorties have failed, the effort put into these
sorties has been, perhaps, even more praiseworthy than that of some of the
most outstanding successes.

3.   It is felt that these reconnaissances give so
clear an insight into the enemy movements that the picture presented is
quite uncanny, and seems to be a preview, or at least a televised version,
of the enemy's movements.

4.   S.H.A.E.F. go on to say that the unmerciful
harrassing which enemy divisions moving up to the front have been receiving,
is entirely due to the information of their whereabouts provided from
Railway sorties.

5.   In particular, attention is drawn to sortie, No.
106G/1948, **flown by F/O Foster**, which was quite invaluable. In addition
to covering the dozen odd stations asked for on the 'Grand Ceinture'
around Paris, this pilot also provided cover of an additional 16 stations.
This additional cover provided S.H.A.E.F. with the complete picture, and
showed them that the enemy was using the inner circle through Montparnasse,
etc., and not the outer circle as had been thought.

6.   Lastly, S.H.A.E.F. state that the reconnaissances
flown for them have been of so high a standard as almost to outstrip the
bounds of praise.

7.   It is requested that the sense of the foregoing
may be brought to the attention of all concerned.

(Signed) P.J.A. Riddle,
Senior Air Staff Officer,
HEADQUARTERS, NO.106 (P.R.) GROUP.

Op. No. 31: Message of congratulation from SHAEF.

This was an even more thrilling game of hide-and-seek than those of
boyhood memories!

The second piece of good fortune was that this happened to be a day
when Frank was in his most 'press on' mood: he just would *not* call it quits.
'Oh, look Kiwi! There's an armoured train! I can see tanks on it – let's do a
run over that section!' That was the mood he was in. If I had ever discovered
what the magic formula was for Franko to be so enthusiastic over the target,
I might have been tempted to apply it to him on other occasions . . . but

that, without a doubt, would have been the end of us, and these tales would never have been told.

Thirdly, it was a big advantage to be over a target that was so close to England, Home and Beauty. Invariably we had hours of battling to escape from Europe, but here we were within sight of the English Channel. We therefore spent a comparatively long time over the city, and knew we had obtained a comprehensive coverage of the railway system. The SHAEF message sums it up.

By the time we left Paris we were tangling with five fighters, which should have been out of ammunition and fuel by then, and I decided that this was my grand opportunity to try a long but reasonably steep dive. I had always wanted to do this, and surely these five were not game enough to follow us out towards England. So down and away we went, straight for home, ears popping, and in a rattling good mood. We will never know the facts, but we suspect that this day's effort probably counted towards the awards to both of us, at the end of the war, of the French Croix de Guerre. Apparently we covered thirty-three of the thirty-four railway stations – I say 'we', but really it was Frank's day.

Back at Benson quite early that same day, Steve asked me if I wished to go to David's funeral. This was an unexpected honour, and I was grateful for his understanding. By the time I was ready, in my No. 1 uniform, the news trickled up from our crewroom that a new crew on 544, Towsey and Kingham, had failed to return. It was a matter of simple arithmetic to determine when a crew was missing: we all saw the blackboard in the crew-room listing the crew and the time of take-off, and we were all reluctant experts at calculating how many hours a Mosquito could remain airborne. When that hour of return came and went, it was bad news if no report had come in from any source. This crew never did return to anywhere.

The visiting party to David's funeral consisted of all the top brass at Benson. I was the boy about the place, but even boys do have a value. We flew in an old Hudson that we had tucked away, and the air commodore, as befitted his rank and position, was pilot. My seat was at the rear, more or less on the floor. The funeral was at the family's estate in Dorset, and the airfield we were aiming for was Zeals. The air-comm., the group captains and the wingcos were talking together with much pointing out of the windows, and next thing my wingco was thrusting a map into my hands, banging his finger up and down on it, and yelling in a stern voice, 'Kiwi! Find out where the so-and-so we are!' – they couldn't pinpoint where we were, and they couldn't find Zeals. So the young flying officer from the other side of the world, who had been playing hide-and-seek over Paris a few hours earlier, then managed to play his part in locating the missing airfield.

The funeral was attended by the workers on the estate and the villagers, as well as members of the family. I did not tag on to the Benson party, but stood on a small grassy knoll and surveyed the scene with tears streaming down my face. The composure of Lady Prunella in particular made an indelible impression on me.

After the service we were invited to the house for tea. The duke, whom I had not met, came to me carrying one of those intricate silver cake-stands loaded with delicacies. He introduced himself, made me sit down again while he stood, and said, 'How good of you to come, Foster; David did enjoy your friendship. How about a few more cakes?' That was the gist of it, and it is a memory I will never lose. How much there was to admire in the bearing and courtesy, and the self-control of this family. Of all the men of this world whom I have met, there is none that holds more of my respect than David did. His friendship enriched my life and he taught me many fine things, and I just wish I had remembered them better, and acted upon more of them.

Five days after the funeral, during which time Frank and I flew two more ops, an experienced crew from our flight went missing, Adcock and Askew; they, too, were killed. On some such occasions, news of the loss of our aircraft and the fate of the men was received in England either from intelligence sources in Europe, or from official German reports, on the actual day of the loss. And then sometimes it was months before any final news trickled into Britain; that state of affairs was thoroughly disquieting, especially for the families of the airmen.

This pilot, Flight Lieutenant Adcock, had chalked up a large number of flying hours, three to four thousand, and had joined the squadron when we did: the saying used to be, 'This chap's been flying since Pontius was a pilot!' For some reason his usual navigator, Lofty South, had not flown with him on this fatal sortie: strange and unfathomable how these losses worked out. The navigator, who lived to fight another day, was a close friend of mine; he had been in the London police force, and had a wife and family. He flew an op. the following day with me as pilot. Our wingco, Steve, came in from his room opposite mine, and asked me if I would please fly with Lofty the day after his pilot had gone missing, because he thought it would be good for the navigator's morale. The idea did not appeal to me in the slightest way: Lofty was a fine chap, and we had been room-mates, but he was big and bulky, and would not be used to the way Frank and I handled our flying. Nevertheless I agreed as gracefully as I could.

The navigator who had flown and not returned, by a coincidence had been temporarily sharing my room. Our room held three beds. At times Joe and Vic, on the other flight, were on leave, and the pressure on mess accommodation resulted in changes being necessary from time to time. That evening I packed up the missing fellow's belongings and wrote to his mother.

The sortie with Lofty was completed satisfactorily the next day, though we had a bit of a sort-out at the start: Lofty wanted to keep his head in the cockpit and study his armful of maps and calculate a good course for me to steer, but I tugged the maps from him and scattered them on the floor and exclaimed: 'You look out all the time, Lofty; screw your head about non-stop, I'll tell you when we're over the target area!' The poor chap was crestfallen, and very quickly sweaty, but this was not the time to change a winning game – and if it was not for sure a winning game, the Foster-Moseley combination was at least making a draw of it up until that time.

My thoughts were that I had done my duty by having Lofty fly with me, but it turned out unexpectedly that Frank was not available for flying the next day, which meant that once again Lofty was my navigator for Op. No. 35, over the French railways. This time a radiator burst and we had to feather the starboard engine. My first and improper thought was that Lofty and I would not be completing an operational flight that day, and the thought pleased me. Lofty knew that Frank and I had returned on one engine twice already, and he made me a fine little speech, this great bulky policeman with the bushy moustache and who seemed a little like a father to me: he said, 'If we have to make a single-engine landing, Kiwi, there's no one I would prefer to be with than you. Just tell me what to do, and I'll do it.' How guilty I felt about my rotten attitude.

As we made a satisfactory landing back at Benson, the wingco's car sped up alongside and as we opened the trapdoor and descended, he shouted to me: 'What the so-and-so are you back for? What's wrong with the kite?' My reply was that he was fortunate to have it back, let alone us with it. So much constant pressure had developed at PRU over these months since D-Day for photo coverage, that keeping sufficient aircraft serviceable was a losing battle – and the same could be said regarding maintaining sufficient aircrew. Wingco bundled Lofty and me with our flying gear into his car, and we tore across the field to our hangar where another Mossie was sitting with its engines ticking over. 'Off you go again, Kiwi! And don't come back so soon this time!' Who wanted the pressures of a squadron commander?

Frank was fit and ready again the next day, and we flew an op. together; for me it was the ninth one in fourteen days. However, the next few days provided some time to relax. I sold the 1934 Austin 10 to a mate on the squadron, and replaced it with a 1933 Riley sedan for £55; it was not as draughty as the tourer with its celluloid side-curtains. Unexpectedly, the relaxation came to an abrupt halt.

On 19 August 1944, Joe and I with a few others sat out on the grass outside our hangar and waited for Vic and Malcolm Moseley, known as 'Mo', to return from their op. They did not return.

Joe and I packed up the gear and possessions of our two friends. Our day was miserable. We agreed that what we missed most were Vic's endless and often ribald Aussie jokes. Wingco came across the passage from his room to commiserate with us. It was obvious that Joe had not lost *his* Aussie humour when he remarked to me after Steve had left us, 'Just another hungry Pom; nearly cleaned us out of cake again!'

Aircrews were supposed to be fit and healthy, and it had always been a mystery to Joe and me how often we used to see Vic popping pills. Once again, not a subject for discussion. But as we went through his drawers and cupboards we were amazed how many packets of medicine we found. We wrapped them up in paper, took them outside to the back of the building and deposited them in a rubbish tin. Photos of girl friends we destroyed, and other small intimate items in Vic's wallet we burnt.

The rule with motor cars was that they had to be immediately impounded when a chap went missing, and they were parked on a field behind a high fence and padlocked gates. There they remained until the estate of the deceased was settled, or until the family claimed them in the case of the missing one turning up as a POW.

Joe and I asked a favour of Steve, which he was not keen to grant, but we prevailed upon him: this was to give us twenty-four hours in which to dispose of the car. We drove over to Benson village and approached a well-known farmer whom we often saw in our mess, and we sold him Vic's Hillman Minx for a reasonable price. We were pleased with our efforts on behalf of our dear mate, and had a few mournful beers at the bar that evening.

Next day, sitting quietly in the crew-room, the squadron adjutant phoned down from his office upstairs, and asked for Joe or Kiwi to come up to Steve's office quickly. Up we both dashed. Steve said Vic had just phoned him up from one of the many temporary hospitals that were dotted all over southern England since the invasion; this was an American one. Vic said his leg was in plaster, and he was a virtual prisoner, but had sneaked out and down the road with the aid of a crutch, and found a public telephone box. 'Come and rescue me!' was the message. This was a shock to the system, but exciting beyond belief. Apparently Mo had also survived, but Vic did not know where he was. He had given Steve the name and hut number of his hospital, and Steve told the two of us to take his RAF car and not to return without Vickers! Off we shot, across the country.

We located the hospital, dispersed over a wide area with the many huts linked up by long covered walkways. We parked the car away from the guarded gate, and reconnoitred the layout until we found Vic's hut. With care, we sneaked up to a small window and peeped in. There was Vickers, sitting up in a bed with his Australian battle-dress top on over pyjamas. The Aussie air force didn't wear 'air force blue', but a blue of nearly a navy colour, and in this way Vic had cleverly identified himself to us. We caught his eye through the window, and he signalled to us towards one end of the hut.

We waited there until he crept out, in his pyjamas plus his jacket and a crutch. 'Let's scoot quick as we can!' he said. Joe, the tough guy, piggybacked

Vic at the run while I carried the crutch. One of Vic's legs was in plaster from the hip to the toes, and Joe reckoned he had also put on weight from the Yankee diet. As soon as we came near to a boundary fence, we two manhandled Vic over it; then Vic and I lay down in the grass while Joe went to bring the car to us. It took him a while to find it, and all sorts of thoughts entered my mind. What kind of a crime was it for an Aussie and a Kiwi to kidnap an Australian patient from an American hospital in England? Vic told me he had no chance of leaving the place in an official manner: he was already in the bad books of his hosts for refusing to receive a medal that was handed out to all the wounded in the beds there. The American habit was to present these 'purple hearts' to all their wounded, but our independent Aussie had tossed it back to them.

On the way back to Benson, our mission accomplished, Vic told us his story. He and Mo had borne a charmed life on ops until this sortie: to my knowledge they had never lost an engine, nor had any bad frights – but this trip had made up for all that. Cannon fire had suddenly peppered them from behind, but they never saw their attacker. The shells struck through the instrument panels, but neither man was hit; but the aircraft then started to break up, and Vic thought it time to bale out. Some sort of confusion prevented this, so Vic, with skill, guided the wreck down along the tops of a forest as bits and pieces broke off. They ended up in a clearing in the woods, still in the cockpit, but not much else of the kite around them. Vic had broken his ankle and Mo also had a disabling wound.

Vic said they had landed in a small no-man's land, right between German and American forces fighting it out, and they were extremely fortunate that it was the Yanks who rescued them. Vic was flown in an aircraft full of wounded soldiers to England, and after having his leg plastered, was securely tucked up in his bed; the down side was that the authorities were too busy to signal anyone that he was safe. Mo finished up somewhere else, and did not return to us for some days.

Our triumphant return to Benson was greeted with enthusiasm. To everything there is a season: we had passed through a time for weeping, and now it was a time to laugh. Wingco declared a 544 party would be held that evening in the mess.

Joe and I took Vic back to our room. This was an unhappy time, because the walking wounded wanted to know where everything was: a difficult question to answer. Our found-again friend was becoming grumpy. Upon hearing about his pills and medicines, Vic stumped off outside, and when he had not come back after a while, we looked for him, and there he was outside with the light of a torch, going through the rubbish tin. Back in the room again, Joe said, in his charming, buck-passing manner, 'Kiwi, I think you should tell your old mate Vickers where his car is; better hand him the cheque at the same time.' This really roused poor old Vic, and his usually good flow of Australian prose became even more descriptive and lengthy. We were not his best friends.

Suffice to say Joe and I had no easy time in persuading the farmer to exchange the car for his cheque. But Vic started to cheer up, and we were all in good spirits as the evening wore on. When midnight approached, the 544 crowd escorted Vic down to station sick quarters. He had two wooden crutches by now, and holding them up to make an 'X', we plopped him into a big comfy armchair, and four of us hoisted the chair and Vic on high; the others formed up in ranks, and we marched along briskly and happily, singing as we went. All was right with the world.

When we reached the sick quarters, the NCO in charge of the building sprang out to the top of the few steps to the double door, and holding up his arms cried, 'Gentlemen! gentlemen! Consider the sick people!' This plea was received merrily: the party-goers gave three rousing cheers for the sick, and upwards and onwards we marched. But someone's judgement was not operating fully, and at the precise moment we would have had Vic and his throne inside the foyer of the building, his crossed crutches struck the top of the doorway: the carrying team had momentum on, and Vic was knocked backwards out of his seat. But because the ranks of troops were tightly packed together, he did not fall to the ground, but was caught and supported by many willing hands. Not every patient at our hospital received such a grand arrival as Harold Rupert Vickers.

That story had a happy ending but, as so often happened in war, a sad aftermath was that, several months later, Malcolm Moseley was crewed up with another 544 pilot, Neville Polley, and they were both killed.

To tell some tales from the 544 story presents a blend of friends, fun and sorrow . . . one laughs or cries . . . and as there is not much point in crying, it's best to try and laugh.

Two quotations complete this chapter:

But you shall die like men and fall like one of the princes.

Psalm 82:7

There taught us how to live: and (oh! too high
the price for knowledge) taught us how to die.

Thomas Tickell, poet, 1686–1740

10
Moscow

As cold waters to a thirsty soul, so is good news from a far country.
Proverbs 25: 25

Taking *The Times* to Mr Winston Churchill
Op. No. 48, 12 October 1944

The black Humber car slid up to the Mosquito aircraft and a king's messenger, aloof and dignified in his dark pin-stripe suit, passed me the diplomatic mailbag. The Humber disappeared swiftly and anonymously. I ran up the two Rolls-Royce engines, waved 'chocks away', winked at my squadron commander on the tarmac, and No. 307 rolled off the dispersal. We were soon airborne and alone.

Except for loading the small mailbag, its cold grey canvas plastered with Foreign Office seals, our take-off from Benson airfield had the appearance of a routine operational flight. The world was not aware that on 12 October 1944, the British prime minister, Mr Winston Churchill, and the Russian dictator, Josef Stalin, were then conferring in Moscow to review progress of the invasion of Europe by the Allies, and to plan the final victory. Top-secret orders to fly this courier mission to Moscow gave me mixed feelings of pride at being selected, but also apprehension at the risks involved. Russia, meaning the USSR, to me meant a vast unknown country whose area occupied more than one-seventh of the land surface of the earth. It was a long way away – the other side of Europe, or at the least, by anyone's definition, it was the eastern extremity of Europe.

The dispatch papers we should be flying back from the conference to the waiting chiefs of staff would be vital to the Allied war effort, and intensive preparation had preceded the flight. Prime Minister Winston Churchill always inspired one to do one's best, especially in wartime Britain, and Frank and I were determined to make this a successful sortie.

Our photo-reconnaissance Mosquitos were the only aircraft capable of a direct non-stop flight. Already proved to be the most versatile twin-engined aircraft in World War II, those used by our squadron were stripped down for extra speed and height and range – not even guns were carried. On our previous forty-seven operational sorties we had penetrated Hitler's Third Reich and the lands pinned down by its Nazi claws to such varied areas as

Norway, Berlin, the Gulf of Danzig, Dresden, Vienna and Italy; but Moscow lay even farther, beyond the Eastern Front.

A man from Air Ministry, suitably forgettable in his dark civvy suit, had detailed my role as 'king's messenger'. The value of the diplomatic papers was jolted sharply into focus when we were told bluntly that they were to be given priority over our lives. This was well emphasized when a bomb was installed in the belly of our Mossie and wired up to a button on the instrument panel. 'Touch the button – no security problem with the mail, neither with the aircraft, nor with anything else, really,' politely murmured Mr X. As it didn't do anything for my morale for Frank and me, as 'crew', to be obviously classified under the heading of 'anything else', I tried thinking about other things.

A Smith & Wesson .38 service revolver was issued to me, together with the necessary webbing and belt to carry it in its holster. Frank and I were given large 'ghouly-chits' to wear round our necks under our clothes. Under its celluloid cover one side was a British flag, the Union Jack, and on the other side written in Russian were instructions to whomsoever found us (or our bodies if we had pushed that button) to contact the government in Moscow. Our verbal instructions were simple indeed: possibly precise, but to our Anglo-Saxon minds delightfully vague. Wherever we found ourselves in Russian-controlled territory, we were to telephone a given number in Moscow. I could not help wondering who would answer such a call, and in what language?

Air-testing No. 307 had shown that the engines were by no means the latest mark (de Havilland produced forty-three marks of the Mosquito by the end of the war), and all photographic, radio and radar equipment had been removed. 'That doesn't make things any easier!' was the thought that came to me. One, only small-scale map of Russian territory was available, and as the Russian armies had pulled up their railways and relaid them elsewhere when the German forces had invaded, navigation had to be simple dead reckoning using the met. officer's estimated wind. Our destination, Moscow's civil airport Vnukova (as it was then spelt), is about twenty miles from the city, and since a prohibited flying area of fifteen miles' radius extended round the capital – aircraft being shot at on sight – any navigational error had to be less than excessive.

Meagre as our information and aids were for the outward trip, I realized they would be even less for the all-important return flight. This was borne out when we learnt that our oxygen supply could not be replenished in Russia, as they didn't bother with such refinements. We could fly fast and far only at high altitude, and that demanded oxygen; without an ample supply I could foresee an eventful return trip.

At take-off, the station AOC handed me a copy of the day's *The Times* for Mr Churchill. The flight into the Baltic was normal: cruise at 30,000ft for the maximum tail wind; across the North Sea over thick cloud, then 'woomph!' a small clump of uncannily accurate anti-aircraft fire suddenly 'rocked the boat'. 'That's Flensburg pooping off again,' snorted Frank. Flak from Flensburg was always the same: prompt, economical and far too close, but under the circumstances an accurate navigational pinpoint. There was less cloud now, but no new German jets this far north, thank God. Some days earlier a Messerschmitt Me 163 had intercepted us near Munich and had made life tedious. Past the island of Bornholm off Sweden, and the eastern Baltic coast reluctantly appeared hazily ahead in the blinding blue sunshine. Through the glare and mist of the autumn day the Russian battles to re-occupy Lithuania and Latvia were raising vast clouds of dust and smoke, while between us and the grappling armies, aerial combats were viewed with detachment. Our oxygen was keeping us up out of harm's way – so far.

Russia still stretched featureless and seemingly forever to the horizon when the navigator advised 'Time to start letting down'; and as the nose dropped, an unmistakable industrial smog such as we were used to over the Ruhr, showed up ahead. 'That *must* be Moscow!' we both exclaimed, and then we spotted the airfield just where it should be. But the intercom suddenly cut in again from Frank, his Midlands accented voice now at urgency pitch: 'Fighters! Open up!' I threw both throttles forward smartly and three Russian 'Yak' fighters dropped astern and out of range: they gave us every intention of shooting us down, and of leaving any questioning or investigating until later. We must land quickly now before they attack again, so it's straight in: no formalities, no circuit, and hoping fervently that the aircraft identification of the airfield authorities was better than that of their fighter pilots – but gently does it, mustn't shake up that wretched bomb. Our copybook touch-down was four hours and forty-five minutes from take-off in England – easily a record, if such things had been fashionable in wartime.

Two jeeps crammed with officers shooting off multi-coloured flares careered along the runway and tucked under our wings out of my sight. This was crazy, and dangerous for all of us for them to be so near our whirling propellers, so I taxied at a scorching pace, smiling to myself at the thought of Air Ministry regulations that forbade an aircraft to taxi at more than 'a fast walking pace'. We screeched round on to the perimeter track with a savage burst of brake and, leaving our would-be escorts behind us in our considerable slipstream, continued at a sufficient speed to win this race, which seemed to have national pride as its prize.

When the dispersal area near the control tower came into view I switched off both engines and we completed our wild dash in an impressive silence. Another vicious stab of brake that pierced the silence as the tyres screeched, and I swung the Mosquito towards the guard of honour which, armed with rifles and fixed bayonets, was drawn up in an impressive semi-circle.

Momentarily I had time to reflect on the discipline and self-control of these troops. They never appeared to flinch, and certainly did not break ranks as they faced up to our spectacular arrival: either they were too alarmed at the consequences of breaking ranks, or they had more confidence in the ability of this racing Mosquito to stop at precisely the right point after its 50mph dash than its pilot had.

In the event, although our arrival was fuelled by a surplus of exuberance coupled with an unnecessary risk, the overall effect was demonstrably dramatic. As a young Kiwi on the other side of Europe I thoroughly enjoyed the few minutes of bravado, and for sure, de Havilland and Rolls-Royce would have smiled in appreciation. Little did I know that our departure would provide even more drama.

Pulling up with a flourish, we quickly exchanged our flying helmets and oxygen masks for our uniform caps, and climbed stiffly down our little ladder. The guards presented arms. A group of Red Army officers strode towards us, flared greatcoats swirling; then they halted, stamping down their high boots, and saluted and bowed as one – an emphatic and impressive welcome. Not to be outdone, Frank and I snapped to attention, threw up our smartest parade-ground salutes and dipped our heads. Our man from the British Military Mission identified himself, and, clutching the mailbag and Mr Churchill's morning newspaper, hurried away to the prime minister.

* * *

Tension lessened; cigarettes were exchanged, and a nuggety major appointed himself spokesman. He grinned and laughed boisterously, gave us a spirited 'thumbs up' and shouted 'Okay!'. These basic elements soon established surprising understanding and camaraderie. Official policy apparently decided we should have no interpreter, and during all the following hours at the airfield we did not hear anyone speak English – surely there was at least one member present who would be monitoring whatever Frank and I said to each other? Major Okay was a formidable character, not tall, but squat and powerful in build and with a ruddy complexion.

Before commencing this courier mission we had been well briefed regarding Russian uniforms, badges of rank and decorations, and various aspects of local customs and courtesies. We had also received an intensive course on the daily and basic servicing of our Mosquito. Our instructions had been detailed to the extent that we had to display complete 'trust', and one aspect of this was that we had to leave our flying gear in the cockpit. Through much miming I managed, I hoped, to explain to Major Okay, who was engineer as well as pilot, that when avoiding the trigger-happy Yaks, our port engine coolant had over-heated to a dangerous level. I was able to point to where the liquid was still leaking down the engine nacelle or cover. You can guess his reply: 'OK', and a hearty 'thumbs up'.

I felt uneasy about leaving our aircraft; the oxygen shortage was bad enough without this engine trouble, and 'home', meaning Benson, was a long way away. . . .

A Time for Toasts

Having breakfasted near London, it was high time to lunch near Moscow. A jeep whisked us to an airfield building, and we sat down with a number of officers – captains, majors and colonels – at one long table. It was about two o'clock.

These Russian hosts of ours were men to be admired. As servicemen in any uniform tend to look, there was a remarkable sameness in their build and colouring. Solid squat men, very broad, with bull-shaped necks emphasized by haircuts that were shorter than Yankee GI cuts. The summer sun had burned their faces and hands to a healthy, ruddy hue. Several had Slav features, and when they laughed their eyes seemed to disappear into slits. Strong, muscular men – hard to tackle or push over, my rugby and wrestling days told me. Their hands were broad, with pudgy fingers. The inherent strength of the USSR was evident in their self-confident bearing and mannerisms, and I believe I understood why Hitler's armies, and Napoleon's before that, had had to cry quits in attempting to subdue Mother Russia.

The meal seemed interminable and the food odd to our taste, but we followed the others and wolfed down each course, including a helping of raw fish heads. In the many, many intervals, chairs were pushed back roughly, cigarettes lit and much vodka consumed. 'Dod nar' (at least that's how it sounded) we chanted in unison with our new comrades: 'Bottoms up', we figured.

Our luncheon companions were decidedly a hard-bitten lot. Most of them were pilots, wearing decorations and campaign medals. One would touch a medal ribbon and shout, say, '*Leningrad!*' and everyone immediately shouted '*Leningrad!*' with even more volume, and then quick as a flash emptied his glass of vodka – in one gulp only, as we learned at the first round. This was obviously a continuing competition of being the first to bang one's empty glass back on to the table. I don't recall who filled all the glasses with such speed and precision, but this aspect of the wining and dining proceeded at a cracking pace. The serving of the food, in great contrast, was a frustratingly prolonged affair.

As inhibitions fell away, pride of nationality made its presence felt. After playing 'follow the leader' to about half a dozen of these Russian toasts, Frank and I had a whispered rehearsal and touched our medal ribbons – and although the particular ribbon was not exactly relevant to the toast, we shouted '*Berlin!*' when we sensed a gap in the successive shouts of our hosts. This one word had a shattering effect on the company, and language barrier or not, they were all apparently incredulous. 'Nyets' were flying about, and there were some derisive guffaws. Russian heads were shaking from side to side in the negative, while we two, stung into action to be on our feet by this time and ably assisted by the fiery vodkas on empty stomachs, were nodding our heads with the utmost vigour in the affirmative manner.

We had certainly been to Berlin, 'the Big Smoke', a few times and had been attacked by fighters in some risky encounters while we were there. My logbook shows, for instance, that we had been attacked by flak and fighters over Berlin on two occasions in the previous month, so the facts were clear in my mind. Of course, the Russians did not call this war 'World War II' or the 'Second World War': to them it was 'The Great Patriotic War', so from their point of view all the emphasis was on the Russian involvement.

By now everyone was on his feet, full glasses of vodka carried at the ready, but disbelief and uncertainty blocking them from being emptied. Our Russian allies had not the faintest idea that British or American aircraft ever flew to the enemy's capital city. A stalemate was approaching, an international one at that, and worse still maybe no more lunch – but Anglo-Saxon inspiration was yet to carry the day. Frank, from years of training as an English football supporter of Coventry, managed to wave his free hand to make me keep time, and in no time at all we had a really good cry ringing out in unison: '*Berlin, Berlin, Berlin!*' I was able with a spare segment of my mind to draw on a superior level of vocal volume from my New Zealand rugby days of shouting Maori Hakas or war-dances, as demonstrated by the 'All Blacks'. It had also been fortunate that operational flying had provided me with aircrew parties at the *White Hart* at Nettlebed, where I often stood on the bar counter and gave what I always thought were excellent renditions of the 'Kamate Kamate' haka. Therefore my vocal chords were in strong form, and the pair of us had no fear as to the local opposition.

And believe it or not, that is how we did convince these worthies of the rightness of our claim. Two or three, of presumably the more easily led amongst the crowd, commenced shouting '*Berlin*' in time with us, and held their glasses on high – the rest capitulated, and Berlin as the prime enemy target was toasted magnificently and unanimously.

From that moment the game swung our way for quite a period. Astonished that we had really been to Berlin, and more interestingly for us, safely back again, right here to prove it, our now worthy allies soon followed us through Regensburg, Danzig, Bergen, Magdeburg, Kiel, Toulouse, Prague, Munich, Cologne, Leipzig, and so on. In short, we sensed we were playing a winning game. Naturally, as good British sports we let the others have a number of Russian battle victories interspersed with our selection.

The question arises whether our hosts ever had discussions at a later date as to where the RAF had *not* been to, around Germany and occupied Europe. To our Western, non-Communist minds, that would have seemed the natural question for discussion: 'Has the RAF *really* been visiting all those places? Are the British and the Americans *really* doing some fighting as well as us, when our State news broadcasts make no mention of such action?'

But there is this other possibility. Although we were in a position of being able to 'converse' with any Russian officers, we never had a chance of a one-to-one conversation. There were always at least two of them, or more, which gave a clear impression that they did not trust one another to exchange facts or views with foreign allies. They seemed fearful of looking as if they were having anything like an intimate parley with us. Maybe none of the gathering *did* query the various possibilities amongst themselves – maybe they were just left with their own individual doubts and questions? I wonder what the Secret Service man, or men, assuming they were present, thought about it . . . . They would have needed to have been exceptionally competent drinkers to think of much at all. However fuddled I was becoming, I still tried to observe if anyone was not keeping up with the play, and I certainly hadn't noticed anyone slacking when the glasses were recharged. Everyone was a willing player, confident in his own ability to last the distance.

We guessed that the last toast was 'to Victory', or something equally desirable. Still copying those remaining on their feet, we hurled our empty glasses over our shoulders against the rough block walls, and extremely satisfying it was, too. It was after five o'clock when an ancient and unexpected Rolls-Royce limousine appeared at the door to take us into Moscow.

Probably the hardest part of the next stage of our journey was mustering the necessary will-power to make any move at all. It became a matter of mind over matter, as our legs seemed to have turned to jelly. A joint effort was required for Frank and me to hoist each other up on our feet after the final toast, and walk unaided to 'our' Rolls. The truth was that I could see no one in a fit state to help us. Nevertheless, we derived a measure of satisfaction in the knowledge that we had kept up with all the toasts, and that when we departed, less than half of the luncheon party was on their feet to embrace us with their farewells. In RAF slang it had been a 'good press-on do', and I choose to think that we kept our end up on the ground as well as in the air. The reports that used to trickle out to us from Transport Command of Mr Churchill's ability to keep up with, or even surpass, 'Uncle Joe' Stalin and his comrades in these hectic and apparently obligatory Russian drinking sessions, made us feel that we too, in our small way, had struck a blow for the cause. I do remember, however, that my eating and drinking and general level of activity the next day were of a somewhat cautious and restricted nature.

Having heaved ourselves up into the roomy interior of the Rolls-Royce, I smiled with a great feeling of well-being at seeing the Union Jack flag flying from the front of the car. Life seemed fair enough.

Interlude: A Variety of Russian Roulette

The road before us was straight, wide, and virtually empty of traffic. The surface was punctuated by monstrous bumps that had the effect of raising our tired bodies, with their overloaded stomachs, a few inches above the soft leather seats. There was no time to relax or feel sorry for the way we felt because to our astonishment, as we looked out of the big windows of the limousine, we saw we were being escorted in close formation by an antiquated bi-plane! These aircraft were used as army ambulances, landing in forward battle areas where two wounded men would be carried out in coffins, one attached to each lower wing. The soldiers presumably recovered their health, or they did not, and in the latter case they did not have to be handled and moved again. An innovative idea.

This aircraft was being handled superbly – the best flying circus I have seen to this day. And even more remarkable – the pilot had dined with us. I gave a petrified look out of my side window as the aircraft side-slipped down to be running alongside me, the wheels just off the road surface, and as he lifted his goggles up to his forehead, there was Major Okay giving me his face-splitting grin and the customary 'thumbs up'. I didn't know whether to laugh or cry – this was horrifying, but also spellbinding in its drama. Whatever the pilot's mixture was of blood and vodka, it was undoubtedly the right mix for this unique demonstration.

The aircraft moved ahead to touch down on the road; it throttled back until the speeding car had nearly caught up with its tailplane, and then with split-second timing this magnificent man lifted his flying machine up and back, over the car, his wheels just missing our windscreen. As we goggled through the small rear window of the Rolls, he touched down on the road and followed us for a while. Every few moments we in the back seat became nearly airborne ourselves as we sped over the bumps. In a sense our driver and us were all part of the action, and intensely involved with every manoeuvre. One tiny mistake by the mad major or a sudden swerve by the chauffeur, and all four of us would have met our end as surely as if I had pushed the 'bomb' button in the Mosquito.

With a finale of devastating sideslips between the telegraph poles along each side of the road, the major gave us his cheeky grin, waved, and peeled away. The skill, the thrills and the danger left me, at least, in a limp and sweaty state; I certainly felt in a more sober condition than I had a little earlier. To reach our quarters and relax proved a great relief.

A Time for Riddles

As Frank at this time was a non-commissioned warrant officer, he and I were housed in separate accommodation that happened to be in different areas of the city. He was escorted away by a pretty blonde Russian girl dressed in a uniform we could not recognize, and she took him to his destination by way of the Moscow underground railway.

The palatial building that was to be my place of residence had originally been built by a wealthy merchant for his mistress during the reign of the Czars – at least, as far as the story could be pieced together. When the war started, the Japanese took it over for some diplomatic use, maybe their embassy, but when Hitler's armies advanced on the capital they decided that discretion was the better part of valour, and evacuated smartly. Incidentally the airport, Vnukova, was near the low-lying Lenin Hills, and that was as close to Moscow as the German advance had reached. This was also the area reached by Napoleon and his armies before their famous retreat.

After the Japanese had concluded their strategic retreat, the British, with commendable opportunism, took over the building. To me, it was semi-oriental in its design and décor: a massive place, but literally with no occupants. And if my bedroom was enormous, the bathroom – or shall we say, the room with the bath in it – was even more huge: one very large marbled room, basically empty, and in one far-flung corner some high curtains, behind which was one huge bath. The dining-room was on a similar scale and exquisitely furnished. I sat in solitary splendour at the head of a long table. Luscious grapes, which my eyes had never seen in Britain during the war, and other fruits, were always on hand in abundance, and it was made known to me that they had been flown up from the Crimea especially for this courier mission. (It would have surprised me greatly if I could have known that in less than four months time Frank and I would be landing our Mosquito in the Crimea, carrying despatches for the Yalta Conference.)

Churchill has commented that some aspects of Russia were 'a riddle wrapped in a mystery inside an enigma', and my short visit puzzled me with conflicting and baffling impressions. But as the years and decades have since rolled by, present events and developments in Russia, and its relationship with the rest of the world, frequently strike me as fitting in with my fleeting opinions and conclusions. The frank joviality and conviviality of the hilarious luncheon party demonstrated the Soviet friendliness, comrades-in-arms acceptance of others as equals, the tremendous good humour, and fun and teasing. But dominating those characteristics were the innate strength and patriotism of those hard and capable men.

These qualities need to be contrasted with the sombre and sinister, even menacing air of the two look-alike OGPU men (later KGB) in their ill-fitting double-breasted blue serge suits who shadowed us constantly. As we stepped outside our gates, guarded by sentries, these two appeared from nowhere and, looking like twin weight-lifters, fell into step and marched along about thirty paces behind us. Apparently we were free to walk where we liked, so we sightsee'd our way round Red Square and the walls of the Kremlin, covering several miles at an outing, setting a brisk pace. We had some satisfaction in seeing our twins mopping sweat from their foreheads from time to time. Navigating ourselves around took much concentration; the Russian alphabet was not recognizable to our eyes, and therefore the various signs did not register with us. We had to memorize every turning we took, and always returned by the same route we had followed on our outward trail. What a blow to our pride if we had had to ask our two 'companions' how to return to 'base'.

Moscow in wartime was a strange sight indeed for our Western eyes. We had been briefed at Benson that no serviceman, non-commissioned, was allowed to visit the capital when on leave, even if they lived there and their families were actually Muscovites: only officers therefore, and there were plenty of them about. Russian military etiquette required all officers to salute all other officers, unlike the British system. This gave rise to a continual saluting process that to us was absurdly ridiculous, especially to a 'Kiwi', which breed has never been noted for a desire to salute anyone; but we turned it into an amusement, and Frank kept up a whispered commentary with his dry wit that kept me in stitches. We decided that everyone's face was tragically serious – little doubt they did not have much to be cheerful about – but no smiles nor looks of acknowledgement could be seen, so our response was to smile at everyone including the innumerable men we were saluting. The effect on the populace was amazing: they turned and stared at us till we were out of sight. Were we men from the moon? How incongruous we were amongst that crowd.

Very few vehicles were to be seen, apart from some long black limousines looking identical to the Buicks and Chryslers and similar American models that I had grown up with in NZ ten years before. Their nameplates said they were 'ZILS' or some such make now forgotten; but for these Russians they were their own manufacture and their own design. The same applied at the airfield, where aircraft identical to Dakotas, the still well-known DC-3s, were proudly pointed out to us as Russian designed and produced.

To comprehend how a harsh dictatorship had so successfully brainwashed its citizens, including officers of the armed forces, into implicitly believing whatever they were told, was a mind-boggling experience for me. This reminds me rather absurdly of the wartime riddle: 'Why was Hitler like an immoral goose?' and the answer was: 'Because he did not keep to his proper gander.' Mind you, here we are looking at the snags in a dictatorship/ Communist state, but how does one explain the following comment given to me in New York a couple of years earlier, from a man who, with his family, was extending superb hospitality to me as an overseas serviceman: 'Sure thing, Son, it was a good thing we Americans invented that Spitfire so your people could win the Battle of Britain!' It was also a good thing that in quiet distant New Zealand my parents had brought me up to be polite to my elders. Propaganda is certainly international. . . .

The traffic also included army trucks and buses that were grossly overloaded, and it wasn't until we were in Cairo about a year later that I witnessed similar congestion on vehicles. The buses on these Moscow streets had passengers on every square inch of space, hanging on with one toe-hold while crowded like sheep in a pen on the large open rear platforms.

As we stood at one intersection, a tall officer approached a bus that was barely moving as it turned the corner. One passenger, a middle-aged peasant-type woman clutching a small sack of shopping, was just managing to hang on right at the edge of the bus step. The officer casually undid the woman's hand with which she was holding the rail, and as she lost her balance and crashed onto the roadway at our feet, he calmly took her place on the bus step as it gathered speed, with never a backward glance. If this was how the officers behaved, how would the troops act if they had been permitted to enter the city? This simple episode sickened both of us.

The poor lady rolled over to the gutter on the edge of which we were standing. We hastened to heave her to her feet, and scrambled about on our knees retrieving and repacking her pathetic articles of shopping into her rough sack. She was dishevelled and grazed, and now and then moaned gently. Why, you may be asking, does this trivial incident warrant a mention? The reason is because of the reaction of everyone else who had either witnessed the affair or who were later arrivals to the scene, and who in the best crowd spirit just wanted to see a bit of the action. On looking up we found we were the centre of a big circle of Muscovites, and we three were the actors on the stage. Who were these strangely dressed foreigners down on their knees with a distressed old woman who was crying? What had they done to her? Where had they come from? What were they doing here at all? Frank and I dusted down the old soul, gave her back her belongings and patted her on the back: but the onlookers stayed exactly where they were, impassive of features and silent. Did they want to see Act II of the performance? 'A riddle wrapped in a mystery inside an enigma', to be sure.

And it was now that for the one and only time our two escorts showed their authority and the results of their training and just waded into the crowd with elbows and massive shoulders until there was a sufficient passage for us to extricate ourselves and continue our walkabout. They never caught our eye, they never said a word to us, and we never thanked them: they were invisible except when they wished to appear, rather like bad angels, it occurred to me.

Another strange sight for us to see were the large squads of burly women marching along with gusto at a cracking pace carrying shovels and grubbers and similar implements. They were the gangs of road repairers and digger-uppers, and they looked truly formidable, both individually and en masse.

Maybe these were the people who had dug up the Russian rail network from the Baltic coast to Moscow, and who no doubt had then relaid it somewhere else, and thereby tested the skills of any intrepid aerial navigators who thought they were going to use maps for map-reading. If their duties were ever to take them to the highway between Vnukova airport and Moscow, we could have assuredly warned them to avoid low-flying aircraft.

The sheer force, and energy, and application of all the people with whom we had any contact made a profound impression on me. We were poles apart in temperament and lifestyles, but there was a feeling of primitive vitality and power emanating from them that gave me a sense of foreboding. If, and when, this vast country ever reaches a state of being able to switch its expenditure and effort on armaments to improve and revitalize the standards of its citizens and its economy, its people could again be a powerful and leading force in the world.

Instead of feeling happy and cheerful, I only had to glance at the street and shop signs that we could not decipher, to instantly feel that we were on some other planet. And the impression is still with me, that we were in effect as far from home as if we had been on the moon. No doubt the uncertainty surrounding the state of serviceability of our Mosquito was coming more and more frequently into my conscious mind, because it was for sure the only means by which we should ever be able to leave this vast, alien land.

Another striking contrast was between the dreary, mostly Slavonic-featured peasants who shuffled about with expressionless faces along the mean and drab wartime streets, and the light, warmth, colour and fantasy of the Bolshoi Imperial Opera whose performances enchanted us as well as Mr Churchill and Mr Stalin. We were privileged to see Tchaikovsky's opera *Eugene Onegin*; it was one of the events of my life, and filled me with joy and happiness. We understood that apart from the army and navy officers and their ladies, the audiences were composed of ordinary citizens who had excelled in their productive efforts in the war factories; this luxury visit to the Bolshoi was offered as a prestigious reward for outstanding service to their country. But while Frank and I shared a box and sat in impressive luxury, part of my mind pictured the old woman flat on her back on the street corner, the ring of impassive bystanders playing out their role. Such contrasts and incongruities – and once following that line of thought, it was only too easy to drop down another cog and find myself reflecting on the complications if the Mosquito was not thoroughly serviceable.

* * *

After the magical atmosphere of the colourful performance, and with the melody of the principal waltz still lilting in my ears, it was a jolt to step outside the building on to the street. Drab and mean the city had looked when we went in – but as we came out, this time our eyes met an unexpected and thrilling sight: the blackness of the night was exploding with brilliant displays of fireworks, the pounding of gun salvoes, and the beat of loud martial music. We learned that all this was to celebrate the freeing – or was it the capturing – of Riga, the capital of Latvia, by the Soviet forces whom we had observed battling below us on our flight from England. The music was broadcast through a network of speakers on high poles or on the corners of tall buildings at most street intersections. There was no question of not hearing it, and clearly this was the media for all the national news and broadcasts. Moreover, as well as the fact that the whole populace had no option but to hear it, there was the further chilling thought that they were prohibited from having access to any other forms of radio receivers.

As the car drove me back to my solitary 'palace' in the middle hours of this unreal night, a feeling swept over me of dread at the possibility of being trapped in this city, in this country, so profoundly different and distant from what I was used to and longed for. . . . The morning could not come quickly enough, but there would still be another twenty-four hours of suspense waiting for the conference papers.

Back at Benson our pre-flight briefing on servicing the aircraft had been given by the squadron senior ground-crew flight sergeant fitters and riggers. All my concentration had been given to learning as much as possible, and I was confident I could make the right decisions in that field, crucial as they might be – crucial to the success of our venture, but also decidedly so to the survival of the crew of Mosquito 307.

The next day, on waking, my mind was instantly filled and occupied with trying to conjecture how much oxygen would be left for us to draw on. Even with taps turned hard off, oxygen always leaks. . . .

'East, West, Time to go Home is Best'

A day later, 14 October 1944, I was tense when Major Okay, brisk and business-like, skidded the jeep to a halt alongside No. 307, and Frank and I tackled the inspection. In the cockpit, a mini-world of precise intimacy to us, our gear had been moved about a little, and I suddenly realized just how much we relied on our RAF groundcrews to carefully maintain and protect this cramped but vital little Mosquito world in which life and death were so evenly balanced. Helmets, oxygen masks, parachutes, inflatable dinghies, Mae West life-jackets, navigation bag (with its lack of maps), and other sundry items had all been moved, and as this started to irritate me something far more important caught my eye. Both engines had recently been run up. Now I was angry: 'Who's been playing with *my* Rolls-Royce Merlin engines that have to get me and my navigator back across all of enemy Europe to Home Sweet Home?'

The port coolant temperature was showing 'normal' – that was a relief admittedly, but the oxygen showed a mere quarter full, and this confirmed my worst fears in this direction. 'Let's get airborne smartly before any more of the precious gas disappears' was my reaction. There would have to be some rather important things unserviceable before I would declare the aircraft U/S: 'Home James! And don't spare the horses' was my Kiwi attitude.

To our astonishment we were issued with a ten page, comprehensive diagrammatic weather report, the heading of which, although it included several lines in Russian, was in 'English' – 'The Central Office of the Hydro Meteorological Services of the USSR'. To be frank I don't think any weather report would have stopped me setting off, and in any case we had to take a chance that landing conditions would be favourable somewhere within range in Britain – but that was the least of my concerns at that stage. The wind would tend to be a westerly: the average wind at 30,000ft is from the west and at a speed of 100mph, and therefore for us in these circumstances a headwind, so the fuel levels would need watching; and without sufficient oxygen to maintain our optimum altitude we would be using more fuel than normal. It would therefore be an interesting trip – what do positive people say? 'Not a problem, but a good challenge.'

The general controlling the airfield presented me with a bottle of vodka and an apology for its weak wartime strength – although the label showed it to be '90% Proof Spirit'. As I read the label, a fleeting thought passed through my mind that we should perhaps be thankful that the copious quantity of vodka we had consumed a few days ago had not been peacetime strength!

Even better than the gift of the spirits was the request from the general that we should demonstrate the qualities of this superior aircraft of ours by 'beating up', or 'buzzing' the place before we set course. 'There will be no Yaks shooting at you this time,' we gathered. Neither before nor since have I been *asked* to do a beat-up, and I relished the opportunity of obeying the orders of such a senior officer; the very thought of it still makes me smile – though in reality it did not turn out to be much of a smiling matter.

This business of 'beating up' a place, as we know, is to fly over at a low level with as much noise and intimidation as possible for the people on the ground. Duke Downie had carried the process to extremes over Benson airfield, and this had earned him castigation from higher authority. Believe me, from my experience of enduring his efforts, any tough guy will fling himself flat out on the deck and cover his head with his hands when subjected to such a beat-up. The unbearable noise, the force of the slipstream as the aircraft passes, and the genuine fear of actually being hit, all this is too much for the human mind and frame to withstand. And that, of course, was the principle behind the German strategy with their Stuka dive-bombers.

The mailbag containing the vital conference decisions was delivered to me. It was, at last, time to start up and be off. A few quick handshakes and some casual salutes, and I moved towards the little metal ladder to mount to the cockpit. Then on an impulse I walked a few steps round behind the wing where there was a Russian groundcrew man. His hat badge appealed to me very much as a souvenir: the badge was a red star with the familiar hammer and sickle imposed on it, affixed to his hat by a small pin crudely soldered to the back of the badge. Not much of a trophy but it took my eye.

We two, hopefully hidden from the little crowd round the front of the aircraft, went into the miming routine. He indicated by drawing his hand across his throat and rolling his eyes out of sight that it would be more than his life was worth. However, he was not aware of the propensity of the Anzacs for collecting souvenirs. I whipped out my trusty pocket knife (and remember at this stage of the proceedings I was wearing my revolver), and the hapless individual wanted to cut and run. But with my knife, in desperation, I sliced off one of my beautifully polished brass buttons from my No. One uniform tunic and tried to make a swap. My victim was looking terrified by this time, but he was still a most capable bargainer, and three of my buttons had to be surrendered in exchange for his one flimsy badge. . . . But the trinket still gives me pleasure.

One last bear-hug with the admirable and invaluable Major Okay and I nipped up to my seat and took the controls.

Because we were away from our base there were no twenty-four-volt battery-carts to plug into, and it was necessary for the motors to start from their own accumulators. The *Pilot's Notes* for a Mosquito give the following instructions at this stage: 'Groundcrew to dope vigorously when starter engaged.' As I pressed the starter button, a Russian airman (but not the one minus a cap badge) commenced pumping the doping primer, but nowhere near energetically enough. This pump was a small affair housed in a tiny doorway in the engine nacelle, and was both hard to get at and reach up to, as well as hard to push in and out. I had demonstrated the action required to these crewmen a few minutes earlier because it meant a great deal to me to ensure that the engines started. Starting on our own 'accs', the action needed to be particularly vigorous.

Major Okay, engineer as well as pilot and stunt-man, knew in a flash what had to be done. Did he ask the airman to try harder or to step aside and let him have a go? Did he what! He immediately showed all the Russian characteristics I was coming to recognize as true to form, and gave the poor unfortunate airman one backward swipe with his powerful arm, knocking him clean off his feet, then grasped the primer with *both* his hands and pumped it in and out at a furious speed. Two things happened: the engine roared into life, and I caught it on the throttle. The major's hands, where they had been too big to move in and out of the little hinged coverplate in the nacelle, were spurting blood all over his face and uniform from the jagged cuts which had been inflicted by the sharp metal on every pump of the primer. He sure was a tough guy, an awesome man: I enjoyed him and appreciated him and I'm sure he knew it. He grinned at me and gave me his last thumbs-up.

The other engine knew better than to play up, and started smoothly. We taxied out and took off impatiently. Being airborne again gave me a surge of relief and anticipation. Foster and Moseley would take a bit of stopping now.

With its maximum fuel load (apart from drop-tanks), the Mossie lumbered into the air as if burdened with the responsibility of the bag and the bomb. As we climbed to circuit height my brain failed to tell me that most of the illegal low-flying and beat-ups I had got away with had been performed with an aircraft nearly empty of fuel – that is, at the conclusion of a sortie when the aircraft was three or four tons lighter.

From 1,000ft altitude I dived over the control tower, on the balcony of which were the general and his staff, and no doubt anyone else who could crowd their way up there – maybe one or two of the Yak pilots wanted a closer look? The fully laden aircraft reacted sluggishly, squashing downwards as I fought to pull it up. For a long moment I contemplated fiasco and disaster due to my own bravado and mis-judgement. I lifted a wing to miss the balcony; a split-second glance told me it was now empty of onlookers.

As this lower wing sunk still further it became entangled with an aerial wire leading down from the tower to a W/T hut situated near the base of the tower. The hut was a low, single-storey affair and the wire wound round the lower wooden wing-tip as a reminder and a souvenir. . . . Frank and I looked at each other, pale-faced and silent for a long time as we climbed away and set course for home.

I am sure that our Russian audience would have instantly agreed that a beat-up like the one we demonstrated was ample: they had changed into reluctant observers, and it is of some comfort to know that even those hardy characters recognized precisely the moment when the best thing to do was to beat a retreat from their viewing point. Major Okay could not have had time to dash over to the control tower and up to the balcony, but I feel sure that if he had been there, he would have stood his ground and given us his airman's gesture. Maybe, on mature reflection, he and I ended up with even score cards.

* * *

The altitude for the return flight was of crucial importance, but our calculations were depressing. Even with no headwind we hadn't the range to reach England unless we flew at more than 22,000ft, where the superchargers cut in; that meant using oxygen, but we had only a little and that supply continued to slowly leak. At lower altitudes we would be easy prey for Russian, and further on, German fighters, as well as flak. Having previously experienced the attack over the middle of Europe by a dozen American fighters, we knew how any single aircraft in European skies seemed to be 'fair game' for any trigger-happy fighter pilots, where recognition came *after* the squeezing of the trigger. There always seemed to be an open shooting season for solitary unarmed aircraft.

Not only did we carry no guns in the interest of extra speed, we were also taking that bomb along for the ride, and as a bonus we had the mail-bag to deliver. Keep away from fighters for as long as possible, ignore any flak, and hope to struggle across the North Sea at a lower altitude: that had to be the plan. We agreed to climb high and use up the oxygen and so get a good start and worry about the rest later. Because you cannot recognize when you are suffering from lack of oxygen, Frank and I continually scrutinized each other for possible symptoms. At 30,000ft a supply failure for less than one minute was fatal, and there was no positive way of knowing when the supply would dwindle out; there is no tell-tale taste or smell, and a lack produces a feeling of well-being and over-confidence similar to the effects of alcohol, so the situation created another challenge.

The first navigation check occurred crossing out over the eastern Baltic coast, and I prayed that cloud would not deny us the necessary pinpoint. Frank calculated our progress before saying quietly, 'We'll never make it at this ground speed.'

'We're going to!' I insisted.

Prudence and training demanded a return to Moscow from this 'point of no return', and even that would be a tight thing relative to the fuel remaining. But going back to where we had come from never entered my reckoning: the all-powerful, ever-deceiving syndrome that 'it couldn't happen to us', coupled with a strong homing instinct, drew us westwards.

When the oxygen gauges showed zero we had no option but to gradually lose height, and unfortunately this resulted in the Mosquito streaming a vapour trail, which arrowed our heading to the enemy world beneath. They knew we were there anyway, by radar, but psychologically one always felt more vulnerable when making trails. On the other hand, other aircraft could also be spotted much more easily, as long as you were looking out for them!

Both engines were running roughly by now; maybe they did not find the quality of the fuel up to their required levels of 100-grade octane. The motors certainly had developed a different feeling. For some unenvied reason, I had become, amongst the crews on the squadron, an unwilling expert on 'engines having funny feelings', with the result that one of my nicknames was 'Single-engine Kiwi'. Confirming this unwanted description, as we neared north Germany, the starboard oil pressure suddenly disappeared and we were fortunate to be able to feather the propeller in time.

Some pilots never did have to feather an engine – and maybe some of those who did not return from ops had one such unsuccessful experience. The net flying time clocked up on one engine in a Mosquito for most pilots was therefore nearly always nil, because when being instructed to fly a Mossie, our instructors talked through the drill but did not fancy actually pressing the button. It was unusual that five of my operational flights had to be completed on one engine.

Staring at the remaining port engine I had a fairly lengthy wonder about the efficiency of the Russian repairs to the coolant system. Flying on one engine forced us to continue losing height with a corresponding loss in speed and miles per gallon. The future didn't seem very cheerful, so I concentrated on the present. This was the very time for my mind, with its mathematical bent, to continually evaluate the fuel gauges, relate this to the distance to go, and see how the equations worked out. The next step was to evaluate how much boost and what rpm to set the engine at in order to obtain maximum range. If one throttled back too much, the plugs were prone to oiling up and a much more immediate challenge would present itself – by then one's mind should have moved into 'parachute' mode.

Lower down we entered turbulent cloud, but on the plus side it was good to have some cover from fighters. Would the Germans let us escape when we were so low and so slow? Not if they knew where we had come from, or if they knew what we were carrying, that was for sure. The port engine started misfiring; perhaps this confirmed that the fuel had not been sufficiently refined for these highly tuned, 'state-of-the-art' engines. On a normal flight we might have considered heading for neutral Sweden, and safety, but now I was engrossed in a personal struggle to deliver those documents to the king's messenger in his Humber motor car.

Conditions became so violently bumpy that I tried letting down further to find the cloud base, although we had no chance of regaining any altitude we lost because a single engine would not give us power for climbing. At 1,000ft through heavy rain we saw the North Sea, grey and inhospitable. The engine was vibrating badly and I told Frank to be prepared to bale out. I hoped I would have time to follow him; far from an easy procedure, but one we had practised diligently in the hangar many times against a stopwatch. I tied the mailbag to my dinghy pack.

While I was intent on instruments and flying a good course, Frank scanned for fighters, or land, in that order. What a shock to suddenly find ourselves just off the German Frisian Islands! Seven months earlier we had struggled our way past these same islands, also flying on something less than one good engine. 'Whew!' I reflected, 'we *are* a sitting duck'; but one more hour of sweaty tension ticked by and I could at last say a silent prayer of thankfulness as we lumbered over the English coast. Even with the anxiety of the fuel shortage I still chose to press on under the lowering rain-clouds

Logbook: 12–14 October 1944, Ops Nos 48 and 49, Moscow courier trip. Note: On No. 49 we were obliged to make our fourth single-engine landing.

BULLETIN D'EXPÉDITION OFFICIELLE

It is hereby certified that the Officially Sealed Bags detailed below contain only Official Correspondence.

From	To	Number of Bags	Bag Nos.	Weight in Kgs.
His Majesty's Secretary of State for Foreign Affairs, LONDON.	Tolstoy. By Mosquito.	One	Tol 6	

Airport of disembarkation................................

To be handed to................................

The above-mentioned .... bags are handed to British Overseas Airways Corporation for conveyance by air to the Airport of disembarkation shown, for disposal as indicated.

(Signature of Despatching Officer)................................

(Stamp of Office of Origin and Date).

Signature of Receiving Officer................................

P.T.O.

Op. No. 48: HM Secretary of State for Foreign Affairs: a bag receipt, known as Operation *Tolstoy*.

towards Benson, comforting myself with the delusion that if the fuel did cut we could crashland without the bomb destroying the documents . . . and us.

Twenty more agonizing minutes, and I brought No. 307 over its base at a height just sufficient to clear the trees, throttled back the one misfiring engine, and eased her down gently, regardless of runway: five hours and thirty-five minutes after our spectacular take-off. The length of aerial wire still trailed from the wing-tip, and that took a little bit of explaining, several times over.

Out of the dusk came friendly fire-engines, crash-tenders, CO's car, and, nosing up to us familiarly, the official Humber. I flicked 'switches off', smiled at the fuel gauges leaning on their zero marks, and said to good old Frank, 'It wasn't a bad sortie Franko!' – then wondered fleetingly why I could hardly get the words out. My mouth opened again, involuntarily this time, and just as I was unbuckling my seat-harness straps I was sick, right down my best uniform, less three of its buttons.

The tension and effort of operational trip No. 49 was over for us.

. . . Diary note: 'Glad to be back. Feel tired but exhilarated.'

The 'message of congratulation' reproduced opposite percolated down to our humble crew-room from the prime minister. It came via Air Ministry, to the air officer commanding No. 106 (PR) Group, to our squadron commander, to our 'B' flight commander, and then to Frank and me who were handed copies of this message, dated 26 October 1944.

The message shown in the illustration should round off this tale, but there is an interesting post-script.

Six months or so later, when the war in Europe was won, Air Ministry informed me by way of our squadron CO, Wing Commander D. W. Steventon, that Mosquito No. 307 had been completely dismantled at Vnukova and every piece photographed before re-assembly. Even the bomb installation had been removed and replaced without blowing anything up – and incidentally, the British opinion of the Russian repairs to the coolant system was that they were first class.

This startling piece of news did not altogether surprise me, but merely confirmed my impressions of the ability and potential of the Russian people. For its part, Air Ministry would not have been surprised at all – and remember, 307 was out of date and minus her equipment before we had been allowed to fly her to the land of our trusty (?), but temporary allies. . . .

COPY.

From :- R.A.F.Station, Benson, Oxon.

To :- W/Cmdr Watts. Officer Commanding No.544 Squadron (2 Copies)

Date :- 28th October, 1944.

Ref :- BEN/705/P1.

MESSAGE OF CONGRATULATION.

The Station Commander adds his thanks and congratulations, and forwards with pleasure letter received from Headquarters No.106 (PR) Group 106G/55/Air. dated 26th October,1944.

(Signed) T.Henderson, F/Lt.
for Group Captain, Commanding
R.A.F. Station, Benson.

"The following message of congratulations from the Prime Minister has been received from Air Ministry:

"The Prime Minister wishes to convey his thanks to all those concerned both in the air and on the ground in the operation of this most successful courier service between the United Kingdom and U.S.S.R. and Middle East during his recent journey abroad thus enabling him to keep in such close and continuous touch with London Headquarters.

It is thought that this striking instance of the enterprise and efficiency of the Royal Air Force was not lost upon the official Soviet circles to whom it became known"

2.   It is felt that all concerned in the planning and carrying out of this operation are to be congratulated on the efficiency with which the service was run.

3.   The A.O.C. wishes,in particular, to thank and congratulate Wing Commander Watts and Wing Commander Steventon. The excellent performance of 544 Squadron is highly commended.

4.   It is requested that you will bring the foregoing to the notice of all concerned.

Copies to O.C.s "A" & "B" Flights.
    "   " Air Crew Order Books.
    "   " Ground Crew Order Books.

Ops Nos 48–49: message of congratulation from the Prime Minister, Mr W. Churchill.

11

When Twenty-Four Hours is Enough

Where there is no vision the people perish.
Proverbs 29:18

Ops Nos 50, 51 and 52, 22, 23, & 24 December 1944

Towards the end of 1944, six months after Allied forces had landed in Normandy to commence the liberation of Europe from the control of the Nazis, their armies had still not been able to reach the River Rhine and to enter Germany. During this period, when the weather usually seemed to be mostly stormy, yet foggy on other days, Frank and I flew Ops Nos 50, 51 and 52. These were shorter trips to the western parts of Germany, with the Luftwaffe still intercepting us.

Just when the Allies did seem to be gathering momentum in their advance, the Germans, under the command of Field Marshal Gerd von Rundstedt, launched a counter offensive, appropriately called 'Autumn Mist', on 16 December. This was a supreme and last-ditch effort to swing the battles and the overall strategic situation to their advantage. Their breakthrough into Belgium, called 'The Battle of the Bulge', was of the greatest concern to the Allied Command.

At this crucial time as the end of December approached, an extensive high-pressure system remained stationary over western Europe, and the weather was brilliantly clear: clear, that is, except for Britain, where the fog was so dense and widespread that for a few days no aerial sorties could be carried out by bombers or fighters or by anything else over the battlegrounds across the English Channel. It became imperative for the Allies to urgently obtain the complete picture of the whole battle area as well as the activities along the routes used for supplies and reinforcements. Obviously the only sure way to obtain this vital information was by aerial photo-reconnaissance – but Benson airfield was as heavily enveloped in fog as ever it could be, and the same conditions applied to virtually all of Britain. Basically, all flying was scrubbed.

The unusual intensity of the fog was well proven when on one of these foggy mornings, a group of us – myself, together with my Aussie room-mates, Joe and Vic, and our three navigators – decided to walk across the airfield to the perimeter track on the other side, in order to take a short cut to the *Riverside*. This aptly named establishment was a small roadside café where we aircrew were often privileged to be able to buy a real fresh egg – just never seen in wartime – which, on toast, we used to consume with relish. No doubt the fact that the serving of real eggs was illegal added to the scrumptious taste.

Such a successful sortie was always a real delight for the three 'Black Troops', as our 'Pommie' colleagues enjoyed calling us – in response to which we, taking a lead from quick-witted Joe, referred to these 'pukka types' as 'the natives'. Although our navigators consisted of two Englishmen and one Scotsman, they were our loyal and ever-faithful camp followers, and it was my belief that we were the tightest-knit little band to be found in PRU.

All the highly trained and carefully chosen PRU aircrew tended to form a collective unit comprised of supreme individualists. The two Spits and two Mossie squadrons had a certain number of pilots, and less than half that number of navigators. Every pilot was captain of his aircraft, and there were no large crews to form friendships together. Because the casualty rate was extraordinarily high, at times a fresh crew was posted to Benson; they would be sent on an op. in the next day or so, and if they failed to return we might not even have had the opportunity to be introduced. Add to this the fact that each pilot had the freedom to choose his own route to and from his targets in Europe, and that a high proportion of the pilots were, in the first place, original and unique characters, and it is not surprising that Benson was crewed by such an independent company. It was natural for Joe and Vic and myself, from the other side of the world, to be room-mates and to become the closest of friends, the best of cobbers, and also for our navigators to stick with us. So we revelled in the fact that we were a band of brothers, until operations took their inevitable toll.

On this particular foggy day, even after continuous and argumentative discussions en route, instead of arriving on the perimeter track near the unofficial exit through the hedge to the café, we found ourselves nearly 90 degrees off track, and even then could not unanimously agree whether we should turn right or left. That's how foggy it was. The picture is still clear to me of big Joe saying, with many Aussie embellishments: 'It's as I keep telling you jokers, there's no point in our carrying these navigators around with us – they are always more lost than we are!' The continual *'cri de coeur'* of all navigators to their pilots was, 'A good navigator is never lost; he just doesn't know where he is for a while!'

Thursday, 21 December

As squadron entertainments officer I was doing my part in organizing the station Christmas dance, to be held on 27 December, and during that day of organizing, the fog produced a false imitation of lifting – just a whisker here and there. From some bases further north, a large force of US 8th Air Force Flying Fortress and Liberator four-engined bombers had managed to become airborne and had completed their missions over the battlefield supply area. On their return over Britain their bases were absolutely 10/10s clamped down with fog, but by some quirk of weather, Benson suddenly displayed a slight clearance of the 'dreaded menace' and many units were diverted to our airfield: we were literally invaded by hundreds of Yanks. Benson, both village and airfield, lies just across the road from the River Thames, which usually helped to generate its own good share of mists and fog. But the powers controlling the weather conditions must have decided that we were all too smug sheltering behind this fog, unable to operate, and that a liberal dose of Yankees would shake us out of our complacency.

That was probably an accurate assessment. It was startling and dramatic to have dozens of 'Forts' and 'Libs' landing from all directions and parking all over the place in an untidy sprawl. And if our meticulously tidy and well-organized airfield looked different, it was a mere nothing compared to how our messes looked. The bomber crews, and there were ten men to a crew, were spread around our airmen's mess and the sergeants' mess, and in our officers' mess we were probably completely outnumbered by our American visitors. In their flying gear they sat or lay on the floors in our formal ante-room – the corridors and even the cloakrooms were similarly occupied, and even that inner sanctum, the Ladies' Room, had been made available to help accommodate the invasion.

In a minor way it *was* as if we had been invaded from another planet. We had men in our mess in leather flying jackets and flying boots for a start, and a large number of them were smokers, many with strong-smelling cigars. Most noticeable of all, perhaps, were the louder voices with their twangy accents and North American expletives and blasphemies, limited in variety and repetitive as they always were to British ears. How they used their eating irons was good for a curious and disbelieving stare, and even my sojourn in Canada and the States for a year did not stop me from being intrigued watching a big husky Yank trying to tackle crackly bacon and soft scrambled dried eggs by stabbing at it with a fork.

A theory formed in my mind that the reason citizens of the good old US of A did so many things differently from Britain had sprung from their basic act of independence from British rule. The rule in vogue then was to create a challenge to see how many things could be done differently, and starting with the use of the knife and fork, the idea quickly spread to driving vehicles on the right side of the road instead of the left, spelling words like 'colour' differently, changing the pronunciation of words like 'dance', designing electrical appliances with different voltages, limiting baggage on airlines by measurement rather than by weight, reducing their gallon to 5/6 of an imperial one, and so on . . . and why not, perhaps? My mother had often drummed into me that variety is the spice of life.

For all their apparent differences, these men of the USAAF were indeed splendid men. We, at this élite establishment of Benson, had to admit to admiring their airmanship in landing their big four-engined bombers at a strange base after an operational flight, in conditions that were marginal. Some of these aircraft were damaged, some landed on three engines, and it was obvious from looking at these kites that some of the crews had been wounded. It was never disclosed if any were killed from amongst the crews that landed at Benson.

No doubt this enforced liaison between American and RAF personnel resulted in a much deeper mutual understanding and respect. Also there would have been no doubt in the minds of all these Americans that Britain was clearly a separate identity from Europe; indeed, they could see this by looking out of their aircraft windows every time they crossed and re-crossed the English Channel or the North Sea. More effectively they could *feel* this every time they strolled into any English pub, or when they went to London on leave . . . they did not need lectures explaining why they were helping to defend this land of the 'Limeys' from that dictator in Europe.

By the end of this 21 December, two decisions were made that affected me. First, the Christmas dance was cancelled because of the increasing pressure on all our operational structure to obtain vital results at a time of unusually contrary and dangerous weather conditions; and second, Frank and I were detailed for a transit trip to Italy the next day. We therefore did not see the mass fly-off of the American bombers that were serviceable. It was apparently a spectacular sight and, once again, well executed – if they managed not to collide with each other either on the ground or in the air, then it was indeed a well executed operation.

Friday, 22 December

Operation No. 53 was a long-range job, our longest trip yet – six hours and ten minutes – the target areas as listed in the log entry being well east on the map of Europe. If a PRU Mosquito survived the outward trip to cover the required targets, there then remained the long haul back to England, and this return trip was usually against the prevailing westerly headwind, and enemy flak and fighters waited for us all the way back across Europe. These trips that penetrated so far into the Third Reich had resulted in the failure of PRU Mossies to arrive back at base on several recent occasions. Whereas sorties by bombers or fighters or torpedo-bombers could achieve the objectives for which they had been briefed, and *then* fail to return to base, photo-reconnaissance demanded a return to base with satisfactory pictures before the objective was accomplished.

With the advent of transit trips, many of the risks and difficulties arising from these 'Eastern' sorties had been almost nullified. As the Allied armies slowly fought their way northwards up Italy against a dogged German defence and the rigours of winter campaigning, it had become possible in the last few months for us to photograph those areas to the east that were at the extremity of our fuel range. Instead of battling our way back to England, we could now turn south, 'left hand down a bit', and take the softer option of flying down to southern Italy. Rome had fallen to the Allied advance on 4 June 1944, and Florence two months later.

On this particular trip, for example, we turned south from East Prussia (now Poland), over Germany, Czechoslovakia, Hungary, Yugoslavia and so down to Italy. Our track took us east of Vienna, not far from Budapest; this was the long way round, but at least we had more chance to live to fight another day. Once landed in southern Italy at an advanced air base, we spent the night, refuelled in the morning, and flew back to England, covering some targets en route for which we had been briefed before leaving Benson.

Our transit stop was at San Severo airfield on the Foggia Plains. The whole set-up appealed to me, as an outdoor type of Kiwi. I enjoyed the primitiveness of it all, the roughness I suppose, and the casual but competent approach of everyone there; informality was the key word. The overall appearance was one of general chaos – as war *is*, in its raw state. The Americans, who shared the landing strip with the RAF and the SAAF, had laid down rolls of linked chain metal to form a firm but flexible runway: in the heat of summer this made for a less bumpy and rutty ride, and in the rains and bogs of winter it kept aircraft out of the churned-up sea of mud on each side of the strip. This metal strip was narrow, and there was no leeway in having to keep a true straight line for both take-offs and landings: one wheel into the mud, and the aircraft was immovable.

British maintenance crews towed away bogged and damaged aircraft with big tractors, and sometimes tractors towed tractors when the first tractor was itself bogged down. Eventually, by a process of cannibalization, the Brits would repair and rebuild the aircraft until they were again fit for flying. Our friends the Yanks, however, had a different approach, their habit being to leave the pranged plane exactly where it was. Whereas the British would haul it back off the metal strip so it did not project over the strip surface and become a hazard to everyone else attempting to land, the Americans made no effort at all to salvage their aircraft – they even left the clocks unstripped from the instrument panels. A British erk would soon be hovering over it with his screwdriver at the ready. 'Plenty more so-and-so new aircraft from where this came from!' was 'Uncle Sam's' attitude – a vastly different principle from the way in which I had been brought up.

In summer, if taxiing was required, our Rolls-Royce Merlin 'in-line' engines with their liquid coolant systems soon boiled after landing in such heat. That was sufficient to make the kite U/S, so the 'gen' was to stop immediately after landing. If you were fortunate and stopped at the right spot, you could let the aircraft run a few yards on to an adjacent, but small area of chain metal.

The snag was that this area was still precariously near to where other aircraft could prang into your kite when they were landing. The drill I worked out, as a matter of preserving the Mosquito in one piece, was to arrive down at the strip very promptly in the morning before the heat of the day built up. Then start up, point the aircraft back down the metal strip – don't bother with running-up and checking the engines – let the brakes off, open up the throttles smartly and hope to be airborne before the coolant overheated. This procedure, harum-scarum as it may have been, also tended to avoid the inevitable congestion of kites trying to both land and take off from both ends of the one strip more or less at the same time, another procedure that is not covered in any *Pilot's Notes*.

It was always pleasant to arrive at San Severo, good old 'terra firma', but it was also very satisfactory to be safely airborne and off again. At times like that, I always felt more content and confident when we were airborne with an adequate supply of fuel, and thus to a large extent, masters of our own destiny.

On this trip, being wintertime and the field a veritable sea of mud, once again we took off in the opposite direction to that in which we had landed. In other words, no importance could be given to where the wind was coming from. To coax a well-fuelled Mossie to become airborne down-wind or even across-wind, especially in high temperatures, presented a challenge which for me, at least, brought forth maximum pilot effort, evidenced by an obvious quickening of the pulse.

Perhaps it would be helpful to point out that these Italian take-offs were somewhat impeded by a self-made difficulty that once again was not catered for in the *Pilot's Notes*: we were always tempted, and I always succumbed, to purchase for a very small amount of lire, a fairly sizable cask of local vino, namely Vermouth. This we eagerly took back with us as a prize, but the difficulty was to fit it into the tiny cramped cockpit that had not been designed with this particular cargo in mind. The task was not made easier by the fact that we had to draw the bung so it did not pop with the changes in pressure; therefore the cask had to stay level, from Italy to England.

We also used to poke into the few odd corners some good-sized bags of oranges and almonds, and, when they were in season, several bunches of delicious grapes. What a shambles it would have been if we had been intercepted by a Bf 109 or an Fw 190.

Having been blessed by surviving the war against all the odds, it is strange in these present days to reflect how carefully we all have to prepare our documentation before we travel from one country to another: tickets, money, passports and visas, insurance policies and all sorts of other papers. But there were Frank and I lobbing about all over Europe and beyond, with nothing more than we needed to carry with us in an English village. No Customs at Benson, nobody to worry about our little cargo; on the contrary, everyone delighted to see it, and hoping they ranked highly enough in the list of friends to be able to participate in the sharing and consuming thereof. San Severo was cold that evening of 22 December, and we were well tired. We just wanted to take the jeep to Foggia and find our quarters for the night at the officers' club. How different the conditions were now, compared with the hot summers. On those starry nights we used to sleep up on the open roof under mosquito netting.

Frank and I had said to each other that we would have a small sample tasting of the vino before retiring. However, we were invited to walk round the town by 'our man from Benson' who was stationed at Foggia for a period to organize transit crews like ourselves. Incidentally, he had not been wasting his time, because it was through his good offices that we had been able to buy the vino at such an attractive price. He reckoned the empty cask was worth what we had paid for it plus the contents. So off we went.

The town was still in a state of disrepair and damage that had not been made good, and the inhabitants had seen enough of war, one way and another. The German armies had moved down through their country, and then the Allied Armies of varied nationalities, including the New Zealanders, were still in the process of slowly rolling back the Nazis in the opposite direction.

Our walk quickly became a search for a suitable bar. Scarcely any business or retail premises were in existence, and when we did at last spot a cramped entrance to a cellar, down we went. There we found a very pleasant, tiny bar, lit with a couple of paraffin lamps, but with a remarkable range of drinks available. We were the only customers, and were welcomed. As soon as we had received our wines, the old chap behind the counter called his wife to take his place, and then another middle-aged man appeared. One produced a piano-accordian and the other a fiddle, and they played us some beautiful music: any tune we cared to nominate, but the interesting thing for me was that their opening piece was a lively and lengthy rendition of *Lily Marlene*.

Several notices were on the walls, and they were printed in German, and some pictures that had been taken out of current German magazines were also displayed. Obviously not too long ago this little drinking 'hole' had resounded to German music, and the patron and his wife had entertained the troops according to their tastes. They had not yet switched over in their minds, or in their repertoire, to the change in the occupying forces. This was

150

interesting, and although we had thought we were tired, there was something unique and enjoyable about the few hours we spent in this 'music-box'.

We sang many of the tunes – English, Scottish, Welsh, Irish, Italian – and made attempts with some stirring German ones. With us shouting drinks to the landlady and the two musicians fairly frequently, they too joined in with the singing. The little gathering was good fun and it gave me, at least, considerable pleasure to sing the last number, that was, of course, 'The Maori Farewell'. Before we struggled up the rickety stairway we were given coffee and some warm rolls. . . . How much better it was to be stamping along the middle of the broken and muddy little street in war-torn Italy than to be a prisoner-of-war in the German Fatherland, or even a broken and dead body on some remote hillside in eastern Europe.

Saturday, 23 December

Operation No. 54: we are airborne via Rome for a 'look-see' at the sights, and targets in northern Italy, landing back at Benson after three hours and fifty-five minutes. The smuggled fruits from the Adriatic coast arrived in perfect condition. We found it had been a busy day at Benson, and Joe and I did not catch up with each other until late in the day. He said to me as we retired to our room fairly early that evening, 'It's been a real beaut of a press-on day here, Kiwi! Bags of flap, mate. And I suppose you've been sunning yourself down there with the "Eyeties", looking at the sheilas! Bring back any vino?'

One of our squadron, Pilot Officer Hayes, had crash-landed today at the end of our runway, and the Mosquito had burned away to nothing; but he and his navigator had walked (run?) away. At that time our definition of a good landing was one from which you could walk away. Some time previously I had watched one of our Mossies crash after a belly-landing, and once again the crew, apart from minor burns, were OK; but even with our modern appliances spraying on all the foam chemicals available, the kite ended up as charred embers, a ghastly and unbelievable sight that upset my stomach. When things had cooled down sufficiently for us to approach the scene of the crash, all that remained was an outline of the shape of the fuselage and the wings, made by the tiny charred embers. The largest part left was part of a propellor boss, and it was hardly bigger than one's hand.

Sunday, 24 December

Operation No. 55: this was our third op. in as many days, another four hours and fifty minutes, and a fairly solid effort to the east parts of the Reich with satisfactory results. The day after an op. we pilots could visit the

Photographic-Interpretation Section and be shown some of our photos, as well as a print showing all photos taken in relation to the various targets. The complete result was there in black and white, one can say, and showed to a precise degree the success of the sortie. We could also obtain selected photos, and my collection is still of interest.

The Christmas Eve side of things was clearly non-existent, and my diary note for that day was 'quiet and lonely'. And in the space in the diary at the end of that week I have filled in: 'three Spits missing; one is Flt Lt Noel Whaley, a New Zealander with a DFC' – though I never knew the man, or anything about him.

Monday, 25 December

Some trips went out: I saw them off and gave the 'thumbs up'. These last few days had still been poor visibility, but just workable. Today, Christmas Day, the fog clamped down again completely and made landings impossible. All our returning kites were therefore diverted to other fields where conditions were fractionally better at the time. Then the vehicular traffic from our base took a long time to drive through the fog and return with the precious magazines from the cameras of these diverted aircraft.

Our squadron wing commander, 'pulling his rank' and breaking all the rules, who literally seemed to know every bend in the River Thames and every lock along it, most skilfully flew his Mosquito nearly to Benson airfield; but failing to reach the field itself, then managed the miracle of landing his aircraft, undamaged, on a riverside meadow. Every factor made it impossible for it to be flown out, and a rescue expedition somehow or other semi-dismantled it, and thus the Mossie returned to base by road in due course. But Steve did arrive back at the mess in time for festive celebrations. The rest of us, displaying a goodly chunk of our human nature, took rather a dim view of his exploit, at the time.

After waving 'cheerio and good luck' to our friends taking off in the morning, I helped in entertaining Frank, then still a warrant officer, and the others from the sergeants' mess – that is, sergeants, flight sergeants and warrant officers – in our mess. At lunchtime, as tradition has it, the officers who were available helped to serve the airmen their Christmas dinner in their mess. The relaxed camaraderie of this infrequent opportunity for informality with the airmen one knew was most enjoyable, and particularly for me with those in the groundcrew of 544 Squadron. Some of the corporals and airmen were old enough to be my father, and we had a good bond. (The excellent opportunity to view all the pretty Waafs was also much appreciated!)

Tuesday, 26 December

Operation No. 56: these targets in the west part of Germany were relevant to the Battle of the Bulge situation. Conditions over Europe gave clear, bright blue sky with exceptional visibility: 'Good vis', we called it. Britain, on the other hand, was blanketed with dense fog, including our base, where it was definitely 'Duff vis'. Apart from Spits and Mossies from Benson, we understood that no other Allied aircraft from any area of Britain had been out on ops during the previous couple of days. We learnt in hindsight that there was continued tremendous pressure from the highest level for PRU to obtain photos of the supply areas of the German armies, regardless of the weather conditions.

On this foggy morning when we looked out of our windows, it looked for sure that no aircraft would be leaving the ground today, certainly from our part of the woods – even the birds were not flying. My mind was already relaxed into imagining another pleasant sortie across the airfield to the *Riverside* to enjoy an egg and chips, followed by some snooker in the mess, and then a pint of best bitter as an aperitif before lunch. After the hectic last few days, was I starting to look at this fog as a shield, protecting me from the rigours and risks of war?

Prior to D-Day, 6 June 1944, fog had always precluded us from flying, but with the exigencies of the invasion demands, weather had since been left out of consideration in arranging sorties of PRU aircraft from Benson – that is to say, every factor except 10/10s fog. Up to my Operation No. 18, a real foggy day therefore had been secretly welcomed as a *Riverside* day of tranquillity and fellowship. No Ops! The following lines from John Keats' *Ode To Autumn* often used to spring into my relaxed and carefree mind on those safe and golden days:

> Seasons of mists and mellow fruitfulness,
> Close bosom-friend of the maturing sun.

But any such reverie for this particular day was shattered by the tannoy in the mess dining-room calling all crews to the ops room. This had never happened before in my time, but the message was: 'Mosquitos and Spitfires will be taking off today. It is expected that by the time they return to Britain, landing conditions will be suitable *somewhere*': such was the urgency for SHAEF to obtain, at any cost, aerial pictures showing what von Runstedt and his armies were doing on the ground, and what supplies and reinforcements were en route to them.

My ops hours now totalled 221 hours and 20 minutes, and the balance in my 'bank of experience' was steadily accumulating – and a good thing too.

Fear death? – to feel the fog in my throat,
The mist in my face.
By Robert Browning

Ops Nos 56 and 57: 26 and 28 December 1944

. . . Still Tuesday, 26 December: all the serviceable aircraft from our 'B' Flight were detailed for ops today, to ensure coverage of a wide area.

As Frank and I were being briefed in the ops room regarding our targets, and receiving the usual 'escape aids' and bank notes in the currencies of the countries we would be flying over, my mind was also wrestling with another matter: was it even possible, with zero visibility, to point a Mosquito along a runway that you could not see, keep it straight, and build up to a speed of 170mph before lifting it off the deck? The Mosquito had a notorious tendency to swing violently to the left on take-off, and therefore the throttles couldn't both be opened right up until about a third of the run had been completed. Imagine yourself driving a high-speed car along a motorway at 170mph, using your feet as well as your hands to steer it, in the densest fog.

The airfield had all its night-flying lighting turned on, and a jeep with flashing lights led us round the perimeter track. At one stage the driver ran off the tarmac because he could not define its edges, and one of our wheels also slid down the side of the track into the soft wet grass as we were busily engaged trying to follow the jeep. Fortunately with a burst of throttle we regained the hard surface. Our guide left us at the end of the longest runway – there was no wind when such a heavy fog persisted, therefore we did not have to take it into account. We were left on our own, positioned between the first pair of sodium flare-path lights; the second and succeeding pairs to right and left were not visible to either of us.

No point in delaying the agony: ease the throttles forward, and hope for the best. Frank called out the speed from the ASI to me, and co-ordinating that information with everything I had ever learnt about instrument flying, I used my best judgement to lift the aircraft off as early as I dared. In less than twenty seconds we shot up out of the murk and darkness of ground level into vivid blue sky over a perfectly flat sheet of dazzling white cloud – the top of the fog.

What a beautiful, serene world of peace. Wishing that I could quell my strong gut feeling of agitation as to where and how we were later going to pierce the world of darkness beneath us, I forced my mind to concentrate on the job ahead: targets, flak, fighters, and the occasional quick glances at the instrument panel. The English coast was soon left behind, and the sheet of fog stopped along a straight line parallel with the coast. The Continent was yet again having an exceptionally clear day, and there would be no problems for the Germans to muster their fighters in the sky.

This trip did not involve any great distance to cover; no long-range fuel tanks were fitted, and my judgement told me to use a few more revs, which gave us a little more speed than on longer trips. Knowing we were cruising that little bit faster made me feel better – and 'safer', psychologically anyway, and that was good for morale. Somewhat to my surprise the sortie was uneventful and successful thus far; with only the PRU unarmed aircraft flying over the Continent, we had fully expected the enemy fighters to aim for a field day. But maybe knowing that Britain was virtually 100 per cent fog-bound had induced the Luftwaffe to have an easy day.

We allowed ourselves to relax coming back in a gentle dive over the Channel. The sun blazed down, there was no wind, and the air was as calm as it is possible to be. But just as we made contact on the R/T to report in to the English south coast, we could see the ominous white sheet of fog stretching into the distance like a giant ice-field. . . . Now where would we be diverted to?

'Tangmere' was given to us as our destination. This famous airfield was not far away from us, but from where we were, nothing could be seen but the layer of white cloud. As we let down in its direction, I called them up and was told to circle and wait above the cloud as there was a queue of our Mossies waiting to land in conditions of 'pretty duff vis'. Usually the English trait of understatement, especially evident amongst aircrew in the RAF, gave me some amusement and enjoyment, but this report, expected as it was, gave me a pang in the stomach.

Our trip so far had kept us airborne about four hours, so there was no worry in my mind that fuel would run short – we should be down in just a few minutes, surely. Against the backdrop of the blinding white cloud layer, made even more so by the rays of the lowering mid-winter sun, we could see three of our aircraft circling around on one another's tails. Over the R/T the ground controller was talking down the leading Mosquito, but nothing positive seemed to be happening; obviously the pilot trying to land was not finding it easy. I flew up and down off the coast, becoming conscious of the return of the feeling of apprehension that had had to be smothered after our take-off. The VHF channels were busy, and it was 'not on' for me to interrupt the dialogue between the controller and the pilot attempting to land.

Suddenly and surprisingly I spotted a tiny hole in the cloud. This layer was only about 300 to 400ft thick, the same as it had been that morning, and there through the hole we glimpsed a part of an airfield. What a fluke! My immediate reaction was to land on it. I throttled back sharply; the Mosquito glided like the proverbial brick, and jerking down the undercarriage lever, plus some flap, we were on the ground and taxiing up to the control tower in no time at all. If any second thoughts came to me at all, they were that 'the Benson crowd' over at Tangmere, just a very few miles

Logbook: 26 December 1944, Op. No. 56. Landed at Thorney Island and Tangmere on the English south coast. *Foggy*!

away, would be as pleased and relieved as we were to have one aircraft safely on the deck.

The whole airfield was like a ghost town – not a speck of life or activity. The 10/10 fog had certainly convinced everyone here that their airfield, Thorney Island, was well and truly 'closed'. I found it spooky that such a front-line place could appear so deserted. But what a relief to be on the deck! That was my main thought. A second reflection was that I had been quite a clever fellow to pull off such an opportune landing.

We parked as close as possible to the control-tower door and Frank jumped down to make contact with Tangmere and tell them the good news that we were 'next door' (the distance between the two fields was only about eight miles as the Mosquito flies). Frank managed to rouse some action. The personnel were astounded that any aircraft had been able to land there, let alone a Mosquito, and as it was only one day after Christmas, it was a major shock to their systems.

Frank had his shock too. On being connected by telephone to Tangmere control, it was our own 'wingco' who spoke to him and said, 'It's best that we are all together, so just fly over here and join us. The vis is not too good – and whatever daylight is left, it's rapidly fading, so *make it snappy!*' Frank did well not to faint with the news; he dashed out, ducking round the flailing propellers that I had kept going because I expected to be told where to park, clambered up our folding ladder, and pulled it in after him: all in record time.

Airborne again, we shot up through what was now a layer of dense blackness. For the second time we experienced the spell-binding impact of being transformed into the startlingly vivid world of white and blue, which in its turn was changing rapidly, as the blinding dazzle of the setting sun changed into shafts of softer light.

Ascending into this realm of serene beauty, we were just in time to see the last of the three circling Mosquitos disappearing from view as it commenced its circuit and landing. We had to wait and listen on the R/T with a growing anxiety to the difficulties encountered by the pilot as the darkness of the dusk deepened before he eventually touched down on 'terra firma'. The saying used to be: 'the firmer it is, the less terror I have.'

At long last it was our turn, and No. 791 was the only aircraft left in the air over the British Isles. The feeling in my stomach, and in my throat, reinforced that thought.

Both Frank and I had been as much surprised that it had been our wingco who had given us the order to fly over from Thorney Island as we had been by the content of the instruction. We knew that Steve had not been airborne that day. When Benson had been advised by the met. people that Tangmere was going to be the most likely place for the PRU aircraft to use as a return base that day, a road convoy had been organized, and it had taken *all day* for the vehicles to crawl through the fog from Benson down to the south coast. Maintenance ground crew, photographic developers and first phase interpreters were amongst those making up the expedition – everyone whose services were essential to keeping 'the circus on the road': that is, keeping SHAEF supplied with the photo-intelligence necessary to combat the enemy advances. Wing Commander Steventon had travelled down with the road convoy.

When wingco took over the microphone at control to talk me in to a landing, my spirits were given a welcome lift. We had been well trained in flying circuits and approaches on instruments, but in 1944 there were nothing like the facilities that are available these days for assisting aircraft to land in poor visibility. Every month pilot and navigator did practice exercises: QGHs by W/T and VHF and beam approaches using Gee. Sometimes we did these in our Mossies and sometimes in an Oxford, a training type of twin-engined aircraft; but these exercises were always over our own familiar airfield. Basically the technique depended on skilful and meticulous flying, coupled with timing the various directions of flying, to the second, and flying at an exact speed at an exact height. It was a mathematical equation, and as such it was perfect . . . in theory. (Regular 'flying' in the link trainer was also a compulsory exercise. My link hours then totalled ninety.)

This particular evening, and under these adverse conditions, we found that the approach to Tangmere airfield (which we had never seen) necessitated us flying south until we could be sure we were over the sea. Then we had to let down in altitude with extreme care, watching the altimeter recording height, until it levelled off sharply. This levelling off was completed after we had left behind our solitary world of overwhelming loneliness above the sheet of fog, and after a few moments of gently dropping down through this layer. At that precise moment the glassy surface of the sea could then just be discerned. The sea was so ultra calm and murky in the early evening darkness that I was never 100 per cent sure how many feet clearance we had from its surface. But making this judgement was vital: if it was only by a matter of inches, the wing-tip must not be dipped into the water as we executed the steep turn, with the wings nearly vertical, that was required for us to head on to the given course that led us to the airfield and the approach to the runway.

Tangmere lay a mere six miles inland from the coast, so at the very slowest flying speed of a Mosquito that distance could be covered in two minutes. Although I was keyed up and fairly apprehensive, I thought to myself that this short distance shouldn't present us with too much bother.

The heading we were on took us slap over the seaside resort town of Bognor Regis; in fact we had to dodge round the clock tower on the way inland. My morale dropped as we fleetingly saw the scared faces of the townspeople staring up at the terrifyingly low and noisy aircraft nearly brushing their chimney pots: flying immediately under the cloud base, we could, by jinking about, just miss the tall trees – I recognized some as elms. We timed our run keeping a constant air speed, throttled back, lowered the undercart, applied some degree of flap, and hoped the runway with its sodium flarepath would loom up in front of us ... but it didn't. Either we would spot the runway at an angle to us, and it was too late to change direction to fly down it, or we would not see it till perhaps half of its length had been covered.

One abortive attempt after another was followed by opening up to full throttle and pulling the labouring aircraft up through the cloud while straining tensely to see what obstacles lay ahead. Once on top of the cloud layer it was the same old rigmarole of heading out to sea for a measured time, letting down gingerly, performing another perilous turn towards land, and trying a repeat approach. On every attempt I tried to increase my concentration and effort, and to include some input learned from the previous failures. The fuel gauges were now flickering on their 'empty' marks ... and each time we skimmed over Bognor at about 170 to 180mph, I dreaded seeing the pale, upturned, staring faces of the fascinated onlookers. Street lamps now lit up their faces, and the whole fleeting scene struck me as weird and ghoulish, a scene from a nightmare.

Regulations and common sense demanded that nearing any landing, aircrew must be tightly buckled into their seats. However, good old dependable Frank volunteered to unstrap himself from his seat, to the right and slightly behind the pilot, and to lie down in the nose on his stomach (from which position he usually operated the cameras) in order to gain a few more feet of precious visibility. In self-preservation I agreed to this move. What sort of horrifying ride he had, with nothing more than a thin, small panel of perspex between his face and the almost hidden, dark, unfriendly world rushing closely by beneath, was not good for me to dwell on. Many times since the war, maybe after a drink or two, Frank has persisted in thanking me 'for saving his life', and each time I have emphasized that of course it was my great desire to keep him alive to return to his dear wife and children; but the truth was that whatever I did in times of peril was ultimately a matter of my self-preservation, and he just happened to be there for the ride.

Part of my mind was grappling with the question of why the fuel situation looked so grim. It did not seem normal to be so dangerously low after having been airborne for just five hours. But the part of my brain working on this problem soon told me that we had cruised around Germany at higher revs than usual, and also all these abortive attempts at landing had resulted in many bursts of full throttle as we climbed away from deck level every time. In short, there was not to be any clutching at straws under the self-delusion that the fuel gauges had all gone U/S.

159

After the first couple of abortive approaches I gave up the idea of lining up on the runway: anywhere on the field seemed more than adequately acceptable. But our last effort was the worst so far, because as we let down ready to land with throttles off, instead of runway, the control tower materialized in front of us. We had to do a steep climbing turn, retracting the undercart as soon as I had a hand free from having the right one on the control column, and the left one pushing the throttles open wide and holding them there. No instructor had ever told me how a pilot needed three hands. A massive and peculiar sweat burst out from me. My neck and shoulders felt as if they were ejecting squirts of liquid, and so much ran off my head, under my helmet and mask and into my eyes, that when we yet again shot up through that hateful cloud I had to spend some moments wiping my eyes clear before they could focus on the instruments again.

The strong possibility that the engines would stop at any second due to lack of fuel was now over-crowding my mind. A wave of desperation swept over me: 'How hard did one have to try? Was this a fair go?' I can still conjure up this thought with chilling clarity. This was a vividly new experience for my body and my mind; I was getting near the end of my tether. All at once it became perfectly clear what had to be done; it was time for an instant decision – why hadn't this brainwave come to me before?

I called up wingco. By this time, the state of affairs being how it was, all pretence of keeping the R/T chatter formal and correct had gone out the window; no holds barred – anything went.

'Wingco! I can't try any more, the fuel is due to cut so we're going to belly-land on the beach!' How easy this is going to be I thought to myself. How smooth and firm and inviting the beach had looked every time we had crossed it. I selected a suitable-looking strip and prepared to action my plan, feeling confident of my ability to execute a satisfactory precautionary landing with the wheels up. The edge of the sea-shore could just be distinguished from our low altitude.

'Kiwi! You silly fool! The beach is full of *mines*! It's mined!' cried out my squadron commander, 'Climb away quick!'

From being bathed in a hot sweat my body was now drenched in cold moisture. I clenched my teeth to stop shivering. But I had calmed down – in fact felt relaxed – and carried out yet another approach procedure in a frighteningly automatic daze.

Oh! The irony of it. With the fuel showing empty, and the evening darkness enhanced by the fog, we arrived over the end of the runway at the right speed and the right height and completed a perfect wheeler landing. When we pulled up, nothing was to be seen in any direction, so we stayed where we were until a convoy of crash tender, fire-engine, and even an ambulance for good measure, all found us several minutes later.

Wednesday, 27 December

A respite for Foster and Moseley. Slept all day. Conditions still foggy but not as bad. Benson still 'out', but several trips set off from Tangmere where our own groundcrews had now arrived to perform the necessary inspections.

Thursday, 28 December

Operation No. 57: airborne again. A short trip to Germany of three hours and thirty minutes, but that afternoon we and all the others of our 'flying circus' could not be landed at Tangmere because of 10/10 fog! Maybe our prolonged performance two days before had given someone the idea that it could be a lengthy business for a Mosquito to land on that airfield, in the dark, and in fog? Once again the aircraft flew, and the road convoy struggled its tedious way, well up north, this time to Northcotes airfield, near Grimsby in Lincolnshire. The fog was determined to give us all a run for our money, and Benson certainly was not allowing us to return to our 'homes' there.

In the late afternoon a few of us went into town searching for the all-important 'good feed', as we 'black troops' called a good (wartime) meal. I was still wearing the same battle-dress and flying boots in which I had left Benson. I had no toilet gear and therefore hadn't shaved, although I did invest in a toothbrush. . . . Had it been *me* who had frowned somewhat at those untidy and scruffy Yanks who had lobbed down amongst us at Benson just those few days ago? It seemed an age.

Friday, 29 December

No ops trip, and it was still too foggy to fly back to Benson. We helped serve the mess staff their dinner – but for we aircrew the so-called festive season was a dead duck.

Saturday, 30 December

At long last we managed to fly ourselves back to Benson, which at that time was assuredly the acme of 'Home Sweet Home'. We had done five ops in one week, twenty-four hours of them altogether – and *that's* the meaning of 'when twenty-four hours is enough'. I had truly had enough adrenalin flow to last me for a while. My diary entry for that day merely records: 'Pressed on for the evening!'

12

Yalta – The Mails are Delayed

No more will we falter
From Malta to Yalta
We mustn't alter!
Winston Churchill to Franklin D. Roosevelt, early in 1945.
(They met in Malta before going to Yalta, in the Crimea.)

Ops Nos 59, 60 & 61, 2, 3 & 4 February 1945

A long and arduous seven months after D-Day saw the year 1944 come to a conclusion. In the latter part of that turbulent period, and extending into the first month of the new year, the Allies had freed from German rule many of the European capital cities that Hitler's forces had occupied: Athens, Belgrade, Brussels, Budapest, Paris and Warsaw – Copenhagen, Oslo, Prague and The Hague still awaited their now inevitable freedom from the Nazi tyranny. At the beginning of the year 1945 the first lines in my new diary read: 'Hope this volume will provide many more pleasant happenings, and fewer unpleasant ones.'

War is a torrid mix of good news and bad, both from the intimate personal level of the individual who is playing his small part, and from the broad sweep of a worldwide perspective. In the eastern regions of Europe the Russians were advancing westwards at an accelerating rate, and millions of German refugees were trying to escape before the invading Red Armies. German concentration camps and slave-labour camps were hurriedly emptied and the occupants forced to flee towards the west. Tens of thousands of these victims died or were exterminated as the brutal treks continued in bitter and freezing conditions.

In the German naval port of Kiel, a Russian submarine sank a German ship that had carried 8,000 soldiers and refugees from East Prussia. Fewer than 2,000 survived. No other single maritime disaster equalled this horrifying total of victims.

Even in temperate Britain it was an unusually cold winter, so much so that we ran round the airfield for the express purpose of trying to warm ourselves up. Snow covered the ground for days, and I often skidded off my

162

bike. Most days began with 20° frosts, and travel by road and rail was difficult and disrupted. Some of our fellows who went to Scotland at New Year had to stand in trains for more than twenty hours. At this time Vic and Joe were in London on leave, and sitting around the cold crew-room wasn't much fun; I found that playing plenty of strenuous badminton became much more profitable. It was a surprise for me, one day, to find myself detailed as station orderly officer, for the first time in fifteen months; I couldn't complain about that. As ever, correspondence occupied many of my personal hours; the diary tells me that I had just received letter No. 95, while I was writing No. 77 to my parents.

When my room-mates came back, we were happy and elated to learn that Joe had received the DFC, and Alec, his navigator, a DFM. The chap who had sold me my Riley-9 Monaco car, a pilot on 540, received a bar to his DFC. All that good news was tempered with the announcement that poor Jimmy Crow, who had been beaten to death the previous month, had been posthumously awarded his DSO, which was a high honour, especially for a navigator.

Frank and I had to fly Op. No. 58 that same day, and when we returned and had been debriefed, I went to look for Joe. It wasn't long after mid-afternoon, but the bar was open, and a good crowd gathered. The sergeant-barman caught my eye as a mate of Joe's, and leaning his head forward he whispered to me that 'Old Joe' – everyone, of whatever rank, high or low, referred to Norman Milton Burfield in that style –'might need a hand from you; he has already had more than twenty beers!' So after a drink for the road, Joe decided to come back with me to the room. He seemed pretty good, all things considered; he said he felt like relaxing in the bath, and toddled down the passage. Some time later a frantic knocking at our door revealed a batman who had seen floods of water coming from under our bathroom door. I rushed off to investigate. Joe had taken all his clothes off all right, except his black uniform socks. He had omitted to turn off the taps, and was amusing himself by swilling his feet about and watching the streaks of black dye as they flowed over the sides of the bath and out the doorway. The rescue mission accomplished, Joe was easily persuaded to 'hit the pit' as he called it. After a few hours' sleep he awoke as fresh as a daisy, and carried on with some more mild celebrations in the evening.

A couple of days later, when Frank was out of action with a cold, Joe and I had our first chance to fly an air-test together. We had good fun, and it was an opportunity for me to observe how tenderly and neatly this big, rough-looking man handled the smooth and responsive Mosquito. The conditions reminded me of Canada when we landed on a snow-covered runway.

The snow was around, off and on, for several weeks. One report said it was the coldest winter for 130 years. Spring seemed well out of reach, but Frank and I were about to fly a trip that would unexpectedly take us more or less to the French Riviera and to a touch of real Mediterranean spring. . . .

A day before we learned about our spring outing, a small party of six of us, including myself, were fortunate enough to win places in a draw to pay a day's visit to the de Havilland Aircraft Company's factory. This jaunt came as a pleasant surprise. A Waaf driver drove us in a Humber shooting brake through snow and fog across to Hatfield; the directors of the company welcomed us, and arranged a comprehensive tour of the entire factory, showing us exactly how a Mosquito was put together.

A magnificent lunch was next on the agenda, accompanied by an equally outstanding selection of drinks. As our hosts said to us: 'None of you is flying today; indeed you are not even driving. Drink up, and have an enjoyable time with us.' This we did, with gusto. I learned much that day, and I also believe the directors may have picked up a few points about their famous product from our answers to their questions. Before setting off into the gloom to Benson, we were invited to a special hangar where we were shown, in confidence, a new aircraft: it looked superb, an even sleeker version of the Mosquito, with two engines, but a single-seater, and aptly named the 'Hornet'. Unfortunately this progeny of the Mosquito did not reach the operational stage before the war ended.

That evening Vic and I drove the car to some quiet fields and amused ourselves taking some unofficial pot-shots with our revolvers. We both agreed it was exhilarating being out amongst the quiet snowed-in landscape. No-one else existed – we had it all to ourselves – time stood still; we both sensed how good our friendship was without a word being said.

We were eager and stimulated the next day to hear about a big trip, similar to the Moscow expedition, which had been given to 544 to organize and complete. Once again the Big Three were due to confer, and it was our task to fly to and fro as couriers with the diplomatic mails. Mr Churchill and Mr Roosevelt, together with the Allied commanders, held a pre-meeting in Malta, where they met on board USS *Quincy*. The meeting of the two Allied leaders with Josef Stalin was to discuss policy for the final phase of the war, and how the post-war world should be governed. The venue this time was Yalta, a seaside resort on the Black Sea coast of the Crimea. The nearest suitable airfield, and therefore our destination, was Saki, located some distance from the conference centre. The first meeting of the Big Three had been at Teheran in Persia (Iran), in November 1943.

Frank and I spent a full day on the briefing and the preparation for the trip. All the local snow had thawed and been cleared, and we took that as a helpful sign, and were in cheery spirits at the prospect of a challenging trip in a new direction. The Crimean peninsula was not much further distant than Moscow, but a direct flight would have been on the unhealthy side, passing unnecessarily over the heart of the Third Reich. It was obvious from a glance at the map that the alternative was to use the established and familiar base at San Severo on the Foggia Plain, as an excellent halfway staging post. Using that more peaceful route we thought we should both, with a modicum of good fortune, be able to give more attention to the navigation, especially on the second leg that was fresh territory for us. Our track from Italy would transverse Albania, Yugoslavia, Bulgaria and a corner of Romania, before crossing the Black Sea. These flights would again demonstrate to me how many countries are packed into this Continent of Europe.

With the memory of the attack by the Yak fighters over Moscow, we knew we had to be alert and aware of our exact position when approaching the Crimean coast. No navigational aids were available: we had to rely on dead reckoning and our own eyesight and savvy. Our briefing told us that in addition to a defence by fighter planes, many units of the Soviet Navy would be patrolling the shorelines. My private thought at that early stage was that we would aim to approach the coast at a good high altitude and get the lie of the land, and the whereabouts of the ships, before we made a swift descent to the airfield.

Once again I was sworn in as a 'king's messenger', and checked out with my revolver in its holster attached to the webbing belt. For this trip we flew in a squadron aircraft with which we were pleasantly familiar: it was a Mark XVI, No. 500, which we had already flown on five ops trips. The photographic equipment was stripped out, but obviously the British authorities did not expect the Russians to have any facilities to dismantle our kite this time, as they had been able to do at Moscow. Probably they did not even have the desire to do so at this late stage of the war.

On the second day of February, following the receipt of the mail-bag from the anonymous, impeccably dressed gentleman, and giving my signature in exchange, we 'cracked off', as the diary has it, and taxied away from the little group of well-wishers. This atmosphere had a noticeable touch of adventure in it for me, and I'm sure I was smiling as we took off, and dipped our wings over our hangar as we set course.

Our track was not quite a straight line direct to San Severo: we put a slight bend in it towards the west, just to make sure we did not become tangled up with any stray fighters near the battle lines below, where the American and British armies were pushing back the German defenders. We had the fuel and the time to reduce the usual tensions of our normal sorties. Not too far away from Mont Blanc we set our final course, and landed at San Severo airfield after a pleasant flight of three hours and thirty-five minutes. We knew many of the personnel stationed there by this time, and they made us happily at home.

The next morning we were airborne again on our hush-hush mission. At this moment no one had any inkling of where we were heading, and if they did know, no one knew why. We carried this secret with us as we set course approximately north-east. Once more we sheered off slightly from a direct course: international borders generally never entered our calculations, and basically Frank drew straight lines from point A to point B, but what we did in this case was to head a little south so as to reach the Black Sea as early as possible, but at the same time making allowance to keep fifty to sixty miles away from both the Greek and Turkish borders. I personally always felt less uncomfortable over water, compared with flying over war-torn lands.

Leaving the east coast of Italy, we crossed the narrow Adriatic Sea and transversed the three Balkan countries. Our route, which happened to coincide with some sightseeing of places of interest, took us over Sofia. We chose to fly at 26,000ft, which at that season of the year kept us just below the altitude at which con-trails would have betrayed our presence more than our judgement told us was desirable.

My mood was a mixture of tension due to the responsibility of the purpose of the trip, added to the anxiety of finding and landing safely on a foreign and unknown airfield. On the other hand, I was relaxed because we were not battling our way in or out of Germany, and that made a pleasant change. As the Black Sea coast came into view, my relaxed mood took control, and without saying anything to Frank, I deliberately edged the aircraft 'left hand down a bit', and slowly turned more northwards. The Transylvanian Alps made an entrancing sight to the north – a long white line of tall mountains highlighted by a brilliant winter sun gleaming on the peaks. Frank told me they were about 190 miles distant from us, a lonely little speck in the empty sky – they looked to be close to us.

The reason why I deflected us to the north was to satisfy a long-held desire to prove the legend that the River Danube, the longest river in Europe, only appeared blue in colour to those in love. The music of *The Blue Danube* waltz has always been a favourite of mine, and here we were, up in the deep blue yonder, one might say, not too far away from the vast, sprawling mouth of this mighty waterway. Maybe a unique opportunity to make the test – surely the Air Ministry could allow us a few gallons of petrol? And surely even a king's messenger has to undertake a scientific investigation when the chance presents itself? The river entered the Black Sea over the Bulgarian border and along the Romanian coast. I carried out my inspection, and concluded with a compromise: the Danube was a bluish-grey.

As we turned directly towards our destination, we both referred to the fact that we were about a half-hour's flying time away from Odessa. This place was in our minds because it was the only suggestion given to us officially as to where to head for if we had troubles in that part of the world and could not reach Saki airfield. The last place I wished to be in, at that moment, was Odessa – so let's press on smartly and forget about it.

It was less than 300 miles to the Crimea now, and we commenced letting down gently. It was obvious that we could not maintain a high and, it was to be hoped, much safer altitude, because our clear blue sky had gone, and towards the horizon all was now thick grey cloud. We continued with our shallow dive to be sure we could get under the cloud base while we were positive we were over water, and therefore away from land with its hills and mountains. My plan of spotting naval ships from a great height was cancelled, and we now faced some hard and nervy work.

Our cruising altitude of 26,000ft quickly reduced to 15,000, to 10,000, and then we levelled off in bumpy cloud at 5,000ft. Here we had a crew conference: how sure could Frank be of where we were in relation to the shoreline? We could not stay where we were, so down again, but more gingerly this time at this reducing altitude. Frank was confident we were still well out to sea, and close to being on track. We skirmished about, losing some more height, then levelled off and peered into the swirling gloom. There was no one to help us but ourselves – though the situation was no worse than on many other previous occasions. Nevertheless, on other trips we did not have to worry about Soviet vessels protecting their president from unidentified intruders.

At the moment we did break cloud, we were at a reasonable height, about 1,500ft. Nothing but angry grey sea, and black and grey cloud ahead: no glimpse of land, and no ships. On we go. And then the land loomed up, and we were spot on: three cheers for Frank; why did I ever worry? We glimpsed two destroyer-class warships patrolling side by side further down the coast, and then were directly approaching the airfield. It stood out from the stark white snow-covered countryside because of the big transport aircraft parked around its perimeters. We landed in a 'Benson special' – that is, we did no circuit, just spotted which direction the wind-sock indicated, and dragged the aircraft over the boundary from a low level, using plenty of throttle before cutting the power and touching down. The Mosquito arrived unannounced and probably observed by only a few sharp eyes and ears. Three hours and twenty minutes . . . the adventure was on track so far.

Saki is situated close to the south-western coast of the diamond-shaped peninsula, and Yalta, the conference centre, is on the south-eastern coast; the distance between them, as the Mosquito flies, is a mere fifty or sixty miles. However, wintry conditions had made the road between the two places so difficult even for four-wheel-drive vehicles to use, that we later heard it had taken nearly as long for our dispatches to travel along this road, as it had taken us to fly them to Saki. At Saki, as in Moscow, we felt a long way from home; not quite as far east as when in Moscow, nevertheless further to the east than, say, Suez.

The set-up here was entirely different from that at Moscow. Here, everything was white and wintry, which tended to make the whole place appear shoddy and dilapidated; but the big difference was the presence of

American and RAF transport aircraft with their crews. Both Mr Churchill and Mr Roosevelt had been flown up separately in their own aircraft from the Mediterranean area.

Our mailbag was handed over, and the Mosquito left, to be checked over by some British groundcrew. I felt relieved of immediate responsibilities and looked forward to proceedings.

Before we left the airfield itself, an American pilot came up and told us the latest news. The Russians had placed a large number of armed guards around every aircraft, and these rakish-looking tough guys certainly looked the part, to my eyes. An American colonel, maybe their senior officer, had reported to the Russian general in charge of the airfield – remember a general was in charge of the Moscow Airfield – that a couple of bottles of best rye whisky had gone missing from his aircraft. A short time after that report, the general called on the colonel, gave him some bottles of vodka, and said, 'I am sorry. It will not happen again. The guard in question has just been shot.' I believe that is exactly how our friend Major Okay would have dealt with the situation – and you can bet there was no more pilfering.

The quarters were austere but adequate. However, while unpacking my pyjamas and toilet-gear from my small travelling bag, I was approached by an English-speaking Russian man who, in rather a halting fashion, offered me the company of a Russian lady for the night. (What secrets of the speedy Mossie did they wish to worm out?) Our hosts were excelling themselves in looking after their guests, but I politely declined. By comparison, I think that if by chance any Russian airman had lobbed down at Benson for a night, he would have found the accommodation palatial, but the conveniences apparently so freely available in his country would have been sadly lacking.

For me that evening at Saki was, nevertheless, a howling success. Considering myself a reasonable expert in the mysteries of drinking vodka toasts in Russia, I tried to slow things down a bit, and also, learning from the past, made every effort to eat fatty foods such as cheese straws, which custom the locals practised assiduously.

The meal, as expected, lasted more or less the entire evening. The occupants of the next table to where I had been placed fascinated me considerably. By studying them and their uniforms, and by now and then finding some Russian who knew a few words of English, I discovered they were a quartet of merchant marine captains. This was not exceptional on its own, but what so intrigued me that I probably stared too much at them, was the fact that all four had large pointed dark beards and heavy moustaches. They could have been the Marx brothers with false whiskers attached. Was their hirsute appearance part of their uniform? I wondered to myself.

Inevitably the foursome, probably tired of my staring, beckoned me to come over and join them, and I did so. Now I was up against the vodka ritual as played by experts, and we had a most enjoyable and hilarious night. From start to finish of the entire evening, a big band played music, and finding this absolutely to my liking, I walked over to the band leader and made a request: as ever, it was *The Blue Danube* I wished to hear. The background noise – a continuous uproar in Russian, English and louder American – was terrific, and the only way I could pass the band my request was to hum and sing the opening bars of the tune. Ah! What smiles of triumph from the players: they were on to it in a trice.

An amusing aspect of this was that they played it in waltz time all right, but at a furious pace so that it was hard to recognize. For the remainder of the evening, every now and then, they would play it again. This was the cue for my sea captains to stamp and cheer and clap and laugh. Worse, they all took it in turns to thump me resoundingly on the back. I seemed to be as popular with them as if I had composed the music . . . . I remember attempting to draw a map in order to place Australia and New Zealand for them. It was encouraging, and surprised me, to find that they had a good knowledge of our part of the world. We parted the best of comrades, and they all gave me a genuine Russian bear-hug.

Next morning, bright and early in this invigorating air, Frank and I prepared for our return trip. The aircraft was all OK as far as it looked and sounded to me. We took possession of the precious mailbags once again, three this time, and with them all the weight of their responsibilities was on my back. Off we went, back along a similar route to the outward trip, and with no alarms until we reached the Adriatic Sea. There we ran into dense storm clouds that reached our altitude of 26,000ft and higher.

The descent was not easy, and we had to call up San Severo and use the descent-through-cloud procedure in order to avoid the high ground that is not far away from those plains. The airfield is only about fifteen miles in from the coast, but that factor did not help us. Eventually we landed in torrential rainstorms under a low cloud base of a bare 400ft, and with visibility less than the length of the runway. The flight had taken three and three-quarter hours.

Our friends at the airfield drove us into the nearby town of Foggia. We felt tired and went to our beds at an early hour. Maybe the previous late night was catching up with us. Nevertheless the note in the diary is optimistic and records: 'Everything is going to schedule OK – wizzo!'

Yalta – But We Do Falter!

The base at San Severo had a useful met. service, and they predicted thoroughly bad weather with low cloud for our return trip to England. Apparently once we had crossed the Alps into France the same system persisted over the Channel and the southern parts of England. Even so, no thought of staying put occurred to me. We were all fired up to complete our courier run – only one quarter to go now, so off we went: if we had to be in duff weather conditions anywhere, Benson was the best place to handle them. Pick up the Thames, locate the Wittenham Clumps, and we'd be right.

About an hour-and-a-half later we were watching the Alps come into view ahead of us as we flew up northern Italy. I was just thinking it was good-oh not to be too near those jagged, icy peaks, when the starboard engine packed up completely in the shortest space of time we had ever experienced. For the fifth time in my tour I had to quickly feather the engine, and as a result of this, aided by our near-full load of fuel, we had to gradually lose height. From a perfectly comfortable situation five minutes earlier, we now faced cloud ahead of us, and the highest peaks were rapidly coming up to our level.

It was not a pretty picture. We weaved around in a gentle fashion in order to fly along the valleys, rather than wondering if we were going to clear a peak or not. My mental picture was not the best, either. We also had this valuable cargo as the number two consideration. Certainly its prompt arrival in London was of grave importance, but I have to say that two human lives of great interest to me squeezed into first place. If we continued onwards, how would we fare at a low altitude for the rest of the trip, in poor visibility after we had cleared the alpine regions? Again, although the Germans had been well pushed out of France, the invasion battlefront ran somewhere from the Swiss border up through Belgium and Holland, and we did not want to be wandering about like a lame duck near anybody's keen-eyed fighters. And an even more dismal thought also soon came to me, that the other engine was quite capable of failing, too: experience was shouting to me that they were missing the expert attention of the fitters at Benson. What sort of a pickle would we be in then, in cloud, at maybe an altitude not high enough from which to bale out? To these dismal thoughts I had to add the mailbag factor.

By this time we were clear of the high country and were still flying our original course, which was bringing us near Lyons, at which pin-point we had planned to set course to bring us to a suitable landmark on the south coast of England. Because it was necessary to avoid flying over London and its environs, we always set course from England, and crossed the coast again on the homeward trip, at some distinct point on the coast; from there we could set one direct course to Benson. Beachy Head, near Eastbourne, was often the right choice.

All things considered, and trying to assess the situation from the aspect of how to ensure the safety of the mailbags and their early arrival in London, it looked a more prudent proposition to contemplate landing somewhere in the southern part of France, and hopefully close enough to RAF engineers capable of repairing our aircraft. The lowering cloud that was now visible ahead of us, although no obstacle to our flying on a single engine, would preclude our finding a suitable landing-field. And apart from visually identifying such a field as being staffed by the British, we would not know whether Americans or French were in control. Many airfields had been bombed and strafed during the last few months, as we well knew. It was a time to make the right decision.

All right then, let's call up on the VHF and see who is on the air. It did not seem a suitable idea for Frank to try his W/T, because it was highly unlikely, at this lower altitude and at this distance, that we could make contact with Benson or any other base in Britain. Also, it was on my mind that the enemy just might know about 'Filter 77' flying back from Yalta, and in that case they would be trying their hardest to locate us – at the least they would be listening out for us. Although our VHF radius was fairly limited, actually all we wanted was someone to speak English to us; my schoolboy French was not then in fluent working order.

I chose the channel, and made my call: nothing dramatic, just a plea for contact, and after a few tries we were pleased to raise a Frenchman speaking halting English. I said we required a large field with engineering facilities, and preferably not lying under low cloud. He gave us a coded reference, which Frank's navigation material disclosed as Istres; it lay to the north of Marseilles, in the Camargue region, so we turned on to a southerly course just before we would have entered cloud. Sunshine and clear skies now lay ahead – but we had no idea what else. My feelings were disquieting ones, to the tune that we had made a proper mess of things – though perhaps that was a harsh judgement: although it did not suit me to be beaten, I had no doubts we were handling the situation satisfactorily enough up to this point.

Istres was easy to find: situated on the huge delta formed around the mouth of the River Rhone, the airfield stretched for miles; it is still the most extensive airfield in France. Coloured a red-brick hue, it is probably a unique site, at least as far as Europe is considered. When we first saw it, all the buildings around its perimeters had been demolished or damaged during the fighting to remove the German forces.

Becoming, of necessity, more experienced in single-engine landings, we circled round and inspected the surface for any obvious damage. We saw no signs of life – the moon-like area appeared deserted, but we made our approach and landed somewhere out in the middle of the vast spaces. We had been airborne for two and three-quarter hours.

What we could not evaluate from our brief inspection was the fact that the surface was not flat as an airfield usually is. Slight, gentle rises in the ground occurred, and the result of this feature was that we could not see anything on the edges of the plain – in fact we could see nothing but the red dusty ground spreading in all directions. This could have been funny really, but humour was not the present mood. With only one engine it is impossible to taxi, except in a tight circle, so we had to stay where we were until the explorers found us – at least, we assumed the man answering us on the radio was in the vicinity. It occurred to us that anyone on the field possibly not noting our one engine would be waiting for us to taxi around and find them: a deadlock situation.

After a stagnant period I asked Frank to push down our boarding-ladder, and to dismount. I was ready to follow him down, throwing the mailbags to him, and positioning the awkward revolver more comfortably about my person, with the plan of walking in any direction to locate the perimeter track. But before clambering down the steps my tired mind told me to call up on the same VHF channel as before and attempt to explain the impasse. This I did, and with some success: apparently a jeep was doing its best to find us, so I called to Frank to wait.

Eventually this ridiculous situation was untangled. Frank was left in charge of the aircraft, and I trundled away with the bags in the battered old jeep. It gave me a much-needed boost to be taken to an RAF officer who, sitting in the doorway of a semi-derelict hut, was smoking perfumed French cigarettes and sipping a glass of vermouth with the bottle beside him. He appeared to be on his own, and it surprised me to see that this officer was a wing commander. He was an administrative officer who was responsible for over-seeing the mixture of French civilians and German POWs who had the gigantic task of starting to clear away the rubble, and of organizing things sufficiently to enable the airfield to function somewhat more normally than it appeared to do at that moment.

Out on the field, Frank was supervising the towing of our Mosquito to suitable accommodation, and he arrived later on. In the meantime I was turning things over in my mind, sorting out the next step to take. This wingco seemed to have slotted into his environment so well that I doubted his ability to come to grips with the urgency of our circumstances; and he in his turn probably thought that we two would be happy to be sidelined from the war for a while, and to make the most of the relaxed status quo. So why get too het up?

I made my decision, and asked our host to please come and have a little walk with me away from the buildings. I rambled on about the need for Allied leaders to confer from time to time. I did not mention the names of the three leaders, nor that the location was the Crimea. All this news was still unknown to the world in general, and it was not my wish to be the person who announced it. At the same time this phlegmatic Englishman had to be activated in some fashion. I told him we had flown dispatches around Europe some months earlier.

Next I told him that these mailbags were more precious than his life, and he did at least show sufficient reaction to that to bother to give me a glance.

He seemed an unemotional man, and rather put out that we had chosen his little kingdom to which to bring our problems. Lastly, I informed him of the codeword of the priority granted to me as a king's messenger, and which was to be used in contacting my base immediately.

'I can't go and use that sort of priority!' he expostulated, showing a spark of interest at the possibility of his involvement in the scheme of things: 'I'll get the sack!' 'You don't have to,' was my retort. 'I will sign a chit for you declaring it is *my* responsibility; but if you do not agree, then your career in the RAF will be on the line.' He took the route of least resistance.

We walked to another hut where the signals section had their set-up. Scattered about the airfield was a small number of RAF personnel, and this particular corporal jumped to in a gratifying manner when I quoted the priority code. It was his big moment to dispatch that signal; I patted him on the back and gave him a wink on the quiet. It was a considerable relief when my message was on its way to Benson. Now they knew where we were, and that the mailbags were still safely with us.

My message also said that we would send Frank with the bags by the fastest available means and route, after Benson had given me the order to action that plan. As yet, Frank did not know he was going to be promoted to acting king's messenger. He would be keen to go back and see his wife, I thought, and as a bonus I was going to lumber him with the revolver. My duty would be to stick with the aircraft and attempt to have it repaired. Then I would fly it back myself. To tell the truth, I was starting to look forward to all this.

As we walked away from the signals room, I asked what could be done to stow the mailbags away as safely as possible. That was my next anxiety: how could I stick with the rough, ugly, bulky things for twenty-four hours a day? By good fortune, this was one item that was dealt with as quickly and effectively as I could have wished for. The CO – if that is what he was, as he was certainly the senior officer for miles around – said his 'office' had an enormous safe that his men had been unable to destroy or move, and he had the keys. It looked imposing to me, at least six foot high and might have weighed tons, and so impregnable did it look that I thought it preferable not to draw attention to it by requesting a guard to be posted. When it was opened, I could easily see why our friend did not wish it to be taken away: it was like a miniature cellar, nearly full of bottles of all descriptions. 'Have to keep things somewhere,' the custodian of the cellar said to me apologetically. He wasn't too keen, but I prevailed, and managed to obtain a scribbled receipt from him for the mailbags. I'll bet these were the most valuable items ever to have been in that safe.

After those few hectic hours, life struck me as more than tolerable, and full of promise. With time to look around and appreciate all the good things, it was good-oh to be alive – and it was particularly agreeable to be right here, I reflected. The skies were brilliant in their blueness, the atmosphere had a clarity I had not experienced since leaving New Zealand, and the warmth of the golden sun was a pleasure to my skin. This was more like it: stay here for a while and we would become sunburnt. Of course! This was early spring! We had been too occupied to realize that. The wingco sent us off in a jeep to settle in our quarters. Frank and I were together, which was a helpful gesture, and a pleasant change for both of us. Our billets were spacious and comfortable. We strolled along the road and found the delightful village of Istres.

This was a most attractive little place, and the inhabitants surprisingly welcoming; probably never since have I found such a friendly and kind attitude towards me from Frenchmen and women. We both revelled in the ambience generated by the people and the surroundings, had our share of vermouths and muscats, and wandered back to our beds in contented mood. Right then, it didn't seem such a bad war.

Up at first light the following morning, we were pleased to be able to promptly organize a DC-3, a Dakota transport aircraft that would take Frank and the cargo back to England. But while we were completing those arrangements in the wingco's HQ, the corporal from signals dashed in waving a sheet of paper and full of his news: Benson had signalled for Frank to remain with me. We were to 'expedite' the repairs to our Mosquito (some chance! I thought), and the mailbags were to be handed over to one of the 544 Mossies that had already taken off in the dark and would be with us about two hours after its departure. This was rousing stuff, and pleased Frank enormously: he had not been grateful for my promoting him to the role of messenger and custodian of the bags. He also said to me, in an aside, and quite unnecessarily I thought, that he had better stay and keep an eye on me.

Whatever our reactions to the message, the wingco was at last impressed that three dirty old mailbags could cause such a stir, and looked at us in a different and slightly puzzled manner. All of a sudden the cry came to mount the jeep and scamper out to the middle of the field, because one of our immaculate sky-blue Mosquitos had just made an unheralded swoop over us. We grabbed the bags with relish, jumped into the transport, and raced off to find our saviours before they too became lost in the wide-open spaces.

What joy! And what efficiency emanated from that clean and polished Mosquito with its Rolls-Royce Merlins idling away like sweet music. Our mates did not need to refuel: they just stopped where they were, opened their entrance hatch, and while the propellers whirled, I made my way to the hatch and had a short, shouted conversation.

Almost at the same time as our signal had been received at Benson, SHAEF had succeeded in locating us – as soon as our ETA at Benson had come and gone they had been contacting stations right across the parts of Europe where we might have been. They had been keen to trace those bags all right; the whole affair had caused a real stir, we were told. Steve passed a confirming message that the squadron was desperately short of serviceable aircraft, and therefore we were not to dilly-dally down on the Riviera. Frank told me Steve was just being jealous.

Up went the wayward bags, into the clutching hands of the navigator, and almost before I could get clear, the pilot swung his kite around in a flurry and took off in the direction of home. It had been an exhilarating episode, and now that was that.

From feeling as if we were unwanted, broken-down intruders at Istres, we were now treated as VIPs, and nothing was too good for us; we were even invited to crack a bottle of my choice from the multipurpose safe as a gesture of fond farewell to the mailbags. The only task left was to arrange for the repairs to our kite . . . and the sense of urgency seemed to evaporate a little. . . .

It was impossible for me to determine who was in charge of the repairs; it never became clear even as to which nationality had the major say. The engineering depot was miles away from our quarters, and we had to borrow any old truck to travel there. The opportunity and novelty of working on such a fine breed of aircraft and engine as the de Havilland Mosquito, acted like a magnet to all and sundry around the neighbourhood. Even when drinking at the tiny bars in the village late at night, some unlikely type would want to engage me in conversation on the subject of how they were the brains behind making it airworthy again. I started to have serious doubts as to whether we would ever fly the thing away. But a stronger, much happier feeling, which overpowered those doubts, was that of intensely enjoying every day and every evening. We became 'locals', and my French began to flourish until Frank, especially when he had mellowed after a few drinks, thought, quite mistakenly, that nothing was beyond me in the linguistic direction.

Having seen the precious cargo off and away, Frank and I checked that work was proceeding on the repairs, and spent a happy day walking round the countryside and eating and drinking in the village. We sat out in the sun at the edge of a lake where the blue waters sparkled with joy. What a bonus for us to experience this foretaste of spring in such a peaceful area, and peopled by men, women and children who for some deep-seated reason that they themselves probably could not have explained, treated us as heroes and important visitors. After an evening meal, we enjoyed the camaraderie of a visit to the local cinema in the company of many of the villagers. The clear starlit nights were as good as the days, and our walk back to our billets was a grand finale to a thoroughly successful day. Frank, my stodgy old English married man, even felt inspired to tell me what wizard perfumes the French girls used!

The next day we again made an early start because we planned to go to Marseilles and back. After checking the aircraft and making sure that progress was being made, we called at signals, and drawing a blank there, felt we were all clear for the day. The weather looked superb and settled, and we struck out. No regular transport was available, but this did not dismay us: walking was a pleasure, and we were content for a long time. A local Frenchman stopped and offered us a ride for a few miles in his old car. The obliging fellow made it his business to stop a huge American Army lorry before he turned off to his own destination. He asked the two black soldiers to give us a lift right into the city of Marseilles. They were helpful, too. We learned that the distance by road between Istres and Marseilles was thirty-five miles; they also told us that it was impossible to buy any meals or food in the city. On top of all the recent good news, this negative item of information affected our spirits somewhat.

Sure enough, we did not find any food. Marseilles had always interested me from my young days of reading. Had not the Count of Monte Cristo been so unfairly imprisoned in the formidable Château d'If? We found our way down to the old harbour, and I relished the view of the island prison. Around the waterfront was a continuous string of tiny bars, and we reconnoitred the nearest one. Men were munching away at something edible. To start the ball rolling, and to make it easy for both parties, we requested 'Two beers, please'. With the beers we were served a small portion of a fresh stick of crusty bread. We wolfed that down as quickly as the small glasses of beer, and asked for a repeat order. What a disappointment! The beers came over the counter smartly enough, but no bread. We downed the beers and left. Obviously, plenty of beer available, but tucker strictly rationed: we had received the message, loud and clear. Our brains were struggling to get up speed into operational mode again.

On this fresh and radiant spring morning, in such a romantic place, our appetite for food was so demanding that we were near to committing some act of felony in order to obtain some sustenance. All my past experience of life told me I could not last much longer without a feed. Then Frank came up with an idea: let's try the adjacent bar, and see if any bread comes along with the first beer. This plan worked splendidly, and we hurried from bar to bar, cramming the tasty bread into us before emptying the beers and moving on to the next premises.

It is not recorded how many weak, war-time-strength beers we drank; the thing was that after a long time we were not quite so hungry as we had been, and for some reason my efforts at conversing in French began to improve. My nervousness left me, and when we took up position on the stools in one particular bar, a useful conversation built up with an attractive barmaid. Frank thought it would be a good idea to stay there for a while drinking several beers, and forgo the bread. However, once we had proved to

Madame that we were serious and worthwhile clients, I piped up with a fluency that surprised me, and brought up the subject of food.

This was not met with a smile; on the contrary the lady's face took on an anxious expression. Nevertheless, she ducked out the back and came back rather furtively with two bigger hunks of bread into which she had cut a slit; these were filled with scraps of tomato and gherkins and tiny pieces of cheese. This action brought smiles all round, and more beer, and we shouted her a drink of vermouth. This simple gesture involved a lot of mime and much elementary French before she got the hang of what a 'shout' meant. But, in an intelligent and business-like manner, she cottoned on fast to the principle – so well, in fact, that the shout became part of the routine each time we ordered 'two beers please, Madame'. In our turn, we laid down our ground rules, to the effect that we only bought the beer if more food scraps accompanied it.

At a later stage, with a flash of memory, I proposed a toast to 'L'Entente Cordiale!' It did me good to see how impressed my old friend Frank was at the way things were proceeding. It was clear to me he thought he had a clever captain, and that is never a bad idea for a navigator to pick up when considering his pilot.

Our enjoyable routine was shattered when Madame's husband returned to his premises, presumably through a rear door. He did not give any of us a pleasant greeting as he entered the bar: looking around at our no doubt flushed and cheery faces, he dismissed his wife to the back rooms. We were coming near to the end of our stay, in any case, but we thought that to show goodwill to the patron and his charming wife, we would order one more round. With the beers were two final breads and fillings that Monsieur le patron dumped in front of us. I took a good bite of mine and chewed away, but for the first time the contents were horrible. In answer to my question as to what sort of meat this was supposed to be, we received the grumpy reply from the surly one: 'Catsmeat!' As one, Frank and I jumped off our perches, kept sufficient control to gulp down our beers, and rushed outside into the warm sunshine. Our appetites were more than satisfied for several hours.

We walked around most of the central parts of this fine city. The people were friendly, well dressed and attractive. The daylight was waning when we commenced walking out of the city towards the north. The return journey involved seven separate rides in a tram, a bus, a car and four lorries. The diary says it all: 'A grand day indeed.'

The next day was 8 February, and we relaxed on the airfield. To our surprise, a French Army engineer found us just after lunch, and said that in his opinion our Mosquito was ready for an air-test. Our previous inspections and inquiries had led us to believe that the task would take much longer. One of the problems had been the dismantling and refitting of the starboard spinner, and as soon as I saw it, I could see how it had been

177

YEAR 1945		AIRCRAFT		PILOT, OR 1ST PILOT	2ND PILOT, PUPIL, OR PASSENGER	DUTY (INCLUDING RESULTS AND REMARKS)	SINGLE-ENGINE AIRCRAFT				MULTI-ENGINE AIRCRAFT						PASSEN-GER	INSTR/CLOUD FLYING (Incl. in Cols. (1) to (10))	
MONTH	DATE	Type	No.				DAY Dual (1)	DAY Pilot (2)	NIGHT Dual (3)	NIGHT Pilot (4)	Dual (5)	DAY 1st Pilot (6)	2nd Pilot (7)	Dual (8)	NIGHT 1st Pilot (9)	2nd Pilot (10)	(11)	Dual (12)	Pilot (13)
				—	—	TOTALS BROUGHT FORWARD	37.05	19.55	2.40	.20		108.40	67.15	3.10	7.45	8.20	1	96.35	46.80	30.
JAN.	3.	OXFORD	6082	SELF	W/O MOSELEY F/S BAYLIS.	W/T QGH's. BEAM.						1.10	3.10	7.45	8.20	1	96.35	46.80	.30
JAN.	5.	MOSQUITO III	503	SELF	W/O MOSELEY.	GEE BEAM GYRO CIRCUITS.						1.15							
JAN.	8.	MOSQUITO III	503	SELF	W/O MOSELEY.	GEE BEAM I.F.						1.30							.30
JAN.	9.	MOSQUITO XVI	500	SELF	W/O MOSELEY.	OPS. STETTIN-POLITZ. 323						4.36							
JAN.	10.	MOSQUITO XVII	798	SELF	P/O SKINGLEY.	AIR TEST (CF.P.1.A).						1.00							
JAN.	14.	MOSQUITO XVI	500	SELF	C/P HAYNES.	GEE TEST.						.50							
JAN.	15.	MOSQUITO XVI	500	SELF	F/L BUTCHART	GEE TEST 8 QGH'S						1.80							
JAN.	17.	MOSQUITO XVII	652	GEE	F/L BURFIELD.	AIR TEST. 35000.						2.00							.16
JAN.	28.	MOSQUITO XVI	807	SELF	W/O MOSELEY.	AIR TEST.						1.40							

SUMMARY FOR MONTH OF JANUARY.
UNIT: 544 SQDN. TYPES: MOSQUITOS OXFORD
DATE: 31 JAN. 1945.
SIGNATURE: ...

C.O. 544 SQN ...

						OPERATIONAL : -					4.35								
						NON-OPS : -					10.26								
						MONTHLY TOTAL : -					15.80								
FEB.	2.	MOSQUITO XVI	580	SELF	W/O MOSELEY.	OPS. BENSON - SPV SEVERO...						3.35							
FEB.	3.	MOSQUITO XVI	580	SELF	W/O MOSELEY.	OPS.						3.20							
FEB.	4.	MOSQUITO XVI	500	SELF	W/O MOSELEY.	OPS. SELL-CRIMEA. (SAXD.)						3.45							
FEB.	5.	MOSQUITO XVI	500	SELF	C/O MOSELEY.	OPS. CRIMEA- SAN SEVERO...						2.45							
FEB.	8.	MOSQUITO XVI	500	SELF	W/O MOSELEY.	AIR TEST.						.45							
FEB.	9.	MOSQUITO XVI	500	SELF	C/O MOSELEY.	ISTRES - BENSON - 3000'.						3.15							.30
						TOTALS CARRIED FORWARD	37.05	39.65	2.40	.20		108.40	87.40	3.10	7.45	8.20	1	96.35	46.80	10.15

GRAND TOTAL [Cols. (1) to (10)]: 697 Hrs. 25 Mins.

Logbook: 2–9 February 1945, Ops Nos 59–62. Courier mission to the Crimea, Russia. Our fifth single-engine landing at Istres airfield, France.

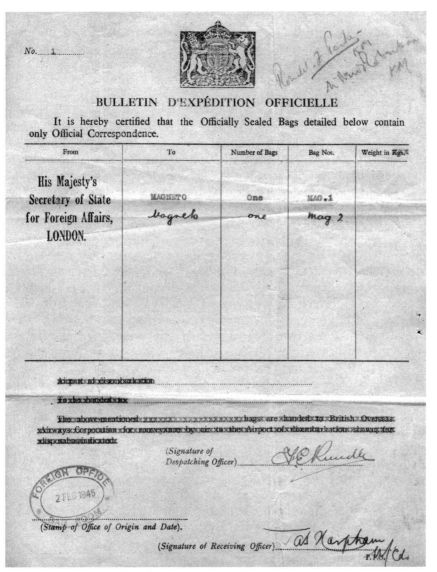

Op. No. 62: Foreign Affairs bag receipt: Operation *Magneto*.

hammered into place; it looked dented and wobbly. No expert authority was available: I had to make the decision. Yes, of course we would test the machine. Frank and I took off, Frank with his fingers crossed, I'll be bound. The spinner and the entire engine vibrated considerably, but all temperatures and pressures were normal. We would fly home, but not that day; much better to have an early start, and have the whole day to cope with any emergency that might arise. Tomorrow was therefore our 'D'-for-Departure Day, and we signalled Benson of our intentions. When we landed, the major insisted that he could not approve the state of the engine without having a flight in the aircraft; I had had a premonition that we would not get away without this request, and how right I was – but I gave him more than his money's worth.

We flew low up the Rhone to Avignon where he was living. We located his wife and a small group of citizens, who waved with a frenzy that only foreigners can attain. As we made successive passes over the balconies of their apartments, waving with their hands and arms was not sufficient for the occasion and they took it in turns to duck inside and come back with scarves and towels and any article with which to make more impressive waves. Each time we came back for another beat-up, more neighbours joined the act, and the whole building quickly caught the festival mood.

Our French ally was thrilled beyond measure, and shrieked with uncontrolled passion. He twisted and turned to such an extent as he tried to see everything and everybody, I thought he would interfere with my controls. I could not manage to interest him in the violent vibrations; indeed, it is doubtful if he ever heard the engines. As we landed again, all his helpers, and other unidentified persons, queued up for a joy-ride. It was picnic day, and I trust that, as far as the RAF was concerned – especially as it was not its fuel being used – 'what the eye did not see, the heart did not grieve over'. It did occur to me that our popularity was soaring.

Whatever plans or ideas Frank and I may have had for that last evening were completely taken out of our hands by the local populace, now extended by the numbers of French engineers, or engineer-admirers. The village of Istres turned on a fête in our honour that night, and the whole party moved through the village, distributing its trade fairly amongst the bars and cafés. At no time during the war did I spend a more memorable night. Why we were apparently so popular still remains a mystery to me. Maybe it was just a joyous reaction to the end of the war for the local people, and just possibly a sign that they appreciated the fact that the British and their allies had liberated their spectacular part of the world.

We drank either vermouth or muscat. This started in a genteel fashion, rather like the aircrew parties; but in similar vein, the evening progressed to a slightly more hectic pace. My practice with the French language had worked wonders, I thought, and the extra confidence in thinking that everyone knew exactly what I was trying to state brought on more reckless confidence. I know that one of the big successes was the toast to 'L'Entente Cordiale!', and another that raised cheer upon cheer was declaring that we considered ourselves as French as the French.

At our briefing for the Crimean trip we had been issued with the currencies used in all the countries we expected to pass over, and obviously this included a good wad of French money. Now I am particular with handling cash, and I truly believed we had paid scrupulously for all our drinks and snacks; but the strange thing was, that when Frank did a re-count next morning of our joint funds (our usual procedure), we were embarrassed to discover we were well in credit. Our French funds amounted to *more* than we had started out with. One of the minor mysteries of the war . . .

The next day we did not feel too big and strong, and although we did our best to be organized for an early take-off, things delayed us. It did not make me feel any better when Frank confided in me that we had entered remarkably well into the spirit of things the previous evening because he had counted us having more than twenty drinks each. They were unusually small glasses though. It was noon when we were airborne: slight headaches, well fed, sunburnt and contented. All we wished for was for the spinner not to fly off on its own. The mandatory beat-up over both the wingco's HQs and the village square ended our farewells.

It would have overtaxed our duff engine, and the spinner, to climb high. Conversely, I did not have sufficient confidence to enjoy the opportunity to low fly across France. We compromised by flying at reduced revs, at around 3,000ft, just high enough to bale out if the worst came to the worst. The trip had its anxieties, but after three-and-a-quarter hours we landed at Benson. Steve dashed over to us, before we could climb down to the ground. 'Is this kite serviceable, Kiwi?' 'No Sir!' He looked disgusted, and hurried off.

Our Black Sea and Mediterranean interludes were over, and it was obvious we were back to Benson, and the war. . . .

13
San Francisco – Open your Golden Gate

PRU at Benson never did have a respite from the intensity of war, and pressure continually mounted, no matter how strongly anyone thought the broad sweep of successful actions must soon terminate hostilities. If one contemplated the inevitable defeat of Germany, there still remained the fanatical Japanese to be conquered, and PRU operations over most of the vast areas of the Pacific, Asia and the Far East had to be further organized and extended.

The operational scene at Benson continued to function smoothly and efficiently. The two Spitfire squadrons and two Mosquito squadrons still coped with the ever-increasing demands for prompt and precise coverage of the targets for attacks by American and British bombers and fighters, and for photographs of the damage caused by those attacks. Losses of aircraft and the casualty rate incurred by pilots and navigators fluctuated from period to period. For some months at a time the development of British aircraft and engines gave them the advantage over the German fighter aircraft, but at other periods the reverse was the case, and certainly from late 1944 until the end of the war, the German jet-fighters were an increasing menace to our operations. The Me 163, which was actually rocket-propelled, and the Me 262 in particular, were both outstanding machines, appreciably faster than any piston-engined aircraft, capable of reaching nearly 600mph (960km/h) compared with our top speed of about 430mph (700km/h). A Benson Mosquito was the first aircraft to encounter the Me 262.

In her book *Evidence in Camera*, Constance Babington Smith MBE, an outstanding photographic interpreter at Medmenham, stated: 'These two jets looked like having disastrous effects on Allied photographic reconnaissance when they began operating in the summer of 1944.' However, during a quiet time of reflection in my room, an idea came to me. If the first pass of a jet did not shoot us down, I would put into operation a hazardous move that would at least give us an even chance of living to fight another day.

A few days before our courier mission to Moscow we had flown Op. No. 47, with targets in the Cologne-Coblenz area of western Germany. It had not been easy going, and in various attacks by non-jet fighters we had tangled with a total of fifteen of them. Because we were comparatively close to England we could afford the time and the petrol to continue these skirmishes and to still cover all our targets.

As we set course for home, Frank, kneeling on his seat with his head in the canopy blister, ever cool, collected, and more importantly, well experienced, said once again: 'Fighter coming up from dead astern – catching us very smartly!' We had our routine. Wait either for the first shots, or (much to be preferred) for the second or two *before* the first shot, and then perform the tightest tight-turn that my mind and arms and legs were capable of. Next came the re-orientation: decide where north-west lay, and aim to manoeuvre round until we were heading towards home, rather than being forced further into the Fatherland.

But this swift interception was by one of the new jets, possibly called up by some of the fighters we had already dealt with. They had eventually dropped away from us as they either ran out of ammunition or their fuel level demanded they scramble back to their base. Running short of fuel was the prime disadvantage of these jets: in the first place they could not stay airborne for too long, and in the second place they were restricted to only a limited number of airfields that had runways of sufficient length for them to use. For that reason we tried to take them away from the area where they found us.

By the time our minds had grasped that this excessive speed must be generated by a jet, I saw him clearly as he overshot us by miles and disappeared out of sight. He had nowhere near our manoeuvrability. I settled down in our north-west direction and concentrated on flying the Mosquito with my fingertips and all my dexterity: this was the only way to squeeze out an extra mile or two per hour, and the standard I attempted to reach was the culmination of all my training and all my experience on the job. At this juncture my mind automatically calculated distance and time to go compared with available fuel, and the result of that equation decided at what revs the throttles should be set. In an instant our enemy found us again and came up fast astern. I doubted if we could expect to avoid him this second time round, so decided to implement my private and drastic plan of action.

For various reasons I had not told Frank of my intentions because the plan was not exactly a morale booster: he either survived with me or he died with me. When he said: 'Now!' meaning, 'Start your steep turn!' I pulled back on one throttle; presumably we went into a spin. Frank, who could not strap himself in when facing backwards, shot up to the blister at the top of the cockpit, and clouds of dust rose up from the floor and crammed into my eyes. Frank's green canvas navigation bag was above my head, and if I did not completely black out, I know I went fuzzy and saw a red mist.

After that I remember throttling back the other engine and easing the aircraft out of its dive. From an altitude of 29,000ft we were just less than 20,000ft, and as we regained straight and level flight, I knew by the position of the sun that we were flying south towards Switzerland (in violent manoeuvres the compass 'topples' and misreads). It was not until the aircraft was climbing again and heading for home that my brain slipped into gear sufficiently for me to study the wings to see if they were still there, or flapping about. On our return I reported my actions, and the aircraft was given a thorough overhaul; fortunately nothing serious had happened to it. Whether my nerve would have let me do a repeat performance was thankfully never put to the test.

Our 544 Squadron was intended, in theory, to have a full strength of twenty crews of two men per crew, but that full complement was never attained during my eighteen months with the squadron; at most, we never exceeded sixteen or seventeen crews at any one time. My casual personal observations show that twenty-two crews or more either failed to return from a trip, or crashed on landing. Because at times a sole survivor was later teamed up with a new pilot or navigator, the total number of men involved was forty-one. The crew killed while seconded to Australia is in addition to this number.

Thirty men from the forty-one were killed; the others either escaped and returned to Britain, or became POWs until the war ended. Two from the 544 casualty list were Kiwis; one was killed and the other suffered as a wounded POW.

From letters from New Zealand, and from meeting New Zealanders from time to time when on leave in London, information about friends circulated on the Kiwi grapevine. In this manner I frequently learned about men who had, for example, lived next door to our family home, or had worked in the same office, or belonged to the same sports clubs. Many times I knew their families and their homes, and therefore I wrote letters of sympathy. Scrappy notes in my diary – by no means an accurate record on this subject – remind me of a couple of dozen such friends who lost their lives flying with the RNZAF, quite apart from those in the army and navy. Although I made no long-term friends amongst aircrew at Benson who were not on my squadron, nearly forty names of companions from the other three squadrons are noted as killed or missing.

These statistics make melancholy reading, but living with the reality over a stressful period merely reflected what had to be accepted as the norm in our way of life then. It was not a subject that came up for any discussion with Frank or Joe or Vic. Although many decorations were awarded to personnel at Benson, that subject also was never one for analysis. Once again, looking at jottings in the diary, the following approximate figures are noted: on 544 Squadron, during my tour, a total of sixteen men earned three DSOs, twelve DFCs, one bar to a DFC, two DFMs, two American DFCs and two French Croix de Guerre.

When Foster and Moseley returned from their eight-day jaunt to faraway foreign places in the early springtime, they were jolted by news from Steve to the effect that they would be ending their tour of operations on 28 March. That was a tour of eighteen months, and up until that time no one had lasted anywhere near as long as that; equally, at no time previously had anyone discussed how or when a tour would terminate. It all took a bit of digesting, and placed us under an extra pressure. Someone told me that our Spitfire pilots had the idea that their tour was supposed to be eighty trips, which would total about 240 ops hours for single-engine aircraft.

Mosquito crews in the two squadrons continued to wonder if they would be posted to the Far East after the job was completed in Europe. The general expectation was that in order to invade Japan and terminate the world war, much demand would be made for photo-recce services. Meanwhile the reducing probability of remaining alive in the face of maximum German effort began to enter the mind of a man confronting death every few days. During that period the bigger picture aroused speculation as to what it might be like flying even longer sorties over seas and jungles against the Japanese.

In rather an anticlimax, I was posted off to a one-week course at Derby, an engine-handling course at the Rolls-Royce headquarters. It was instructive and entertaining, and the numbers attending were small; they included six USAAF single-engine P-51 pilots, and the atmosphere was lively and congenial. We were billeted in a comfortable hotel where we gathered almost every evening and enjoyed fraternizing. During the daytime lectures I felt embarrassed when single-engine flying for Mosquitos came up for discussion. The Yanks were not too keen to hear about engines failing; – and I would have felt the same, had there been only one engine to start with! In the same fashion as at de Havillands, the Rolls-Royce lecturers were most interested to hear from us regarding various aspects of our experiences with their products. The week was beneficial to all participants, and I learnt some useful information. But at the same time I could not relax well: Benson was on my mind, and especially how Joe and Vic were surviving. The end of the war in Europe was not far off now, but I realized I was starting to wonder if my mates and I would be around to cheer at the celebrations.

Returning to Benson at the end of the week, two items of news awaited. The first was that our tour was *not* now a period of eighteen months, but was to conclude when 300 hours had been flown on ops. No explanation was given as to why there was a change of format. At that time Frank and I had about 260 hours, and it wasn't clear to me whether one option was better or worse than the other. But what *was* clear was that first, no one from 544 had ever reached 300 hours; and second, our date of completion would now be extended until after the end of March.

The second item of news was that Joe and Vic and I were going up to Leuchars as a detachment in a week's time to cover Scandinavia and the Baltic. Wingco said Joe, as the biggest of us, would be in charge, and he called a meeting in the hangar for all the squadron's groundcrew as well as we three and our navigators.

When everyone was present, Steve stood on a box and informed the crowd about the small detachment. He said everyone was tired of these 'Black Troops', and they were being banished to the frozen north. He said men and women of all trades would be required to go to Scotland, and he realized that many of them would therefore be leaving their wives and families for a few weeks. He felt it would be best, in the first instance, if he called for volunteers to take two paces forward. What price the Black Troops? *Everyone* present stepped forward . . . a mild sensation. Steve then asked 'Old Joe' if he would like to choose so many fitters, so many riggers, a Waaf driver, and so on: in short, we had the pick of the bunch and, more strikingly, everyone's vote. The feeling all round was overwhelming, and quite sentimental.

Sensing that things in general were moving on, I made a big decision and sold my bicycle at a profit of five shillings, for £3 10s. Ginger Baylis was the lucky buyer. We were able to retain our room in the mess, and that helped our arrangements. A friend of mine from the office days in New Zealand arrived to see me, Ron Williams, then a lieutenant pilot in the Fleet Air Arm. He stayed in the mess for the night, and next morning Steve approached us in the crew-room and asked if I would like to fly an air-test and give my naval friend a ride in a Mossie. How generously and understandingly we were treated; I hope I showed my gratitude enough. We had great fun together in the kite, so much so that we became lost for a while, and had to work hard first of all to find the Thames, and then pinpoint our familiar base again.

After driving Ron into town the next morning to catch his train, Frank and I flew Op. No. 63 into Germany, and No. 64 to the east of Dresden the following day. The day after that we flew ourselves and Vickers up to Leuchars. Frank became a father the same day, and what better idea than to wet his baby daughter Janet's head that evening in the Leuchars' mess.

At Leuchars, we three crews, with our loyal and efficient ground supporters, not forgetting our handsome flying machines, were a complete miniature PR unit. Joe and Vic and I went in a deputation to the Motor Transport Section, and succeeded in obtaining a service car to go with our Waaf driver. A Norwegian army captain became our meteorological officer. Andreas was a fine man, fair and handsome, who had fled from his homeland in an overcrowded fishing-boat to Scotland. When we first met him he was on the serious side. If we were not used to Norwegians, he was not used to Australasians and their habits, and especially their humour.

But in a short space of time we all became good companions, and our trio became a quartet; wherever we went our new friend came too. You can imagine how much leg-pulling occurred. As the early spring days came along we resorted to frisking about on the grass outside our little crew-room. One silly trick we often played was for any two of us to gang up on a third man: one of the pair crept up behind the victim and crouched down on his hands and knees, and the other one then walked up to the victim and, placing a hand on his chest, applied a gentle pressure. The one who had been picked on had no alternative but to attempt to step back, when he would slowly fall backwards over the recumbent body.

The first few times we selected Andreas as the victim he was enraged, and wanted to fight. But strength of numbers kept him in check, and in no time at all he became a fanatical practitioner of this boyhood pastime. Indeed, his enthusiasm for it developed to the extent that we had to fall into the habit of continually looking behind us to see if Andreas had found a conspirator to kneel down against our legs. One day at lunch-time when the mess was crowded, we spotted Andreas and a henchman 'playing' a game in the mess corridor outside the dining-room. Everyone in the vicinity looked on incredulously: whatever had happened to this serious foreign fellow since he had been attached to this Photo-Freddie outfit? But what tickled us enormously was the fact that his victim was a Polish lieutenant. We shall never know if any international scenes grew from this game; probably it is now popular in Norway, and might be played in Poland. When a successful incident had been organized by Andreas, he would roar with laughter, and many a time over the next few weeks, his laughter somewhere within earshot told us he had achieved another success. I hope he did not break too many friendships in the process.

In the manner of all good 544 systems, Joe drew up a 'tennis-ladder' with the names 'Joe', 'Vic' and 'Kiwi'. The one at the top of the ladder flew the next trip, and was then placed at the bottom of the list. The two who did not have the trip that day helped the crew on ops to prepare, waved them 'Cheerio', and waited for their return. The groundcrews excelled themselves in their servicing and maintenance, extending themselves to polishing our aircraft, already spick and span. They knew by now how much I valued a clean windscreen, and someone would still be polishing it after we had climbed up into the cockpit. They took it to heart when I explained how a tiny speck on the glass easily became an enemy fighter when the pressure came on.

Our trips were early in the day in order to photograph near midday, and so we returned early. The groundcrew would pounce on the aircraft as soon as it had returned, and usually they had completed their duties by the middle of the afternoon, polish and all. Joe acknowledged their admirable fervour by announcing in his direct Aussie language that the rest of the day was theirs, and they could push off to Dundee or St. Andrews to enjoy themselves. Everyone else on this large Coastal Command station looked upon our outfit with disbelief and some envy.

At the end of February, Frank, who had recently applied for a commission – he was then a warrant officer – was called down to Benson for his interview. Steve was most co-operative, and sent a Mossie up to Leuchars to collect him and take him down to Benson. The next day it was my turn for an ops trip, and Joe offered me his navigator, Pilot Officer Alec Barron DFM, who readily agreed to make an extra trip with a different pilot. Alec was small and agile, he performed his duties admirably, and did things exactly as I wished. It also demonstrated to me why the Burfield-Barron combination was still alive and kicking. That trip was my No. 65, over the Oslo area, and provided some anxiety with fuel problems.

Both Alec, and Vic's navigator, Mo, had recently obtained their commissions, and I think Frank must have then been lonely in the sergeants' mess. It was excellent news when he, too, became a pilot officer, and at long last the six of us were housed in the same mess; he and I became even closer friends. My promotion to flight lieutenant came through about the same time.

For our little team, that was not all the news, and an entirely unexpected and unsettling item was relayed up to us from Benson, namely that Burfield and Barron, and Foster and Moseley were about to be posted to Transport Command 'for Mosquito trials'. What did that mean? Were our ops over? And why Transport Command? We had no answers; the only line of thought that came to me was that over a period of several months, Steve had selected Frank and me to test-fly the latest modified Mosquito for PRU work. This model had been developed in response to the deployment of jet interceptors by the Luftwaffe. We had flown seven trials. It had extended wings, was lighter and more streamlined, and was designed to fly higher and faster. It was the Mark 32 version, and five production aircraft were built. We had reached nearly 43,000ft in it, but the machine was not particularly easy to fly at that altitude; for one thing, the engines overheated. But now I wondered if Joe and I were going to further this development.

A few more days, and another flap: Joe and Alec were on their way to Transport Command *immediately*. We were sorry to see them depart, and hoped we would soon follow. Vic had fallen in love with Sue Kidner, the beautiful Waaf officer from the Intelligence Section who was attached to our Leuchars unit, and they were planning to be married. Our detachment was coming apart in unforeseen ways. A replacement crew, Burr and Dyson, came up from Benson to bring our strength back to three crews.

Frank and I flew Ops Nos 66, 67 and 68 during the earlier part of March; these trips were over Norway and Denmark. One day a Mosquito from Benson dropped in to refuel, and we learnt that Benson was having a sticky time, mostly due to the German jets; three Spits had just gone missing (by the month's end that total had risen to six). The 544 news was that Ray Hays had been awarded a DFC, but he and his navigator, my friend Lofty South, were killed a mere two weeks later.

On 18 March 1945 I had to fly Op. No. 69 with a different navigator, Flying Officer Grover, but this trip was not successful because the spark plugs oiled up, and we returned after two hours and forty-five minutes. It was a close-run thing.

This No. 69 was my last operational sortie, although neither Frank nor I knew that at the time. My total ops totalled 275 hours, and total Mossie hours then were 430. (The faithful diary also noted that my bank balance had now reached the princely sum of two hundred and fifty pounds!)

Towards the end of March Frank and I were granted leave. Did they wish to make sure we were still in the land of the living when our posting to join Joe and Alec came through? Frank Dodd flew up from Benson to fly us down, ready for leave, packing the four of us into the cockpit for two.

But while on leave I received a telegram to return to Benson the next day. As I was digesting that, another telegram arrived saying: 'Return immediately'. Back at base, Frank and I heard that our posting to Transport Command had come through: our tour of ops was finished, and our gear had already been packed up and flown down from Leuchars. Someone was certainly giving us the 'hurry up'.

The following day we had an exhausting time arranging for our clearances from Benson, my home for eighteen months. Sadly, Vic and I never had the chance to meet again before he was married and returned to Australia, although we both tried. A time of war can take little notice of relationships, and one has to learn to carry a heavy heart.

In the short space of time left before hostilities ceased, some more crews from 544 went missing. The two members of a crew who had been posted to the peace and quiet of Australia for special duties, had been killed in a flying accident.

We left Benson in a rush, with ten pieces of baggage between the two of us. Strangely enough, the date was exactly 28 March! Harrow was our given destination, but fortunately we left most of the baggage at Paddington station, because at Harrow we learnt that Transport Command HQ was in the process of moving to Teddington, and would we please go away and come back again in three days' time. We put the new plan into action with alacrity and placed ourselves on leave.

Frank and I arrived for our interviews on the Saturday of Easter. The diary reminds me that we had 'loads of bumph to fill in, but we were treated like "gen men"; first class news about our posting – may turn out to be terrific!' Yes, the news at the interview was stimulating, to put it mildly. The gentleman who played the leading role was a similar type, in his well-cut suit and in his manner and voice, to the king's messengers I had already met briefly. He told us he was speaking in the strictest of confidence.

At the termination of the war in Europe, an international conference would be held in San Francisco where delegates of some fifty countries would sign a United Nations' Charter. Two of the most suitably experienced Mosquito crews were to fly dispatches on a courier mission to and from the conference and England. The two crews had now been chosen, and we were to proceed to RAF Station Pershore, to be attached to the No. 1 Ferry Unit. A new Mosquito would be issued to each crew, and we were to 'fly them in' and hold ourselves in readiness. The best part was kept to the last: 'Your next instructions will come direct from No. 10 Downing Street.'

On arrival at Pershore, in Worcestershire, we were delighted to be met gleefully by Joe and Alec who had spent much of their recent time on leave. It was just one month since they had left us at Leuchars. Joe kept bursting out into snatches of a popular song: 'San Francisco, Open your Golden Gate!', and continued to warble it from time to time during the next few weeks. I never had the nerve to ask Frank how his sea-twitch would react to a flight over the Atlantic. The whole project filled my mind with restless anticipation: it was a great secret to be holding. At the end of that week yet another newsflash gave us further cause for celebration: Frank and I each received a DFC. We hurried into the town to buy some medal ribbon, and, not having our worthy Rose to do it, plodded away in the evening and sewed them on our uniforms. Both Steve and the good old Adj. from 544 Squadron found time in their hectic lives to write us letters.

It has been commented before, how war news comes both good and bad at the same time. It was just at this time that Air Commodore D. J. Waghorn, the CO at Benson who had flown us to David's funeral, was killed in a flying accident.

Joe flew us to Filton airfield one day, where we collected a brand new Mosquito-XXV. Flying it back to Pershore brought the project a little closer. The senior officers at Pershore were not too pleased to have us at their unit: they saw we tended to be rather a law unto ourselves, even to deciding if and when we wanted to fly our beautiful new machines. While we waited for further instructions we kept our hand in by flying Oxfords and Ansons for a ferry flight; this entailed carrying passengers around many parts of England, and was a relaxing and low-key activity. We four made it as enjoyable as we could, and were popular because we continually volunteered to fly when others were happier to sit and play bridge. All the atmosphere of Benson disappeared forever. We were summoned to a CO's parade, and we were well out of practice for that sort of thing. But Joe did manage to manoeuvre us to

Award of the Distinguished Flying Cross to Flight
Lieutenant Ronald Henry Foster, Royal New Zealand
Air Force - 1945.

Copy of official citation.

"Flight Lieutenant Foster, as a pilot, has
completed numerous reconnaissances. Throughout his
operational tour the high standard of his work has been
reflected in the excellence of the results obtained.
Since the invasion of France he has taken part in a
large number of sorties against enemy railway targets
in all parts of France and Belgium. On the majority of
these, adverse weather has been encountered. This has
often necessitated a descent to a low level to escape
cloud, but despite damage to his aircraft from anti-
aircraft fire on several occasions he has almost
invariably secured excellent photographs. Flight
Lieutenant Foster has also participated in many sorties
to Germany, Czechoslovakia and Norway."

DFC citation.

the rear of the formation marching to a church parade, enabling us to break
off and double back to our billets for an extra hour. Old Vic would have
approved of the way we had learnt from him. These billets were the old
Nissen huts, and we moaned about missing the luxuries of Benson.

We did *not* moan that we were *not* still at Benson. It had come as a major
shock to have our tour of ops terminated at such short notice, and my mind
had not yet adjusted to the change; but we knew only too well how tense the
atmosphere was on PRU at this trying time. The enemy's concentrated
defences over Germany, spearheaded by their jets, made sorties more and

191

more dangerous, and it was hard going, in those latter stages of the war, to penetrate into Germany. Crews were tired from what seemed to be unending tours of operations. It was the air of suspense at this particular time that gave me the feeling later on that it was a good thing the war in the air finished when it did. The overall scene did not appear too auspicious when I had surveyed it from my seat in the Mosquito cockpit, holding the throttles ready to open up.

For at least some Allied aircrew a conscious effort became necessary to keep up morale. In response to my parents' plea for a 'decent photograph', I took time to go to Oxford and have a studio photo taken; when it reached New Zealand my father wrote and asked me why I had to look so sad and serious. I did not reply to that.

Close as the defeat of Hitler then was, more effort and more strain were required to achieve a satisfactory and unconditional surrender. Several authorities have since stated the opinion that if the war had not ended when it did, the jets, particularly the Messerschmitt 262, would have been capable of reversing the advantage in the air that Britain and the USA held so strongly. However, post-war records do show that the Allied Command was in possession of facts relating to the sorry state of Germany's economic situation, and was aware that the German war machine was then close to defeat.

Although his ultimate and complete defeat stared him in the face, Hitler continued to boast that his secret weapons would give Germany the victory. After enduring five and a half years of warfare the British civilian population had experienced enough of danger, death and privation. The testing and production of the V-1 flying bombs had commenced in 1943 at Peenemünde, on the Baltic coast, and that area was a priority target for PRU flights for a long time. However, it was mid-1944 before the first pilotless jet-propelled bombs were launched in an attack. The approximate figures published for these scary weapons show that nearly 9,000 were launched from sites in France. Of these, 2,340 reached the London area, resulting in between 5,000 and 6,000 deaths, and 16,000 seriously injured.

The V-2 rocket also saw the light of day at Peenemünde, as early as late 1942; the Germans called them vengeance weapons, and more than 1,000 were launched against Britain. Before the public had any knowledge of this invention, Frank and I had the uncanny experience of sighting one of the first of these 13 ton, 40ft long monsters launched from Holland: while returning from a sortie, a V-2 shot up nearly vertically, close to the nose of our Mosquito. At debriefing we had to sketch our impressions of the apparition, and no one in the operations room appeared to know anything about these weapons at that stage.

In late 1944 the first of these rocket-bombs, each carrying one ton of explosives, landed on London. These rockets had an unnerving effect on the citizens. A few weeks later one single V-2 hit a Woolworth's store, killing 160 shoppers and injuring 135. Six weeks before the end of the war the last rocket was fired from Holland. These indiscriminate weapons killed nearly 3,000 people in England, and more than 4,000 in Belgium. Other secret weapons being brought to a state of readiness in Germany were fortunately too late to be utilized in this war. Even so, it was only two months before the German surrender that an American bombing raid on the German atomic bomb research plant near Berlin finally put paid to Hitler's efforts in that alarming direction.

By February the Soviet armies were within fifty miles of Berlin. Dresden was bombed by night and by day by 1,200 British and American aircraft. The Allies crossed the Rhine, and were soon only 200 miles from Berlin, where Hitler moved his HQ to underground bunkers, 50ft below. In Belsen, liberating forces found 10,000 unburied bodies.

During April 1945, President Roosevelt died and Harry S Truman became the US president. Two weeks later, Italian partisans shot dead Benito Mussolini and his mistress, before hanging them, upside down. On the last day of that fateful month, Adolf Hitler shot himself dead; his mistress, now married to him, poisoned herself to death. Another hectic seven days, and the Nazis surrendered unconditionally to the Allies.

* * *

Back on peaceful Pershore station, near the tranquil Vale of Evesham dressed in its annual cherry blossoms, and in nearly all the rest of the world, it was announced that the victory in Europe would be celebrated the following day, 8 May, the day known as VE Day. Frank and I were granted leave, and we wondered every day when our call would come to fly the courier mission. My diary records: 'Cannot appreciate the fact that the war in Europe is really finished. Wonder what is going to be my future in the war now?' Frank and I heard we had both been awarded the French Croix de Guerre.

A friend who was a pilot on the flight at Pershore kindly flew me to a convenient airfield for the start of my leave. On this flight, in a slow old Anson, we nearly collided with another aircraft: it was a close shave. Probably all pilots feel the same, but I was always happier when doing the piloting myself. Air Ministry statistics indicated that 'pilot error' was responsible for about 80 per cent of air accidents. After the leave I requested an interview with the wing commander in charge of flying, and pressed him to try and ascertain what was happening to our projected job. The United Nations' Conference was now under way in San Francisco. His immediate reaction was to pack us off on some more leave.

On return from this leave my intuition was already telling me that our Atlantic and trans-American trip had hit a snag, and I went to the wingco

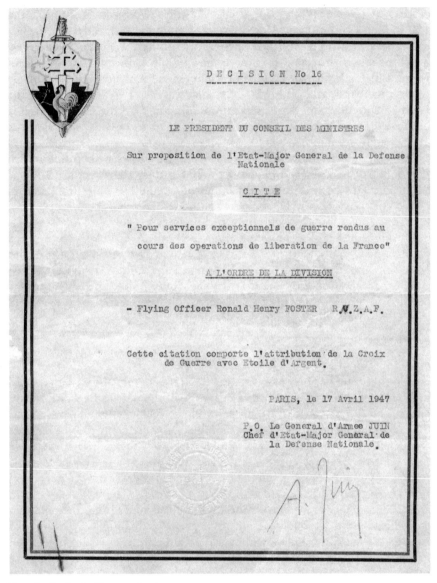

French Croix de Guerre citation.

and told him our strong feelings. He despatched us to Transport Command HQ, telling us to combine that little journey with a 48-hour leave pass. We were having a slack time of it.

At HQ we were again treated most pleasantly, but the news was that the trip was 'off', even though the conference did not end until late June.

Although the British authorities were enthusiastic about the project, the Americans were not. Reading slightly between the lines of what we were told, the Yanks did not have a suitable aircraft, and were not agreeable to using a British Mosquito or British crews. Our beautiful new Mosquito would break all existing records for flying times, and that did not suit all parties. I felt as flat as a pancake.

The man informing us then added that he was indeed sorry that we had been waiting about so long. He also said that if the trip had gone ahead satisfactorily, Joe and I would have been promoted one rank. This was small consolation, but his next offer was most acceptable. 'What do you two wish to do now?' he asked. Joe stepped in quickly and said, with his usual Aussie additions: 'All I want is to get out of here smartly and go back to my wife in

Caricature in Paris at the war end – a taste of light relief (money refunded if not completed within 60 seconds).

x i m
CARICATURISTE
FOLIES-BERGÈRE
P A R I S
1 9 4 5

Australia.' 'And that is what you shall do, Burfield,' said the man who made the prompt decisions.

My answer to his question was that I would enjoy a period of ferrying Mosquitos and any other aircraft to various parts of the world before I returned to New Zealand. And his reply was, 'Back you go to Pershore, and that is what you'll do.' We stood up, shook hands, saluted and departed. There was no more singing about the Golden Gate.

Joe, all the time I knew him in Britain, was the perfect husband, as much as he could be, half a world away, to his pretty Australian wife. He constantly spoke about her to me, and I trust she was the perfect wife for such a fine gentleman. Joe returned to Australia promptly.

After a period experiencing a peculiar contrasting blend of having my life hanging by a thread every now and again while at Benson, yet at the same time enjoying an organized and satisfying routine, my future now looked uncertain and unsure. If, as it appeared, the war against the Japanese was nearing its conclusion, it was dawning on me that a time for war is indeed a time for war; but the future, in a time of no war, looked already to be a decidedly different prospect.

Epilogue

High Flight
Oh, I have slipped the surly bonds of earth,
And danced the skies on laughter-silvered wings;
Sunward I've climbed and joined the tumbling mirth
Of sun-split clouds – and done a hundred things
You have not dreamed of – wheeled and soared and swung
High in the sunlight silence. Hov'ring there,
I've chased the shouting wind along and flung
My eager craft through footless halls of air.
Up, up the long delirious, burning blue
I've topped the wind-swept heights with easy grace,
Where never lark, or even eagle, flew;
And, while with silent, lifting mind I've trod
The high untrespassed sanctity of space,
Put out my hand, and touched the face of God.
John Gillespie Magee, Jr

This poem was published in the *New York Herald Tribune* and in the *RNZAFA News*, Vol. 7, No. 4, to whom thanks are expressed for this reproduction. The author, aged nineteen, an American volunteer with the Royal Canadian Air Force, was killed in action on 11 December 1941.

A Postscript to the Epilogue

Now, sixty years after the events in this book, I am well and truly aware of the beauty and the truth expressed in this epilogue. For some reason, as yet not known to me, the Great Creator God kept me alive, against the odds, during my aerial adventures. But something I *do* know, and I know this with the same sharp clarity as the brilliant blue sky contrasted with that sheer white layer of fog beneath it. . . . Whatever our current view may be of Europe, or this great wide world itself and its future, ultimately there has to be a better way to obtain a permanent peace than by going to war. *Quaero*: let's seek it, remembering that peace embraces more than the mere absence of war.

Glossary

ack-ack anti-aircraft fire
AFC Air Force Cross
AFU Advanced Flying Unit
Allies nations allied against Germany and its supporters in World War II
ante-room the lounge in a mess
ANZAC literally, Australian and N.Z. Army Corps; refers to a New Zealander or an Australian
AOC Air Officer Commanding
ASI air-speed indicator

bags of flap a lot of panic
batman a man or woman in the services acting as an orderly or a servant
beam approach a radio signal to direct the course of an aircraft towards a landing
beat-up a pass over people or objects by an aircraft at an extremely low level
belly landing an emergency landing with the wheels up
Bf 109 Messerschmitt fighter plane
bi-plane an aircraft with two sets of wings, one above the other
buzz the American equivalent of a beat-up

CB Companion of the Order of the Bath
CBE Commander of the Order of the British Empire
civvy civilian
CO Commanding Officer
cobber a friend or a mate

D-Day military code name for the invasion of Europe on 6 June 1944
deck the ground, in flying parlance
DFC Distinguished Flying Cross
DFM Distinguished Flying Medal
dicey-do a risky action
DNCO duties not carried out
drink the sea, or a lake or river
DSO Distinguished Service Order
duff poor: opposite of good

EFTS Elementary Flying Training School
erk an aircraftman, the lowest rank in the RAF
ETA estimated time of arrival

feather to turn the propellor blades edge on into the airflow to reduce resistance
flak anti-aircraft fire
Flt Lt the rank of Flight Lieutenant
Fg Off the rank of Flying Officer
Fw 190 Focke-Wulf 190: German fighter plane

Gee a navigation system
gen information
GI a private soldier in the U.S. Army
gong a medal, or other award
GRS General Reconnaissance School

ITW Initial Training Wing

kite an aircraft
Kiwi a flightless NZ bird, but applied to a New Zealander

LAC the rank of Leading Aircraftman
letting down to descend in altitude

mess a building in which servicemen eat, and sometimes have accommodation
met meteorological
mission USA version of a sortie
Mossie Mosquito aircraft
MVO Member of the Royal Victorian Order

nacelle the cover or shell of an aircraft engine
NCO non-commissioned officer
nyet Russian for 'no'

OGPU former term for Soviet secret police
op. or ops an operational flight against the enemy
OTU Operational Training Unit

perimeter track the boundary road around an airfield
POW prisoner of war
Prang a crash/to damage by impact
press on 1) to continue activity in spite of difficulties
2) to have a drinking session

PRU Photographic Reconnaissance Unit
pukka good, real, genuine

QDM course to steer to transmitting station
QGH procedure to descend through cloud

Reich the former German State
revs revolutions per minute of an engine
RNZAF Royal New Zealand Air Force
rpm revolutions per minute
R/T radio-telephone

SAAF South African Air Force
scrubbed cancelled
SHAEF Supreme Headquarters Allied Expeditionary Force
sheilas young women
sortie operational flight by military aircraft
Spit a Spitfire aircraft

tannoy public address system
ten-tenths = 10/10s complete cloud-cover
type a person *eg* 'a good type'

U-boat German submarine
UN(O) United Nations (Organization)
undercart undercarriage, or wheels of an aircraft
U/S unserviceable
USAAF United States Army Air Force

vapour trails condensation trails behind an aircraft at high altitude
VE-Day Victory in Europe Day
VHF very high frequency: used over R/T
vis visibility – for flying
VJ-Day Victory over Japan Day

Waaf Women's Auxiliary Air Force
wheeler an aircraft landing where the two front wheels touch and the tail is high
wingco a wing commander (Wg Cdr)
W/T wireless telegraphy

Yank (Yankee), inhabitant of the USA

Index

Index of Crews

This Index lists some of the crews who flew for 544 Squadron during the author's sojourn with this distinguished group during 1943, 1944 and 1945.

Many were killed in action, and some were not.
Many have since died; a few are still alive.

The list is unofficial and incomplete. It has been compiled from random diary notes, aided by Frank Moseley and other squadron members. If any of my comrades reading this do not find their names listed, may I humbly proffer my apologies, yet fervently say, 'Well done! Congratulations on still having your feet on terra firma.'